xx: refs to local authority : 39, 41, 86, 209

58 - secularization as "arising religious

66 : "detailed account of previous period is t necessary.

79 : for Finney's world, no distinction twice religious +
        secular reform

— re: big question is who are the targets? — —

220 - quote Johnson: must realize that masters experienced
        disobedience as religious assent ! this very ind,
        suggesting that the workers experienced disobe religious
        dissent as subversive !

REVIVALISM
AND CULTURAL
CHANGE

GEORGE M. THOMAS

REVIVALISM AND CULTURAL CHANGE

*Christianity, Nation Building,
and the Market in the
Nineteenth-Century United States*

THE UNIVERSITY OF CHICAGO PRESS
CHICAGO AND LONDON

George M. Thomas is associate professor of sociology at Arizona State University.

The University of Chicago Press, Chicago 60637
The University of Chicago Press, Ltd., London
© 1989 by The University of Chicago
All rights reserved. Published 1989
Printed in the United States of America

98 97 96 95 94 93 92 91 90 89   5 4 3 2 1

Library of Congress Cataloging-in-Publication Data

Thomas, George M.
    Revivalism and cultural change : Christianity, nation building,
and the market in the nineteenth-century United States / George M.
Thomas.
        p.   cm.
    Bibliography: p.
    Includes index.
    1. Revivals—United States—History—19th century.   2. United States—Politics
and government—19th century.   3. United States—Economic conditions—1865–
1918.   4. Republican Party (U.S. : 1854–)   5. Sociology, Christian—United
States—History—19th century.   6. Christianity and culture—History—19th century.   7. United States—Church history—19th century.   I. Title.
BV3773.T49   1989
306'.6—dc19   88-38578
    ISBN 0-226-79585-3 (alk. paper)   CIP

∞ The paper used in this publication meets
the minimum requirements of the American National
Standard for Information Sciences—Permanence of
Paper for Printed Library Materials, ANSI Z39.48-1984.

This book is printed on acid-free paper.

To Michael and Margaret Thomas

Contents

Preface

In the social scientific literatures on religion and society there seems to be a rather strange gap. On the one hand, there have been great strides in our general theories and insights into religion and society. On the other hand, there are rich interpretive descriptions of religions and religious movements and of how symbol systems are interwoven with everyday life. Yet, when the two levels are brought together, when for example description is put into a larger theoretical frame, simplistic interpretations seem to abound. This is especially true of studies of religious movements. Appeals still routinely are made to some supposed function that movements meet for people in crisis, with little reference to their structure or content. This gap has been closed somewhat with the increased number of historical studies of culture and institutions. Yet, even here religious movements tend not to be treated with the same insights as purportedly more rational political-economic ones.

In this book I pursue a possible solution by interpreting social movements, and especially religious ones, in terms of their theory of reality or their ontology. What is the content and structure of the cosmos that a movement is attempting to build? How is this cosmos related to myths and ideologies of social organization and relationships? What groups and sectors of society will find this cosmos credible and compelling? These questions force us to focus on the historical tradition and content of a movement and the place of that movement in large-scale cultural change.

This book also is part of ongoing work on the role of religion, and culture generally, in constructing, propelling, and reconstructing the modern world. What are the cultural and religious changes involved in the rise of nation–state authority, individualism, and capitalist markets? These dynamics are now properly understood as occurring at a world level. Thus, I have used comparative historical studies in constructing the theoretical model used to interpret the U.S. case. The concept of world culture seems especially important; it is only implicit in much of the book, but in the last chapter I explore its relation to religious movements. Thus, I hope that this book makes some modest contribution to the exciting work in historical and cultural sociology and toward world cultural analysis.

I build a general model of the relation of large-scale cultural change to social movements within historical institutional contexts. I am committed to keeping the two projects of theory construction and historical interpretation together. I take this approach fully aware that it goes against a tradition of grand theorizing and the more recent reactive move toward historical uniqueness. I apologize, more than once, for burdening the reader with theoretical abstraction and historical detail but not for the approach. Substantively, the conjuction of theory and history, I believe, calls into question one commonplace interpretation of religious movements—that they are in some way reactions to crisis. I am not sure if it is going too far to question any utility of the concept of crisis.

In attempting to take seriously the contents, traditions, and historical dynamics of movements, it is necessary to delve in depth into their content and structure. I spend much time (e.g., Chapter 4) in sketching these aspects of nineteenth-century culture, religion, and ideological movements. I discuss theology and practice and make use of religious newspapers as well as party platforms and agendas. Out of this work and within the theoretical framework, I generate three statements that I believe help interpret the changes that were occurring. In Chapter 5 I shift perspective and treat these interpretive statements as causal hypotheses, developing quantitative measures and carrying out statistical tests. I again am aware of the controversy in bringing such different methodologies together; however, I see little advantage in sacralizing any one method but much advantage in using what is appropriate in its circumscribed realm.

Christianity in the United States is a unique but enlightening case. The nineteenth century saw massive changes in culture and political economy. Europe, observers argue, was marked by secularization; the United States by an outpouring of new religious movements. These movements constituted a divide within Christianity as major as secularization or any other change of the century. I hope also that this book will make some contribution to better understanding this great divide. I should note that in the manuscript's long history earlier versions were circulated, and some references to it appeared in print under its working title, "Christianity and Culture in the Nineteenth-Century U.S." Much more needs to be said about the tension between Christianity and culture (especially that of the nineteenth century) beyond the diverse leads of H. Richard Niebuhr, Peter Berger, Jacques Ellul, and T. S. Eliot. But that is a different book.

Constructing general theory, describing historical cultural structures, and carrying out statistical analysis are in tension. I prefer to view them as mutually critical colleagues. I expect sociologists working on social movements and large-scale change to be especially interested in the theorizing; those working in culture and history along with colleagues in religious studies and American religious and political historians to applaud my attempt to describe historical, cultural contexts; and many sociologists, American political economists, and quantitative historians to attend to the testing of specific causal assertions. I appreciate the healthy skepticism each may have of the other and hope each will appreciate the study as a whole and my attempt to interweave these components into one approach. And as always, the reader is encouraged to critically pick and choose out of the attempted whole. It was difficult to find a language that would do justice to all of the subtle nuances of each field. I apologetically warn that the reader will have to be patient with some idiosyncracies and jargon of the different literatures.

This project began with discussions with John Meyer who was the first to refer me to Whitney Cross's *The Burned-over District*. In a class on collective behavior, Francesca Cancian allowed me to organize historical observations of revivals in a long and tedious term paper, which she critically but sympathetically read. I am indebted to Morris Zelditch, Jr., for his model of exactness and his active interest in the project. I owe a profound debt to John Meyer, not only for his guidance in the present work but for the development of my thought generally. I must here rely on understatement. The friendship and many discussions with John Boli also have greatly molded my thinking; he has provided a model for theoretically relevant historical sociology. Francisco Ramirez has played an especially important role in this project. Beyond much substantive input, he was the first to actively encourage, and insist on, the writing of the book. He persevered as a continued encourager and advisor throughout its long history. Bob Wuthnow also contributed advice, critical comments, and timely encouragement. Eldon Ernst and Sandra Sizer provided expert historical judgment. Doug Jardine read and commented on the entire manuscript, and its readability is largely due to his skills. Debbie Sult heroically typed and retyped the many revisions of revisions.

Thanking one's spouse takes a commonplace form, probably because a relationship goes through near universal experiences when one writes a book. Such thanks is important despite the cliches or feeble attempts at doing it in a unique manner. I thought it minimal to give Karen the last sentence or so of the Preface to comment on the project. After quoting Ecclesiastes 12:12 she paused. "Oh. It's too bad. I haven't read it yet."

ONE

Introduction: Sociocultural Change, Revivalism, and Republicanism

Objectives in Studying Revivalism and Change

There are two purposes to this study. The first is to work toward a general theory of sociocultural change with respect to religious and political movements that is based on historical comparisons. To that end, I analyze the historical inter-relations of political-economic expansion, religious movements, and the creation of national authority structures. The second purpose is to use this framework to better understand nineteenth-century revivalism in the United States. Revivalism was central to the constituting of the U.S. polity, and it has shaped subsequent religious-political movements. Moreover, it provides significant insights into the more general processes of social movements and cultural change.

Recurring periods of emotional intensity, popular interest, and political impact, periods known as revivals or awakenings, characterize the history of Christianity in the United States. During the First Great Awakening in the 1730s revivals occurred throughout the colonies. They greatly influenced the rise of revolutionary ideology. The waves of revivals of the Second Great Awakening at the turn of the nineteenth century increased in frequency, breadth, and intensity in the 1820s and eventually spread into the cities. They had profound effects on abolitionism, temperance and nationalism.

Unlike the First Great Awakening, which was viewed as flowing from the sovereign will of God, the "new" nineteenth-century revivalism was considered to be the result of deliberate action by churches and evangelists. Revivals were planned and coordinated among different denominations and towns. A large number of religious newspapers and journals gave regular accounts, usually on page one, of revivals throughout the country. Reports of emotion, tears, testimo-

1

nies, and remade lives included descriptions of whole regions being caught up over a period of weeks in a "spirit of revival." This was the fabric of individual and collective identity, purpose, and solidarity— the framework of a new social order.

A century and a half later, in the mid-1970s, the emergence of new religious movements, a born-again Evangelicalism, and a Christian political conservativism have received much attention as the signs of the most recent "Awakening." Though little is gained by merely labeling and counting awakenings, an historical perspective does improve our understanding of these movements. This is clearly shown in recent historical studies of Evangelicalism (Hunter 1983; Marsden 1987), Christian conservatism (Liebman and Wuthnow 1983), fundamentalism (Marsden 1980), and Christianity in America (Handy 1984; Noll, Hatch, and Marsden 1983).

Complementing the newly established historical perspective, there have also been major theoretical advances. Recent works in the sociology of religion suggest that religious movements are bearers of new cosmologies and ethics. Collective action theory contributes the idea that movements organize and mobilize people and resources for advancing specific claims. If we combine these insights, the image emerges of aggressive religious movements that articulate and attempt to establish a new social order by advancing a specific agenda.

Nevertheless, despite promising developments, these contributions have not had a major impact on the interpretation of religious movements. For example, when interpreting religious movements, scholars commonly revert to the well-worn theme that such movements are rooted in the anxiety, anomie, and alienation that come from rapid change—an approach that I refer to as a crisis-theoretic perspective. For example, the spread of Evangelicalism and the new Christian Right, as with previous waves of revivals and awakenings, are viewed as reactions to rapid sociotechnological change, a breakdown in social organization, or alienation.

The present work grew out of a dissatisfaction with conventional sociological interpretations of religious movements and of their relation to society. This concern quickly expanded to the broader area of cultural change and the rise of social movements. In the research reported here, I make a distinct break with the crisis perspective. I combine elements from the sociology of religion and culture and from collective action theory to construct a model of the effects of change on social movements. I offer the interpretation that religious movements articulate a new moral order and that each attempts to have its version of that order dominate the moral-political universe.

It is not hard to find religious movements locked in a struggle over the construction of a new order. The different branches of the Reformation, the Puritan Revolution of seventeenth-century England, Islam in nineteenth-century Morocco and Indonesia, the twentieth-century Islamic resurgence, liberation theology, and the Christian Right in the United States are all examples of this phenomenon. Are all of these movements using sacred symbols to reject change and "the new" and to regain a traditional society? The usual answer is "yes." Consequently, a conflict is seen between secular groups that embrace social change and religious ones that are against it. Yet, the formula usually applied to religious movements, "It is necessary to take one step backward to take two steps forward," is also true of secular movements in that all attempts at framing change draw on a cultural tradition.

Movements in the United States during the 1970s and 1980s provide a case in point. In the early 1960s, worldwide technological change and political-economic expansion caused a reworking of the moral order. Definitions of citizenship and individual rights were incorporated into the concepts of morality, lifestyle, and personal meaning. This intensification of individualism led to social movements that attempted to define the nature of the primodial value we call "the individual" within modern society. The institutionally prescribed definitions were organized in terms of citizenship, education, knowledge, and the psychological techniques of self-realization, self-esteem, and self-assertion. Alternative definitions were asserted by a spectrum of different groups, from student culture to Eastern mysticism.

In the 1970s, various movements, usually called "liberal humanism," attempted to build aspects of this new individualism into the general culture and the political-legal system. At the same time, other movements, known as "the new Evangelicalism," began to define the citizen as one who is "born-again," not so much to salvation or relative to a Holy God, but to the good life and progress (see Hunter 1983).

There is much conflict between these movements, conflict that focuses on the nature of the individual as citizen with respect to such issues as prayer in schools (the nature of knowledge and education), abortion (the rights of the unborn versus those of the mother), homosexuality (self-choice and the nature and source of sexuality), and evolution versus creation (myths of origin). One set of movements is self-described as "new" while the other is self-described as "traditional." Yet, both attempt to build a new social order by drawing on traditional systems. Liberal humanism legitimates the expansion of citizen rights by alluding to eighteenth-century rationalism and Enlightenment theories of history and the social contract. The Christian

Right legitimates change by integrating the psychology of self-assertion and self-esteem into a nineteenth-century revivalism. This conflict does not reflect the most recent in a long series of revivals that have attempted to reject change and to return to an idyllic past. Rather, it is the natural rivalry of two large groupings, each attempting to define a new moral order, each drawing on different traditions that are built into the constitutive framework of the United States: elements of rationalism and the Enlightenment on the one hand versus elements of America as a moral Christian civilization on the other.

I develop this line of thinking into a general model of how large-scale change results in social movements that articulate new organizations and definitions of individual, society, authority, and cosmos. I then use this model to study empirically revivalism of the nineteenth-century United States. These revivals created the institutional linkages among Protestantism, American society, and the Republican party that now form the context of the twentieth-century Christian Right.

In my view, both a general theoretical perspective and a study of several specific historical cases are necessary for an adequate understanding of revivalism in the United States. The reader should be warned that this study diverges from the large literature on "American religion." While it is a fruitful literature, it has narrowed our understanding by focusing on characteristics and developments unique to the United States. I attempt to interpret religion in the United States from a more general perspective and to use diverse theoretical and historical materials that to date have not been systematically applied to the study of Christianity in America. I develop comparisons of the nineteenth-century United States with other cases and periods and try to answer such questions as: What implications does an understanding of other historical cases have for our interpretation of nineteenth-century revivalism? What aspects of religious dynamics in the United States are applicable to other historical cases? What aspects are unique?

The construction of a general theoretical model is required for ordering and guiding these comparisons. But working inferentially, I find these empirical analyses and comparisons are necessary for the construction of a general theory. The abstract issues involved have often been discussed in specialized "grand theory" monographs. The present work is based on a commitment to developing theory in the context of empirical historical analysis. In particular, the subject of nineteenth-century revivalism has much to contribute to the construction of a general theory.

Summary of the Book

My objectives are pursued in five broad stages, each the subject of a chapter of this book. As an overview of the study, I briefly summarize the arguments of each stage.

An Institutional Model

In chapter 2 I specify and empirically justify a set of concepts, metatheoretical statements, and propositions for interpreting the relationship of large-scale change to religious and political movements. These elements are set forth informally, but I refer to them as an institutional "model." A variety of historical examples are presented to give substance to the abstract theory, to demonstrate its scope, and to develop a comparative empirical basis for examining the nineteenth-century United States.

Substantively, this institutional model describes how a cultural order defines reality (it is a world view or ontology), and how it guides and justifies action (it is an accounting system). Generally speaking, a cultural order *constitutes* action. The model then focuses on cultural change and the process by which a new order, with restructured knowledge, emerges to challenge the old. Such change can give rise to a large number of social movements. Some movements react negatively to the change, but my core argument is that generally they accept and articulate the new cultural reality; they emerge to specify a "new order of things" in terms of concrete rules of social organization.

An Institutional Analysis of Market Penetration

Chapter 3 narrows the focus of the institutional model to the type of large-scale change that took place in the United States early in the nineteenth century. Growth and incorporation in the national polity occurred primarily through the expansion of local markets into national and international ones. Instead of growing crops for their local regions, farmers sold to merchants who shipped to major centers such as New York, New Orleans, or even Europe. Local populations became oriented to national issues and politics, at the expense of local obligations and authority. This type of political-economic expansion is referred to as economic rationalization, or, more descriptively, as market penetration because local communities are incorporated into (penetrated by) a larger market. Market penetration fundamentally transforms everyday life, resulting in social movements that embrace this change and organize to build a new life.

Frequently, religion plays a special role in the construction of the new order. Religious movements frame the changes of everyday life and the expansion of the national polity within a reformation or revival of a particular tradition. This revivalism is a reciprocal process whereby a newly emerging order shapes and is shaped by tradition, the new synthesis being labled a "revival."

The way in which market penetration occurs and the type of social movements that emerge have varied from country to country throughout history. They occurred in one way during the rise of capitalism in sixteenth-century Europe; they displayed other characteristics during periods of colonization. They have taken different forms in the northern and southern United States.

Our purpose is not only to understand what happened in the distinctive nineteenth-century United States, but also to understand the dynamics of religious movements and what we are calling market penetration generally, as they occur in cases other than the United States. Therefore, in chapter 3, I use the institutional model developed in chapter 2 and draw on diverse historical examples to develop a "middle-range" theory of market penetration that can be applied to a number of historical cases. From this theory I then generate propositions that are directly related to revivalism in the nineteenth-century United States.

Chapters 2 and 3, therefore, flow in a spiral from generality to specificity. I move from an abstract theory of large-scale change and social movements to a middle-range theory of a particular kind of change, market penetration, which is then narrowed further to a particular historical case. This flow covers much material and asks for the patience of the reader who is primarily interested in the subject of U.S. revivalism. In order to illustrate the argument toward which the theoretical work builds, I summarize in the next section the interpretation of revivalism and its political-economic context that is put forth in chapter 3.

The Political-Economic Context of Revivalism

Nineteenth-century revivalism framed the rules and identities of the expanding market and the national polity. It articulated a cultural order centered on the individual (citizen) as the prime mover. People believed that rational moral action would establish national morality

6

and transform American civilization into the Kingdom of God on earth. Consequently, in the North and Midwest, revivalism was the source of social reform and political movements such as abolitionism, temperance, and Republicanism. The Republican party itself developed an ideology of nationalism, citizenship, and rugged individualism, and throughout the century it drew on revivalist support.

Thus, revivalism was shaped by the individualism and nationalism of political-economic expansion; but it also shaped and organized that expansion by articulating a broad institutional framework. Using the language of the sociology of knowledge, the market, the primary carrier of sociocultural change in this case, was the "plausibility structure" of revivalism. In turn, both the market and revival religion formed a plausibility structure for political ideologies such as Republicanism and Prohibitionism.

Chapter 3 concludes with three interpretive propositions: (1) Wherever one can identify the domination of everyday life by entrepreneurship and the small capitalist enterprise during the nineteenth-century in the United States, one can expect to find outbreaks of revivals and the adherence to a revivalist world view. (2) Wherever one finds a dominance of entrepreneurship, one can expect to find support for Republicanism and Prohibitionism. (3) Wherever one finds a dominance of revival religion, one can expect to find strong support for Republicanism and Prohibitionism.

A question likely to be asked at this point is, "Does this not reduce religion to economics?" The answer is "no." These casual relations are not transhistorical. Thus, in developing the model, I explore different historical cases and different causal directions—including some in which religious change occurs first. Moreover, I describe why I think "material" action is inseparable from the meanings and cultural accounts implicit within it. Systems such as markets are not just material in nature, but are institutions. Political-economic change therefore is not merely "material" change that eventually affects "culture." Political-economic change *is* sociocultural change. Additionally, the cultural order at the start of change shapes the organization and direction of change.

The Social Meaning of Revivalism and Republicanism

This interpretation and its propositions imply that the structure and content of revivalism, Republicanism, and the organization of life within the expanding market are all somewhat similar. The similarity of structures is known technically as isomorphism and can be illustrated by the following description of revivalism and individual farm production.

Within a new democracy, a growing rural community comprising successful merchants, craftsmen, cottage industries, and shopkeepers, surrounded by successful yeoman farmers, might be exposed to a wide variety of preaching. A Calvinistic minister might tell his congregation that they were morally corrupt by nature and slaves to sin, that they did not have the capability to choose good or salvation, that God alone saved, and that He alone caused one to believe. This orthodox Reformation message would run counter to the individual's self-determinism in the everyday life of market and polity, as well as to the corresponding cultural order. The sermon would not make sense. A traveling Methodist revivalist might address the same people in his revival meeting and preach that they were slaves to nothing, that they had the will to choose to do good and to believe, that they controlled their own destiny, and that God would respect each person by not forcing salvation on them—indeed it might be that He could not do so. In the context of their everyday lives and the cultural individualism that characterized those lives, this message would make sense to the people. Thus, the revivalist world was isomorphic with everyday life and the broad cultural order; Calvinism was not.

In chapter 4, I document this isomorphism by describing the nature and structure of revivalism and Republicanism. Revival religion constitutes rational individual action and national progress as manifested in four core elements: (1) radical free will (Arminianism) with shades of antinomianism, (2) rational unity of means and ends exhibited in rational methods of evangelism and spirituality, (3) the expected perfection of each believer in this life, and (4) through the efforts of individuals, the perfecting of the nation, i.e., individuals bring about the millennium.

Republicanism is similar in content. The Republican party arose and coalesced around two complementary themes: the primacy of the "rugged individual" and of the nation. These themes were worked out in debates over free labor, federal citizenship, and national interest in world markets. The second half of chapter 4 describes the ideologies of the Republican and Democratic parties with respect to specific issues. I show that Republicanism was isomorphic with revivalism, whereas the Democratic ideology was not.

As the third stage of the project, chapter 4 is not a formal test of my interpretation of revivalism; the three propositions of the theory are not simply applied deductively. Neither, however, is the chapter a mere narrative. It is rather a "retroductive" attempt to move back and forth between an empirical description and an ordered interpretation of the content and structure of revivalism and Republicanism. It therefore links the general analysis of institutional interrelations with a phenomenological understanding of the movements building those institutions.

Quantitative Analyses

In chapter 5 I treat the three interpretive propositions presented in chapter 3 as causal hypotheses and test them empirically. I develop quantitative measures at the county level of economic entrepreneurship, memberships in revivalistic religious bodies, and voting. I construct statistical models of the three hypotheses—multiple regression panel models. Analyses are carried out for 1870 to 1896 for the counties of two northern and two midwestern states.

The results strongly support the hypotheses relating to the first and third propositions (measures of entrepreneurship do affect indexes of revivalism which in turn affect the Republican vote) and qualified support for the second (entrepreneurship has mixed effects on the Republican vote). Moreover, the results provide a novel description of the pattern of economic organization, denominational memberships, and voting during this period. Of course, the hypotheses and my general interpretation of revivalism are not *proven*. Nevertheless, the statistical findings, when added to the material of chapter 4, increase our confidence in the interpretation and suggest extensions of it. Not only must we document isomorphism, we must also demonstrate that the three structures occurred in the same populations. In this manner, the qualitative work of chapter 4 gives depth to the interpretation; whereas, chapter 5 provides formal statistical support for it.

General Comparisons

Much ground is covered as I move from an abstract theory of sociocultural change and social movements to diverse historical cases that are used to build an interpretation of market forces, and finally focus on these processes in the nineteenth-century United States. In the last chapter I return to more general theoretical and comparative historical concerns. In it I bring the various elements of this study together and attempt to produce a general historical perspective on religious movements.

Using the institutional model based on Wuthnow's (1980) essay on religious movements and world order, I present an overview of historical religious movements. I place nineteenth-century revival religion within this larger framework and compare it with earlier periods (e.g., the Reformation and English Puritanism) and later periods (e.g., twentieth-century religious movements).

An emergent theme that unites the diverse elements of the book is the centrality of dialectical processes wherein manifestly contradictory structures and movements are mutually legitimating. This is so because they are isomorphic with the same cultural order, but constructed upon contradictory components of that order. Contemporary movements, while highly diverse in their views of the transcendent and in their attitudes toward political-economic change, share a common cultural foundation.

This book focuses on specific empirical issues, which I analyze at different levels of abstraction. I examine the nature and institutional context of the particular form of revival religion that swept the United States during the nineteenth century. In the process, I outline the dynamics of social movements that construct a unified cultural order when social life is rationalized by and incorporated into world markets. On a more abstract plane, I am concerned with social factors that causally affect the content of knowledge structures and the role social movements play in that dynamic process.

Moving across levels makes relevant a whole set of metatheoretical and methodological issues, such as the pitfalls of reductionism and the possibility and adequacy of phenomenological bracketing. Although I have put few restrictions on the range of substantive material addressed, I have attempted to mention such general issues only in passing. This decision tends to compartmentalize them from ongoing research, relegating them to "philosophical" discussions which are made irrelevant when the "serious" business of research is undertaken. Compartmentalization can result in the misinterpretation of a given study's implications. For example, I argue that the content of a particular institution within a society, such as the Church, is causally affected by its cultural environment, but this cannot be construed to imply, as is often said in the sociological study of religion, that it is reducible to that environment. Any scientific reductionism is, in the last analysis, an illusion. Similarly, by studying the sociological aspects of change, I do not address the essence and historical meaning of revivalism.

The present study examines the sociological aspects of the relation between Christianity and culture, and is indebted to previous studies of the conflict between Christianity and society (e.g., Ellul 1978, 1975; Berger 1967; Niebuhr 1951). The cultural mythology of a society constitutes an ontology that is morally binding on the institutions of the society, delineating legitimate meaning, activity, and organization. Christianity as an institution in society is positioned within this context. When the propositions of Christianity and its cultural environment conflict, Christianity loses legitimacy relative to the assumed cultural myth. Social movements and long-term trends "within Christianity" are often grounded in the rhetoric of the "external" culture; they legitimate proposed change by linking it to the external structure. Such movements often move beyond modifying Christianity and claim that their particular vision of change is the true nature of a whole new order. Thus, nineteenth-century revivalism actively used the broad cultural myths of individualism to forge an extremely individualistic Christianity; this "revival" of "true" Christianity, however, was not just the revival of the Church, but the reconstituting of the individual and the nation.

Any social movement, therefore, must be interpreted in terms of the cultural knowledge on which that movement is based: What is the content and structure of the world that a movement is attempting to build? How is this cosmos related to the cultural myths of the society? What groups or sectors of society will find this ontology credible and compelling? My theoretical approach is thus to interpret religious movements in terms of the cultural knowledge that they presuppose and on which they are built. I locate that knowledge within the social structure and develop and test hypotheses relating movement support to those areas of society. This approach requires a detailed treatment of the general nature of institutional change with a focus on political-economic rationalization.

TWO

An Institutional Model of Cultural Change and Social Movements

Large-Scale Change and Social Movements

In this chapter I develop a general model of how sociocultural change gives rise to and is fueled by social movements. Despite important differences in theoretical approaches, previous interpretations of social movements, especially of religious ones, have tended to rely on conceptions of strain or crisis: These movements are thought to be class reactions to oppression, the frustration of interest, or the loss of social control (e.g., Niebhur 1929; Stinchcombe 1961; Cohn 1957; Johnson 1978); or to result from social disorganization and anomie (e.g., Carroll 1975; Wallace 1956; Chirot and Ragin 1975; McLoughlin 1978; Smelser 1962; Turner 1982; Douglas and Tipton 1983); or to be caused by some form of relative deprivation (Glock 1964).

According to these arguments, culture is a system of generalized goals and values that maintain the social order. A social movement results from a traumatic crisis at some level of structural strain or breakdown, what conflict theorists refer to as a loss of hegemony and social control. In these views individuals, stripped of generalized meaning and values, search frantically for personal meaning and control, aggregating into social movements. To be sure, there is much debate over whether these movements result from material versus cultural strains, from a breakdown in social control versus a consensual moral order, or from material versus status interests. Yet, most approaches regard social movements as the aggregation of individual attempts to deal with some form of crisis.

Two developments, one in collective action theory and one in the sociology of religion, suggest more promising lines of analysis. Theories of collective action and social movements such as resource mobilization theory have moved away from interpretations based on strain, breakdown, crisis, or the lack of elite hegemony (Ramirez 1987; Jenkins 1983; Turner 1982). Tilly (1978), for example, conceptualizes collective movements as routine aspects of competition within a polity over resources and positions of power.

This approach has been very fruitful; unfortunately it relegates culture (and religion as an aspect of culture) to an insignificant role in the collective action process. Religion *as an organization* might be used to mobilize people, it is agreed, but religious symbols and beliefs are tangential. Theorists in this perspective recognize that movements claim to have legitimate demands, but they do not address the cultural frame and origin of the demands nor of their legitimacy. They therefore have not been able to account for why individuals commit personal resources and time to a new movement—that is, how they overcome the free rider problem. What is needed is a more aggressive view of culture (and religion) as playing an integral part in constituting movement demands and stimulating individual participation (cf. Douglas 1986).

Recent developments in the sociology of religion are potentially corrective. Many theorists view religion as defining the reality of everyday life within a sacred worldview and instilling an ethos that impels people to action (Douglas 1966; Berger and Luckmann 1966; Geertz 1973, 1980). They see religious movements as carriers of different cosmologies and ethics, as symbolized by specific claims and issues. For example, numerous studies have shown the ways in which religious symbols are used to frame and construct social change (e.g., Geertz 1968, 1973; Liebman and Wuthnow 1983; Lincoln 1985; Robertson 1978; Thrupp 1970; Walton 1984; Walzer 1965). Some studies are rich in historical depth and detail. Yet, in addressing the formation of movements, most continue to rely on the ideas of dislocation, structural strain, anomie, and psychological anxiety. They relate the religious aspects of these movements and their accompanying emotional intensity to such sources and to a longing for a traditional past or a secure objectivity in the midst of change.

The present work builds on the innovative leads of these theorists. I take from collective action theory the idea that movements are routine aspects of social life; they organize and mobilize around specific goals and claims. From the sociology of religion I take the description of how religious-cultural systems constitute action and collective goals. A religious movement is one mobilized to work on the cultural frame. It is a carrier of a particular worldview or ontology. Such movements use religious symbols to construct a new social order, not in the abstract, but in their specific claims and demands. Thus, movements are in competition with each other and with established organizations to institute their own vision of the cultural order.[1]

To develop this perspective and to apply it to nineteenth-century revivalism, one needs to ask many questions and define many concepts. How does a religious-cultural order constitute everyday life? What is the process by which a new order emerges to challenge the old? How do new definitions of reality result in movements that embrace change and mobilize as its carriers? How do such movements incorporate specific demands for change within religious symbols? This chapter addresses these questions. The reader interested primarily in U.S. revivalism can view this material as a clarification of the concepts and approach used in later chapters. For those interested more generally in social change processes, I present the concepts and propositions of this chapter as a model of cultural change and religious-political movements.

Institutional Order: Rules, Ontology, and Knowledge
Institutional Rules Constitute Action: Coinherence

A cultural order is a set of institutionalized rules that infuse people and their actions with meaning and value. Weber (1968, 32) states that a legitimate (institutional) order includes or entails "determinable maxims" that are held by the collective to "define a model or to be binding." Binding or exemplary rules define and prescribe: They constitute actor and action as well as regulate them. By reference to rules, one evaluates and chooses identities and courses of action. Taken as a whole, these rules comprise an accounting system that people use to guide and justify action (Burke 1950; Mills 1940). Thus, one orients oneself and one's action to institutional rules not only in the interest of "social order" but also in the interest of meaning.

Moreover, action is *assumed* to be meaningful; one assumes that others are oriented to rules. In this sense, action carries with it the rules that constitute its meaning (Goffman 1967, 1974). Thus, a pattern of interaction and the shared rules that are used to interpret and guide it do not comprise two disparate levels of social action and cultural values. The two analytically distinguishable aspects are "coinherent." For example, in the previous chapter I mentioned that markets are not just "material" action but also are institutions. By this I mean that markets and market action are constituted by cultural rules. For instance, exchanging commodities for profit is meaningful and of value only in the context of the acceptance of certain objects as commodities that are to be bought and sold, the autonomy and rationality of the individual, intentionality and self-interest, inviolable contracts, abstract law, and a this-worldly methodical ethos (Polanyi 1944; Weber 1961; Collins 1986, 19–44; Wuthnow 1987). Exchange for profit, the epitome of material action, is a cultural action, an acting out of meaning.

Institutional Order Is An Ontology

An institutional order is not merely an inventory of rules or accounts. It is a classification scheme. It is composed of categories or types of *entities*—types of people, groups, things, and events (Schutz 1967; Douglas 1966). This scheme of things is a map of reality that is used in practice to interpret identities and action.[2] Consequently, an institutional order is fundamentally a knowledge system or theory of reality—an ontology. Categories, rules, and accounts are embedded in the structure and organization of reality. They have a "facticity" about them (Berger and Luckmann 1966; Berger and Pullberg 1965) and are accepted as the imposed conditions of life and nature (Geertz 1973). They are accepted as knowledge. Thus, meaningful action not only assumes specific rules but also fundamental assertions about reality and existence.[3]

Look again at the cultural rules constituting market behavior. They are rules about the existence, nature, and interrelations of entities: Individuals exist and are independent from social groups; individuals are capable of complex rational calculation; nature can be made into commodities for exchange that have a quantifiable value or price; contracts exist; legal definitions of justice presuppose formally equal individuals; and there is something called the collective good or progress to which all of these things are related.

Consequently, a cultural or institutional order directly shapes action because it depicts reality, and its categories and rules of reality are used as accounts to guide, justify, and interpret people, action, and events. Moreover, the cognitive aspects of this process are intimately related to legitimacy and morality. The institutional order is *cognitively compelling* and *morally binding*. What is fundamentally real cognitively constitutes knowledge and meaning; it morally constitutes what should be and what is legitimate. What is sensical and meaningful is also legitimate and moral. Thus, any moral imperative is rooted in assumptions about reality.[4]

Integration of the Institutional Order:
Isomorphism and Environments

In analyzing a particular historical case such as U.S. revivalism, it is helpful to speak of the economic, political, and religious spheres. For example, the present theory works toward explaining the causal relations among market organization, revival religion, and voting for the Republican party. Following common practice, I conceptualize the cultural order as consisting of various institutional spheres (Marx 1963, 173; Weber 1946) or fields (Bourdieu 1984). An institution may be analyzed in terms of one or more of these spheres. For example, Thanksgiving or Memorial Day may each be studied in terms of the religious sphere, the political sphere, or both. Much evidence has been amassed which shows that the structure of knowledge in each sphere or province of meaning is intimately tied to that of other spheres (e.g., Bourdieu 1984; Douglas 1973).[5]

How are diverse institutional spheres related to each other? How do changes in one affect changes in the others? How is a specific situation integrated in the broader cultural order? The first two questions are most directly relevant to our present study, but the latter is more fundamental. I therefore will discuss integration generally and then draw out the implications for integration across social spheres.[6]

An insight of Durkheim (and of structural anthropology) is that the cultural order carries its own logic of integration. It is an integrated structure in that the categories of the classification scheme are delineated and related by rules that (1) define each category in relation to the others, and (2) describe the nature of each relation. In short, the cultural ontology depicts entities in a coherent, structured relationship to each other and an institutional order is characterized by an underlying structure (Levi-Strauss 1962, 1963; Douglas 1966; Durkheim and Mauss 1963).

People use a cultural order to organize and interpret diverse situations and thereby specify rules of action. Rules infuse meaning and value precisely by linking the situation to broader reality. Because situation-specific rules are rooted in the cultural order, the underlying structure is reproduced throughout social life and across situations and institutional spheres (Douglas, 1973; Levi-Strauss, 1962, 1963). The common underlying structure, as emphasized, is an ontology—an assumed structure of reality. It also can be metaphoric; it is used holistically as a model to structure diverse aspects of life. It also can be mythic; it is an explanatory story about the themes and rules of life.[7]

This underlying structure is not more abstract than the classification system nor does it lie at some "higher" (or deeper) level.[8] Any situation-specific rule is an integral part of the structure. It is helpful to view an institutional order analogously as a picture or gestalt in which a figure is set against a background. The figure is placed in relief against the background, but it is an integral part of the picture as a whole. Situation-specific rules, like a figure set against its ground, are used in practice in the context of the underlying cultural structure, *of which the specific rules are an integral part.* It is in this sense that all culture is circular, from primitive classification to modern science.

Both action and rules are seen as legitimate when they fit into the broad underlying structure. Thus, specific action in a given situation is legitimated only if rules or accounts can be appropriated from the institutional context. Rules themselves are seen as legitimate or not depending on whether they fit into the underlying structure. Processes from face-to-face interaction to formal lawmaking are governed by the principle that rules must fit the underlying structure in order to make sense and be legitimate. Thus, not only particular actions and rules, but institutions and organizations within society are defined as legitimate by reference to the institutional order. At all levels this remains both a cognitive and a moral process. What the underlying ontology defines as real and sensical is what should be and thus is morally binding for social organization and interaction.

When analyzing an institution (or institutional sphere), it is helpful to shift our terminology, for example, from cultural "context" to cultural "environment." The classification system used as an interpretive ground can be conceptualized as an environment for institutions. Interaction and organization within a particular institution (the "figure") conforms to its environment (the "ground") and is said to be legitimate. The knowledge and rules of a particular institution are an integral part of the cultural order as a whole; yet, from the point of view of action within the institution, the larger order stands as an external environment.[9] Because the same ontology or underlying rule structure is being worked out and specified in each institutional sphere, there is congruence or similarity of structures across diverse spheres.

In general, if the knowledge of an institution conforms to environmental myths, it is defined as sensible and legitimate. If it does not fulfill external cultural requirements, it loses legitimacy and credibility. The fundamental cultural structure is binding on the specific categories and rules of an institution; if the specific does not fit the general, then it is defined as illegitimate (Meyer and Scott 1983).

The cultural environment of an institutional sphere imposes requisites on institutions by stipulating the type of structure that characterizes legitimate organizations (e.g., bureaucracy), the types of entities (e.g., individuals), the style of action of the entities (e.g., rationality), and the general type of authority present (e.g., rational-legal). For example, established psychologies dictate to schools the essence of who an individual is, how a given person—typed according to, for example, personality or learning speed—is to learn, and how authority is to be manifested and limited in the classroom. More generally, the cultural myth of rationality requires that all organizations adopt formal structures and strategies that correspond to a rational calculation of means and ends, independent of the actual relevance and efficiency of such ritualized organization (Meyer and Rowan 1983).

Theorists refer to the similarity of structure through different levels and across institutional spheres by several names. Because of its frequent use in sociology, I use the term *isomorphism* (see, for example, Wuthnow 1987).[10] Recall the example of the Calvinist and revivalist preachers in the expanding agrarian regions of the United States. Calvinism is incongruent with the emerging cultural order of market expansion, whereas the revivalist message is isomorphic with it—primarily in terms of the self-determination of the individual. Lack of isomorphism causes not only problems of meaning but also leaves the institution open to charges of immorality and illegitimacy.

In summary, a cultural or institutional order is integrated according to an underlying structure. The fundamental structure is an ontology (a cultural myth or metaphor) that is a binding context or environment for institutions and institutional spheres. While emphasizing that there is a unity and therefore a circularity between a given institution and its context, I speak analytically of an institution's *external* cultural *environment* as being *applied to* the organization of and the activity within the institution. This application process results in specific rules that reproduce the broader structure. In this process the structure of the external ontology causally affects the structure and organization of knowledge within a given institutional sphere. Organizations, institutions, and institutional spheres therefore tend toward isomorphism with the structure of their cultural environment, and therefore with each other. This application process is not some conscious intellectual labor toward consistency. It occurs through everyday interpretative action and includes both cognitive and moral aspects. The environmental order is morally binding and isomorphism defines legitimacy.

Formal Organization and Ritual

Social movements in general and religious ones in particular are marked by emotional intensity. Members of religious movements seem to be caught up in the truth and power of their beliefs. The emotionalism of revivalism is famous. Nevertheless, movements are quickly organized and successful ones evolve into formal organizations. For example, the institution of revivalism became organized within particular religious denominations. Similarly, nationalism was formally incorporated into the Republican party.

It often is assumed that this routinization within formal organization marks a loss of religious intensity, validity, and social impact; that people no longer are caught up in the religious ethos that impels them to action but are diverted instead to maintaining organizations. Yet, revivalism, I will show, maintained its social impact throughout the nineteenth century. I think this is so because religion as an ontology shapes everyday life, and therefore its formalization need not diminish its relevance and impact. Long after the waves of emotionalism have past, formal organization preserves the ontology by encoding it in concrete rules. Because this argument is relevant to interpreting the formalization of revivalism, let me sketch it out.

Formal organization lies at the interface of cultural structure and everyday activity. Formal rules and definitions are the immediate, concrete frame of activity. They also are ritual-like codes for the categories and rules of the institutional order. In other words, formal organization is shaped by the cultural environment, and cultural categories and rules are built into its offices. For example, the increasing instrumental rationality of the Western sociocultural order results in the rationalization and bureaucratization of formal organization across the range of institutional spheres (Weber 1930; Ellul 1964). Bureaucracy is a ritualistic adaptation to the institutional environment that may in some cases be instrumentally inefficient and counterproductive but which produces legitimacy. Therefore, organizations tend to be isomorphic with broad cultural order and with each other (Meyer and Scott 1983).[11]

The specification of a cultural order within formal organization (and in concomitant identities and rules of interaction) narrows the potential versions and uses of the cultural order.[12] At times, one particular formal organization becomes _equated_ with the metaphoric categories: A particular organization or institution becomes _the_ carrier of sociocultural reality. For example, Illich (1970) critically describes the equating of process (social institutions organized as means) with substance (abstract, valued goals) as the "institutionalization of values" in a particular formal organization or organizational setting:

> Medical treatment is mistaken for health care, social work for the improvement of community life, police protection for safety, military poise for national security, the rat race for productive work. Health, learning, dignity, independence, and creative endeavor are defined as little more than the performance of the institutions which claim to serve these ends. . . .
> (P. 1)

Isomorphism is especially rigid when a formal organization is institutionalized as the embodiment of the larger myth. Other possible organizations of everyday life might be consistent with the institutional order, but its specification in an already given institution excludes these alternatives. This is manifested in practice by an institutional bias against the exploration of alternatives, change, and movements organized for change.[13]

Thus, while more rigid and seemingly at odds with substantive validity (as evidenced by Illich's tone), formal organization does preserve the cultural order, building it into specific rules of action. While such a situation might lack a spontaneous, emotional ethos, individuals will act out the moral imperatives of the order, not necessarily out of emotional fervor but by the routine orientation to institutionalized rules (Weber 1968).[14]

Institutional Dynamics: Rethinking Elective Affinity

The United States in the nineteenth century was a society undergoing an extended period of dramatic change and experiencing the construction of a new religious system. The symbiotic relation between religious-cultural order and the organization of everyday life can produce a degree of bias against change. It is misleading, however, to focus on this negative aspect because cultural order is quite dynamic. Moreover, the complex interrelations emphasized in the institutional model are laid bare by the examination of such change as we find in the United States at this time. We are able to assess the institutional model by observing patterns of change and inferring flows of causation over time.

A modification of an aspect of cultural order causes changes throughout the system. This modification can be viewed as a change in the ground (the broad cultural order) causing change in the figure (a particular institution). Given the fact that one institution is part of the environment of another (the basic unity of figure and ground), change within an institution will modify the environment of other institutions. Through this modification of its environment, any other institution will tend toward isomorphism with the change. Such ripple effects are not mechanical or automatic nor will all institutions feel the environmental effects at the same time. Much depends on the historical links among the institutions as well as the ability of some to buffer themselves from all but major environmental changes.[15]

As an example, and to anticipate the argument in the following chapters, political-economic change in the early nineteenth-century United States radically restructured its cultural order. As this restructuring was specified in all areas of social life, religion in the form of revivalism became a special, although not the sole, carrier of the new order. This is reflected in (1) the direct relation of political-economic change to the emergence of revivalism and (2) the direct effect of revivalism on the rise of Republican nationalism.

The argument can be illustrated by showing how it agrees with Weber's theory of the religious roots of rationalization and capitalism and how it modifies the dynamics of his theory. Weber views religious systems as having an economic ethic: the "practical impulses for action which are founded in the psychological and pragmatic contexts of religions" (1946, 267). It is a religiously structured "way of life." Likewise, the organization of economic activity and of everyday life carries with it an ethos or spirit. For example, referring to the goal of increasing capital accumulation, Weber states, "Truly what is here preached is not simply a means of making ones way in the world, but a peculiar ethic. The infraction of its rules is treated not as foolishness but as forgetfulness of duty" (1930, 51). Thus, an ethos is a set of moral imperatives, attitudes, and moods (cf. Geertz 1973). On the one hand, an ethos can devolve from a religious and cultural order, and on the other hand, an ethos can be built up out of the life experiences of a group.[16]

An ethic is the primary mechanism by which religion affects social action and organization. When an ethos devolving from a religion and one generated from a style of life are similar, they are said to have an elective affinity. In general, there is a tendency toward the natural selection of ethics across institutional spheres and lifestyles that have an elective affinity.

Weber (1930) argues that the rise of rational society and economy in the West was due to the fact that the ethos of Protestantism was similar in many respects to the ethos (spirit) of rational capitalistic/

bureaucratic organization. The social-psychological aspects of the argument have been the most popular and most generally applied: A new ethos (the Protestant ethic) drives people (Protestants) to transform everyday life (methodical work and capitalist enterprise). For example, one of the most insightful interpretations of nineteenth-century revivalism, that by John Hammond (1979), is that revivalism created an ethos that motivated individuals to participate in the abolition movement and Republicanism.

Yet, Weber's early work also includes institutional elements, and, as Collins (1986, 19–44) has pointed out, Weber's (1961) "last" theory of cultural and economic rationalization is even more institutionalist (see also Poggi 1983). Weber delineates the institutional—not the social-psychological—prerequisites of rational, capitalistic organization: free markets including that of labor, rationalized technology and organization, and entrepreneurial enterprises. The Protestant Reformation contributed to the institutionalization of these elements by redefining the individual as the center of activity and value attainment, free from identities embedded in traditional feudal hierarchies. Individual activity in economic and political life became the vehicle for working out salvation and religious identities. The construction of a rational, disciplined life no longer took place in the monastery but was transformed into the rationalization of everyday action. These transformations together with rational law, state bureaucracy, and citizenship provided the basis of capitalism.

This institutionalist interpretation appears to be satisfactory historically, but, with no replacement for the earlier social-psychological emphasis and the related idea of elective affinity, the dynamics are left vague. Any systematization of the theory tends to end up a chronology of the various conditions of capitalism (e.g., Collins 1986, 19–44).

The present model agrees with Weber's institutional framework but fills in the dynamics. The modifications can be viewed as a rethinking of elective affinity based on the structured ontology basic to culture. Elective affinity is not simply a similarity of attitudes and motivational imperatives, it is also an *isomorphism of ontologies.* The implicit ontologies of Protestantism and capitalism are by no means identical in content, but they do have a high degree of *structural similarity:* the autonomy of the individual as a rational decision-making entity; the importance and nondualistic nature of individual action and rational calculation; the demystification of nature; and the expansion of secular authority.

The Protestant *ethic* impelled believers to carry out rationalized activity. Possibly more importantly, Protestant *ontology* defined a reality

[handwritten annotation in top margin: W's argument is that "bad" is is necessity to work or status; nothing moral about it]

in which rational activity and organization, including capitalism, made sense and came to be morally binding. Moreover, because the ontology is collectively defined as valid, it affects social action even if an individual is not a believing Protestant (which fits the evidence better than a social- psychological interpretation).

The key Weberian idea is therefore further articulated: The reorganization of culture had important consequences for the rationalization of authority and economy. The destruction of the dominant metaphor of traditional hierarchy and the construction of Protestant rational individualism laid the ontology underlying rational institutions, including both capitalism and state authority (Meyer et al. 1987; Poggi 1983; Walzer 1965). And so, culture was structured by an inner-worldly practical rationality that was myth and metaphor for increasing levels of rationalization.[17]

Environmental Dynamics and Social Movements

The theory so far describes how a cultural environment affects the structure of an institution and how one institution affects another. As formulated by structural anthropologists, the tendency toward isomorphism is cognitive in nature: Perception of the assumed reality of one institution is used to conceptualize and shape that of another. Consequently, the general metaphor is cognitively transposed onto all levels of perception and social organization. In fact, we can document change in one institution and map subsequent effects on others without reference to individual or collective action. Yet, the mechanisms of the production of isomorphism need to be identified. Moreover, the interpretive use of rules and accounts is social in that they are collectively shared and managed by social institutions. The construction of specific rules of the underlying structure, the production of isomorphism, and thus the causal flow of change are carried out by people through collective action and social movements.

Environmental change can decrease the isomorphism between an institution and its environment, resulting in delegitimation. There are several different reactions within an institution to illegitimacy. Those groups that embrace cultural change try to modify the institution to make it congruent with the newly emerging order. It is often the case that these groups first raise charges of illegitimacy. Thus, if there is initially no structure within the institutional sphere that is congruent with the environment, a social movement will emerge to create one. The ontology implicit in the movement's demands rarely is a completely new one but a blending of various old and new elements.

Additionally, there often are several different movements, each espousing a slightly different solution to the legitimacy problem. From the point of view of a particular institution, a social movement uses the environmental myths to work on change internal to the institution—the figure in our earlier metaphor. Given the institutional bias against change and against movements attempting change or otherwise competing with groups in power, such movements gain leverage by grounding their claims in the newly emerging cultural order. From the point of view of the larger order, these movements articulate specific aspects of it—they are working on the frame. Groups, by advancing specific claims, shape further change in the institutional order. Thus, for example a nineteenth-century revivalist and a contemporary member of the new Christian Right are revitalizing the church *and* reworking the cultural order. The school administrator who is using new psychological studies to improve curriculum is also expanding cultural conceptions of the student and supporting certain psychological theories.

Other factions may refuse any change, and working within a different (possibly older) structure, they will attempt to modify the demands of the new cultural myth or buffer the institution from it, or both. Looking at the institution as a whole, there will be movements attempting both internal and external change although different people are in the different movements.

These ideas can be summarized more formally. I distinguish degrees of congruence or isomorphism between an institution and its cultural environment and relate them to corresponding levels of an institution's legitimacy. The greater the isomorphism between an institution and its environment, the more legitimate is its knowledge structure. Low levels of legitimacy lead to the development of an isomorphic structure by factions internal to an institution. Low levels of legitimacy also lead to attempts by other factions to change the cultural environment or buffer the institution from the environment, or both. The idea of constructing a new order is at times explicit in the ideology of a movement while at other times it is implicit in the pursuit of specific goals. In either case, the new cultural ontology is specified in the demands and collective action of such movements.[18]

Carrier movements attempt to organize social life according to changes in the institutional order, and they compete for the support of authorities and the public (Zald and McCarthy 1987). In the absence of coercion, or when analytically controlling for levels of power and force (Tilly 1978), and given a number of competing social movements, each with their own version of the cultural order, that version which is most legitimate (that which is most isomorphic with the sociocultural order) is the one most supported by the public. When there are various groups carrying a range of different knowledge structures, again controlling for power, that group whose ontology and corresponding claims are most isomorphic with the environmental myth will be most successful in attracting adherents and mobilizing resources. In short, there is a tendency toward the more legitimate and isomorphic structures.

This conception of the dynamics of legitimacy is similar to the idea of plausibility structure (Berger and Luckmann 1966), for a knowledge system will be cognitively and morally acceptable when it is plausible relative to material social interaction. The institutionalist model, however, emphasizes that plausibility structure also includes cultural rules—the interpretative knowledge—that are implicit in the organization of everyday interaction. Structural isomorphism is therefore a key aspect of what is or is not cognitively plausible and morally imperative.

A new movement, even one at odds with those in power, then, will be most successful in mobilizing populations or subgroups precisely where its claims make the most sense—where they are most isomorphic with the organization of everyday life and the corresponding cultural order. A social movement will find little support within a group, short of coercion, that is firmly linked to older, traditional structures, and will be most successful among those groups and populations where similar plausibility structures are emerging. It appears, then, that cultural structures in conferring legitimacy make mobilization of populations and resources easier, not simply in terms of organizational capacity but directly through social and material support.

As an example, the Protestant Reformation as a social movement was most successful in regions coming under the rationalizing authority of territorial princes and undergoing political and economic expansion. Similarly, the fundamentalist Islamic movement and the Majumi party in Indonesia found their greatest support in expanding economic regions among both labor and capitalist classes because these classes, although in conflict, nevertheless presupposed the same rationalized world. This support was not found in the animistic and Hindu-dominated hinterlands that were alien to nationalistic Islam, impersonal state authority, and a rational capitalist world (Geertz 1968). This idea is also seen in the early work of Tilly (1964), who argued that the French Revolution was supported where the structures of urbanization were most present; the counterrevolution occurred in those regions that were less urbanized.

An Example: Twentieth-Century Protestantism

The present work is an application of this formulation to religious movements and political-economic expansion. In order to illustrate the scope of the formulation, I will present an example of cultural change leading to religious movements that is related to yet quite different from the political-economic examples. The liberalization of Protestant theology provides such a case. At the turn of the twentieth century, intellectual life became rooted in an existential humanism. Scholarly work had to take place using its categories. The expansion of a technological-bureaucratic order extended this worldview to large sections of the population (Berger 1967). Ellul (1975) emphasizes that this "plausibility structure" is not so much the material organization of social life as it is everyday life interpreted by cultural definitions. For example, the myths of this modern nexus, such as "progress" and "man coming of age," dominate even though there is little empirical reference to them.

A central feature of this mythology is that empirical, scientific, and historical statements are qualitatively different from faith and theological statements. The latter are seen to comprise an outmoded, irrational style of thought, whereas modern thought is said to be based on rationality and "mature" critical thought—on knowledge. The separation of reason from faith (and truth statements generally) has been a gradual historical process, but disassociation was complete in the existentialism and "bourgeois subjectivity" of late capitalism (e.g, Zaretsky 1976).

In the context of this cultural environment, the traditional propositions of Christianity became unacceptable and illegitimate. Two types of movements resulted. Both types accepted the core dichotomy of faith versus reason as well as the mythology generally. The first type, liberalism,accommodated the religious tradition to the new cultural myth. Early in the century, theologians such as Bultmann "translated" Christianity "into terms that made sense within the frame of reference of an existential anthropology" (Berger 1967, 6). Later, these theologians became popular at the mass level, as exemplified by writers such as Harvey Cox. Berger states that in the face of these shared definitions, traditional transcendental "religious lore" became irrelevant to the person in the street, leading to the conclusion that "the remedy lies in reinterpreting the tradition so that it *will* be relevant (that is, subjectively meaningful and practically applicable)" (p. 7).

Liberalism, then, was a movement that applied an existentialist ontology that had emerged as Protestantism's cultural environment. It redefined faith and meaning as subjective concepts that could not be apprehended by conventional reason (e.g. Tillich 1959; cf. Bellah 1970). Ultimate reality (truth) became unknowable apart from an irrational leap as defined by existentialism (or the more mundane) "bourgeois subjectivity").

A second set of movements attempted to maintain Christian statements of faith and theology in the face of delegitimation. Two primary movements developed: neoorthodoxy and fundamentalism. Neoorthodoxy rejected liberalism and much of the sociocultural myth. Nevertheless, it accepted the faith-reason dichotomy built into the cultural environment. Faith and theological statements are distinct from historical and empirical statements. The former deal with the meaning of history, not just with the "facts." One affirms these statements from subjective experience, not by rational discourse. Fundamentalism, unlike neoorthodoxy, maintained the historicity of scripture and theology, but the discussion of truth and the basis of belief still were in the context of the core cultural separation of faith and reason. Fundamentalism denied reason any significant role in the discussion of faith, which was relegated to emotions and subjectivity.

Fundamentalism and neoorthodoxy illustrate that given the subtleties of syncretism and the pressures toward isomorphism, even those groups that take a stand against a movement's applying a new cultural order to an institution often accommodate and conform to that very order.

Therefore, as the propositions and "reasonable faith" of Christianity lost credibility within the cultural myth, different sets of movements emerged. One applied the external structure and translated Christian symbols into a system congruent with the modern myth of humanism. The other attempted to maintain its propositions but used the external myth to structure its defense. As the sociocultural environment continues to change, these movements might modify their theologies, and new syntheses will emerge, as exemplified in subsequent new religious movements.

Competition and Formal Organization

Revivalism was not the only religious movement in nineteenth-century United States; spiritualism, Mormonism, transcendentalism, adventism, and numerous utopian communities all emerged in the same context. Republicanism was not the only new party. The Prohibition and Greenback parties also attempted to organize revivalistic nationalism. Indeed, many observers cite the large number of movements as evidence of cultural breakdown and of a frantic search for meaning.

The institutional model modifies this imagery of individual action building upward to culture; it focuses rather on flows of meaning moving downward from a new cultural order. As already noted, large-scale change generally results in more than one movement or faction that make claims on the institution. These movements embrace change as a source of meaning, each articulating their own vision of the new order. They might focus on different specific issues and strategies, and they may even be in violent disagreement on particular issues, but they all are oriented to the same underlying ontology.[19]

We may refer to a set, range, or "family" of movements operating from the same cultural ontology. Whatever their differences, they share (to varying extents) the same knowledge structure and the same claims to legitimacy. Serious disputes over particulars may be put aside in attempting to restructure the institution, or such disagreements may cause serious problems. Through the process described, one movement often will come to dominate, and its leadership and organization will become recognized as the core of the movement. This is a continuous process in which leaders of one faction compete with those of other factions within the "family" of movements for control of the movement's organization.

Problems of unity among a diversity of issues and strategies dominate the agenda of movement leaders. Much work has been done on the nature of leadership and the evolution of goals and strategies in protest and reform movements (e.g., Gamson 1975), with recent advances focusing on relative capacities for mobilizing resources (e.g., McCarthy and Zald 1977; Tilly 1978; Zald and McCarthy 1987). In the present model, I add the factor that isomorphism with the underlying ontology is crucial to a leadership's (or a faction's) ability to legitimate goals and strategies and thereby mobilize support. To the extent that their claims, goals, methods, and rhetoric are isomorphic with the sociocultural order of a population, the leadership is able to mobilize that population. In asserting this relationship, I omit physical coercion, but include propaganda used to "convince" the population of isomorphism.

Once a movement achieves some success within the institutional setting, ideological and tactical differences become more salient. Increased disagreement over goals and strategies causes growth of splinter groups and competing movements. It is likely at this point that any threat or loss of momentum will result in one of two possible strategies: (1) One faction, interpreting the movement's decline as a result of internal conflict, will attempt to unify around the core goals, organization, and strategies. (2) Others will view the decline as evidence for the movement's inadequacy and will mobilize around competing organizations and leaders. One cannot predict which strategy will prevail, or even if the movement will survive. In later chapters I will use empirical analyses of the shifts of revivalists between the Republican and Prohibition parties to describe some possible courses of action.

In the face of internal dissent and resistance from other groups, formal organization emerges as a crucial factor within a movement. The control of social organization operates materially to mobilize people and resources efficiently for collective action (e.g., Paige 1975; Tilly 1978; Walton 1984; Wolf 1969). Formal organization also operates culturally because it concretizes and specifies the cultural environment; it embeds collective definitions of group goals, boundaries, and membership into ongoing activity. This is especially effective when an organization is defined as *the* movement and *the* institutional carrier of the new order, when the underlying metaphoric structure is equated with the movement's organization.

Thus, the argument concerning the equating of metaphoric structure with formal organization can be applied to social movements. Movements can gain leverage against institutional bias, groups in power, dissident internal factions, and competing social movements. The equating of a particular movement's organization with the cultural frame effectively controls the legitimate use of cultural rules and limits competing factions and movements from being able to manipulate them legitimately, even if their alternative version is just as isomorphic. Thus, internal dissenting factions, competing social movements, and countermovements are hindered in their competition for resources and people. Attempts to shift goals or strategies are defined as immoral, counterproductive, counterrevolutionary, or as not preserving the true nature of the movement. Countermovements similarly are deemed illicit misuses of the themes and symbols of the new order. This perspective suggests that if one movement out of a family of similar ones comes to be identified as the carrier of the new order (even when others might be comparably isomorphic with the cultural environment), then that movement can more easily mobilize support.

This appears to have occurred with individualistic nation-building movements that arose in part with the support of revivalism in nineteenth-century United States. Several political movements emerged throughout the century: Republicanism, Prohibitionism, the Greenback party, and in some respects Bryan's Democracy. Yet, the initial formalization of revivalistic nationalism in Republicanism tended to equate the Republican party with nationalism. As this linkage became institutionalized, other parties increasingly found it difficult to establish legitimacy by manipulating dominant cultural symbols. We will see short-term shifts of revivalistic groups to and from other parties in the family of movements, but these shifts are in the context of the Republican-revivalism alignment.

Further Considerations: Contradictions, Interest, and Power

Using abstract terms such as cultural order or even concrete ones such as revivalism tends to imply a completely integrated system and static congruence. Yet, I have emphasized the dynamics of isomorphism. So, throughout an entire century of change, it is unlikely that institutions such as rival religion or the Republican party could maintain complete isomorphism with their cultural environment. Several historians in fact argue that the Republican party, because of growing inconsistencies with revivalism, lost its support to the Democrats in 1896. Yet, all cultural orders have contradictions and inconsistencies, and formal rules and organizations tend to create tolerance of them. The Republican party was no exception. In order to lay the basis for assessing the dynamics of revivalism and Republicanism in the elections of the late nineteenth century, I discuss cultural contradictions and the roles of special interests and power in the process of isomorphism.

Contradictions

The institutional model describes how social movements construct a unified cosmos that results in various institutions or institutional spheres becoming isomorphic. People use a knowledge structure as a tool (or, as Burke 1950 points out, as a weapon) to make sense of and to organize other spheres of reality. Isomorphism results without being driven by any psychological goal of consistency. Additionally, the tendency toward isomorphism does not mean that there will be complete consistency at all levels. Contradictions and conflicts exist, including contradictory role expectations and rules, the use of certain rules in some situations but not in others, and the inability to classify an entity or a behavior into one and only one category (Douglas 1966). Contradictions counterintuitively may result from the establishment of isomorphism because of different requirements at various levels of organization. For example, it is known from formal organization studies that instituting rational accounting principles at all levels may create glitches or irrationalities: The rationalization of higher levels of organizational accounting may require activity at a lower level that is nonrational within the task-oriented logic of that level (Scott 1987).

Isomorphism also can create contradictions between institutional spheres. Recall the individualism associated with the market. Individualism in the context of market activity emphasizes the impersonal nature of the individual: abstract civil rights, equality, and freedom from personal obligation, charity, or interdependence. Yet, individualism within the moral and religious sphere is constructed around the primordial, sacred value of the person. Moral individualism is the foundation for elaborating the personal motives and needs of the individual. Political-economic liberalism implies rather harsh business practices in contradiction with moral-religious maxims concerning individual value and fulfillment. Yet, both are dialectically integrated ? within the same ontology.

Contradictions such as these may form the basis of radical change (cf. Marx 1967), but the pervasive metaphor of individualism structures all spheres. It is precisely because the various spheres are isomorphic, albeit focused around different dialectical poles of the structure, that normative contradictions appear. The dialectical tension provides a "dynamic stability" in structure.[20]

While possibly stable, such contradictions usually are compartmentalized in some manner. Often the different sets of contradictory meanings are invoked and used in different institutional settings or situations; thus, the contradictions are edited out of ongoing activity. A person or group that never attempts greater integration will in practice ignore the contradictions by using knowledge contextualized within each separate setting. For example, moral "humanitarian" aspects of individualism are explicitly irrelevant to the "business world" of liberal economy. Attempts at synthesis are manifested in cultural work either to justify or to compartmentalize contradictions. Anomalies, marginal entities and events, and contradictory situations and categories are compartmentalized and buffered by ritual rules (Douglas 1966; see also Hughes 1945; Goffman 1963).[21]

Rational bureaucracy, as ritual and ceremony (Meyer and Rowan 1983), is especially effective in dividing up activity and narrowing attention to small component parts. Formal organization provides a functionally consistent integration of the cultural structure: Cultural inconsistencies are pragmatically worked out in formal rules. Internal glitches are edited out at the accounting level even though heightened rationality at all levels results in a larger number and a greater intensity of such irrationalities. In many cases the internal activity of the organization is "decoupled" from its environment so that while the formal structure continues to be adapted to the environmental structure, the actual activity within the organization is effectively buffered from external demands (e.g., Scott 1987).

When a formal organization, whether as an institution or as a social movement, is established as *the* carrier of the cultural metaphor, inconsistencies may increase proportionally to the greater claims. Yet, the equating of formal organization and metaphoric structure tends to be maintained even in the face of growing inconsistencies between the two. The equating process undermines attempts to document lack of isomorphism and to make charges of illegitimacy. A population's commitment to an organization will therefore allow for continued support even if inconsistencies increase.

For example, a revolutionary movement that changes particular policies once it successfully takes power is often able to maintain popular support by emphasizing that its leadership and party *are* the revolution. Factions that would argue that the successful regime has sold out important aspects of the revolutionary program might be delegitimated as being counterrevolutionary: They are counter to the regime that *is* the revolution. When tension over moral issues divided the Republican party and revivalism, late in the nineteenth century, there might not have been a decline in revivalistic support, as many observers have inferred. The then institutionalized linkage might have been maintained in spite of decreasing isomorphism. At the social-psychological level, "bad faith" operates (Berger and Luckmann 1966): A people may not question lack of isomorphism simply because the leadership or the organization is assumed to be the carrier of the order.

Interest and Power

The institutional order is related to patterns and organizations of exchange and to the collective agency involved in having people carry out action, rather than to particular interests that reside in the exchange process. Put another way, the focus and the integration of cultural rules are not constructed around interests, but around the organization of life within which interests lie. Vested interests embedded in a given pattern of exchange and authority will naturally actively construct and support the corresponding cultural rules, but in doing so, they support the order generally that has implications beyond their particular interest. The institutional order sets limits on action according to its own logic, not according to the logic of any particular interest within the system. An institutional order limits the types of material, organizational, and constitutive interests that can be justified.

The present study emphasizes that an institutional order is sufficient to structure action against material interest—and it does so even to the extent of limiting the interest-motivated action of elites.[22]

Within these limits, classes, status groups, or factions do manipulate and modify cultural rules in order to justify and further their own interests. Interest undeniably affects the selection of cultural rules and themes and shapes the direction of change. Such action can result in a lack of isomorphism and in the existence of contradictions.

As already mentioned, groups in power may resist the institutionalization of a new order if it means loss of power and authority. This is true for all organizations from the family to the church to the academic department. Conservative factions, even those not in power positions, may also resist change because of institutionalized commitment to the traditional structure. Such groups may use the formal organization of commitment or "symbolic annihilation" to delegitimate change. They additionally might use threat or force or actual coercion to resist change, resulting in the repression of social movements and their knowledge claims. If interests within a particular institution successfully resist the application of a new order, that institution will manifest low levels of isomorphism with its environment.

The degree to which power and repression are operating and the manner in which they affect isomorphism must be assessed in any study. The model presented in this chapter describes a somewhat ideal typical situation in which such processes are not major factors or in which they can be analytically taken into account. We thus are able to talk about the relative abilities of competing groups to mobilize members and support within a polity. Moreover, I relate their abilities to the relative isomorphism of their worldview to the population's sociocultural structure. This remains valid when groups are in active conflict. What is invalid is to take a particular point in time as an "end state" of change and argue post hoc that certain prior cultural or structural conditions gave rise to it without filling in the historical dynamic that would have included effects of power and interest.[23]

The focus of this study is on religious memberships and voting behavior in the nineteenth-century United States. Coercion plays a relatively minor role in the religious and political behavior of the northern populations that are examined, making them suitable for a straightforward application of the model. However, in the final chapter, when the findings are placed in a larger perspective and the theory is applied to different historical settings, it is necessary to take coercion into account in order to isolate institutional factors in sociocultural change.

33

THREE

An Institutional Analysis of
Market Penetration

Political-economic expansion lies at the heart of historical sociology. It is the "great transformation" of society from social, communal exchange to rational economic exchange; from feudal, imperial authority and traditional kinship and ecclesiastical structures to the rational bureaucratic state; from the cultural dominance of quasi-religious kinship groupings and loyalties to liberal individualism; from agrarian empires to urban industrial nations. It results in and shapes movements which articulate their specific vision of this change.

The source of political-economic expansion, as with change generally, is found in different institutions depending on sociohistorical conditions. The spheres of economic exchange relations, authority structures, and religion may each be a major generator and shaper of change in different historical contexts. The institutional model developed in chapter 2 does not reduce change and its concomitant social movements to the workings of only one sphere, such as economics; thus it can be applied to diverse cases.

In this chapter I apply the model to changes carried largely by the market, not because this is *the* nature of change, but because this is the case before us. In nineteenth-century United States, the national polity was expanding not only through the settling of new geographic regions but also by the reorientation of social life toward national identity, legal structures, and political participation. While political in its constitutive aspects, this reorientation of communal organization to the national polity was brought about primarily through market forces. Previously local and communal markets were incorporated into a larger and more rationalized one. Let us examine briefly the dramatic market penetration that occurred in nineteenth century United States. Then, I will use this and other historical cases to delineate the general features of market penetration and to conceptualize the rationalization process.

Market Penetration in Nineteenth-Century United States

The English colonies of North America were not settled by corporate political powers. Communities were set up by companies for the primary purpose of carrying on trade and by religious bodies independent from Anglican authority (Sweet 1948). The corporate structure of these institutions soon gave way to self-sufficient families organized within local, community-based proto-capitalistic systems (e.g., Bailyn 1955; Bushman 1967). Consequently, the colonies and new nation were more individualistic in both culture and political economy than Europe. The economy flourished and expanded after independence. A moral communal order of obligations and reciprocity shaped capitalistic exchanges, barn raising and credit at the general store being the romanticized symbols. Growth was, of course, still dependent on the policies of Western Europe. Yet, there were no major economic or military threats facing the United States that drained resources or resulted in a strong militaristic state.

The influx of external (primarily English) investments, technological advances in the area of transportation, and increased foreign trade caused an acceleration of growth in the early nineteenth century, especially in the 1830s and 1840s (Heilbroner 1977; Bruchey 1968; North 1961). Growth above all meant the incorporation of local production and exchange into national and world markets.

A myriad of statistics could be cited to show that, except for short depressions and price deflations such as in the early forties, there was large-scale growth in the short span from 1830 to 1850.[1] One could see the effects of incorporation into the long-distance market and the resulting national frame of reference in all areas of social life. Transportation networks composed of canals, roads, bridges, and later railroads; newspapers; political participation in state and national structures; the articulation of law and an influx of lawyers—all characterized this change. People in local communities were well aware of the broader system. For example, after the town had raised bonds to finance a railroad in 1827, a local paper in Ithaca, New York, editorialized, "There is no reason why the direct route from San Francisco to New York may not be through Ithaca" (quoted in Hays 1957, 6). Moreover, many communities sprang up as creations of the broader market. For example, a planned canal branch or railroad line would lead to the construction of new, sometimes boom-towns (Cross 1950).

These communities did not experience any real "transformation" per se, but developed through market dynamics, although individual families would experience a transformation in their move to the town.

Exchange became governed less by a local communal ethos and more by a monetary system. Family farms continued to dominate the North and Midwest throughout the century. Individual families owned their own land (although there was a sizable proportion of mortgages) and dealt directly with local merchants. But, as both production and the size of the market grew, farms increased in specialization. Town craftsmen, regional manufacturing, and shopkeepers replaced home industry, and a new generation of merchants, manufacturers, lawyers, and clerks appeared. The farmer had to deal with strangers in the form of merchants, commodity dealers, and other middlemen and was forced to make rational decisions in terms of the larger commercial market. Uncertainty was multiplied in the world market. To the fickleness of nature were added unanticipated national and international factors that caused prices to fluctuate seemingly at random. If nature allowed a good crop to be harvested, the farmer still was not sure that the produce could be sold at any sort of reasonable price. Moreover, specialization magnified the consequences of failure. In the context of these market dynamics, the individual farmer bore the responsibility for his own success or failure. The yeoman farmer was incorporated into the national market as the head of a modest enterprise. Despite the uncertainty, however, and because of world conditions and U.S. growth, these farmers were quite successful.

Incorporation into larger market systems and the entrepreneurial enterprise that was its consequence occurred unevenly across regions. Some areas remained locally oriented. Others retained forms of dependent farming (North 1961; Moore 1966). The most obvious contrast was between the North and the South. Market penetration in the South was as complete as in the North, but within the constraints of a plantation system. The control of large quantities of land, capital, and labor by the landed class meant that small farmers produced for a rational market, but were dependent on the landowner through tenancy or sharecropping at the edges of a plantation based on slavery. Individual farmers thus were not incorporated into the larger market as the heads of their own successful agrarian enterprises.

At the time of initial expansion, industry developed primarily outside the South. Small-scale self-employed capitalists accounted for much of the production, which was primarily in textiles (North 1961). A wealthy landowner would invest in a set of mechanized looms, employ a female labor force from neighboring family farms, and build a manufacturing house on a river running through his land.[2] In this manner early manufacturing in the Northeast and Middle Atlantic States remained in the hands of petty, usually domestic, capitalists. Early manufacturing in the West was similar. As these small-scale industries grew, they began to replace the manufacturing that occurred on the family farm. The growing town/farm division of labor led to increased monetarization and, again, the incorporation of social life into impersonal markets.

The rapid economic growth between 1830 and 1850 can be summarized for the northern and midwestern states by three points: (1) Local proto-capitalistic communities were incorporated into the more highly rationalized national world-linked market. This was accompanied by linkages to national political-cultural structures. (2) During early expansion both agriculture and industry were characterized by individual entreprenuers. (3) These changes dominated the North and Midwest, as compared to the South, but they emerged and spread at different rates and to different extents throughout these regions.

Market Penetration as Rationalization
Processes and Concepts

We see, then, that incorporation of a community into a rational market entails fundamental changes in social life and the cultural order. Emerging national institutions govern the economy in place of communal rules. Exchange relations are no longer bound by communal relations, identities, and authority, but become organized around individual choice, rational calculation, and national economic development.

A profusion of conflicting, sometimes violent, social movements emerge. Even the gradualism of Western development did not preclude violent conflict (e.g., Moore 1966; Tilly 1975; Tilly, Tilly, and Tilly 1975). These movements are collective attempts to constitute the rationalized sociocultural order. Historically, they increasingly have been politicized attempts to redefine the collective as a nation and the individual as a citizen, and to reorient activity from local communal rules and identities to a broader, external political order. They appear across the range of social spheres, each possibly emphasizing different if not contradictory aspects of the cultural order. Because the transformation is concerned with the cultural theory of reality, these movements often frame their claims within religious symbols. Not infrequently, explicitly religious movements come to be the primary carriers of the new order, shaping rationalization and being shaped by it. Revivalism in the nineteenth-century United States was just such a case.

The nexus of change as a whole encompasses three interrelated processes. These are the emergence, expansion, and dominance of (1) economic exchange within a rational, capitalistic market; (2) a culture of individualism; and (3) impersonal authority within the nation-state with varying degrees of bureaucratization. By the nineteenth century, these institutions characterized a worldwide system of national polities and markets (Wallerstein 1974b; Thomas et al. 1987).[3]

I have referred to these changes as political-economic expansion in order to include the political-cultural aspects. These transformations have many features. Tilly uses the concept of "urbanization" to refer, in addition to the growth of cities, to "the growth of large-scale, centralized activities, increasing differentiation, the development of rationalization, impersonal rules of conduct, and so on." He notes complementary concepts of "industrialization," "modernization," "centralization," "rationalization," and "the growth of the nation-state" (1964, 11), most of which I use at various points for emphasis. To refer to this change in general, I use interchangeably political-economic expansion and rationalization. Following Weber, by rationalization I mean practical or instrumental rationalization which standardizes social organization as a means to abstract ends.[4] Rationalization therefore includes all of the various specific changes and the three general processes of a rational market, state authority, and individualism. Later in this chapter I also develop a concept of "individuation" in order to focus attention on the centrality of autonomous individual action in a rationalized social structure.

There are also a large number of terms used to refer specifically to the cultural aspects of rationalization. Individualism focuses attention on the primordial value of the individual in the cultural order. Yet, it slights the collective, political aspects. A term such as "individualistic nationalism" is possibly more accurate, even though it unfortunately connotes social-psychological emotionalism, and it might be less appropriate for European cases. The point is that corporate reality, far from being destroyed with the passing of the traditional order, is reorganized in rationalized authority structures. This often is manifested in a centralized bureaucratic state (Thomas and Meyer 1984). Thus, "statism" also can convey important collective aspects. I will use "individualistic nationalism" to describe a rationalized cultural order because it captures the nuances of nineteenth-century United States. I will also refer to it by more focused labels to narrow attention to certain aspects of the process: individualism, nationalism, capitalism, statism.

Culture and the Dominance of Rationality

All institutions do not undergo rationalization concomitantly or uniformly (Weber 1930). One institution might be the original or primary force of rationalization, pushing others in the same direction and possibly hindering rationalization in still others. Nevertheless, political-economic expansion results in practical rationality dominating the sociocultural order and structuring the underlying ontology. The cultural dominance of rationality is due to several factors. Materially, organizing exchange within competitive capitalistic markets and organizing authority within bureaucracies are the most efficient means of mobilizing resources, increasing production, and controlling populations. The advantages of rational technique results in dramatic increases in production, long distance trade, state military power, and the entrenchment of capitalist classes. Thus, the dominance of rationality derives in large part from the power and autonomy of markets, the bourgeoisie, and the state.

Aspects of practical rationality as a cultural order also are crucial in its dominance of society. Weber (1946, 1930) describes the inherently expansionistic logic of this system as the movement toward rationality intensifies with increasing levels of rationalization, resulting in an "iron cage." Ellul (1964, 1975) discusses the inexorable, all-encompassing nature of technique, which results in a "technological society." Relevant points in their analyses can be summarized by noting three relatively autonomous dynamics of rationalized culture.

First, as state power and authority and economic production for long-distance markets increase, not only is traditional substantive value stripped from social relations, but value is reconstituted. Value is redirected from corporate groupings to the individual and is linked to structures outside local community and authority. Thus, the primordial value of the individual becomes located in the national market and polity and is constituted by an increasing number of national institutions such as law, education, and elections. The centralization of authority within the state also undermines local authorities. Value devolves from the collective, the sovereign state, into the smallest rational entity, the individual. This abstract individual is collectivized as the people, and purpose is defined as progress which above all is economic growth but also standardized justice and security.[5]

A second dynamic is that institutions come to be viewed as means to ends rather than ends in themselves. Social life is rationally organized as a series of means which it is assumed eventually produce the collective good. Within rationalized accounting, all structures are evaluated in terms of practical efficiency. As the means-ends linkages become longer through increased specialization and rationalization, value becomes increasingly abstract and distant from everyday life (Simmel 1978). For example, building a bridge might ultimately be linked to progress but the linkage is so distant and abstract that it is rarely invoked in the everyday work of a welder. Therefore practical rationality appears more fundamental and real while substantive discussions of value appear subjective and ethereal (Marcuse 1964).

A third cultural reason for the dominance of instrumental rationality is that as traditional resistance becomes delegitimated, conflict increasingly becomes centered around one of the three aspects of rationalization: the state, market, or individual. For example, criticisms of the authoritarian state are based either on individual rights or on the "self-regulating" market. In both cases, overall rationalization is unquestioned, the issue is through what structures value is to be constructed. Similarly, criticisms of the self-regulated market are based on the need to protect individuals as well as the nation from inequalities. Wherever this criticism prevails, it is universally carried out in the name of the individual and the nation by the state. Thus, conflict tends to increase overall rationality, and whether market, state, or individualism is the main dynamic, rationalization ultimately comes to dominate social organization.

These autonomous dynamics of rationalized culture are important analytically because they point to the content of sociocultural change. They guide us in understanding the new order that will emerge and thereby make interpretable the claims and structure of movements arising out of these changes.

Rationalization in Historical Perspective

The dominance of rationality is not a suprahistorical, predetermined force. It develops through the actions of institutions, groups, and movements. Therefore abstractions and generalizations must be conditionalized and rooted in historical analysis. There has been much study of the transition from traditional to modern societies: of societal rationalization and the rise of market and state and concomitant individualism. I draw on this work and apply it to a broad historical base, giving special attention to Europe's transition from feudalism. My purpose here is to delineate general aspects of rationalization across historical cases and thereby construct a general interpretive framework for this form of social change. I emphasize the similarities across cases, although important differences will be discussed. I will focus on the interplay between market and state in political-economic expansion and the broad themes of rationalized culture, i.e., individualistic nationalism. These dynamics, found generally, will then be used to analyze the nature of political-economic change (what I refer to as individuation) in the United States and its relationship to the individualistic nationalism of revivalism and Republicanism, taking into account the unique conditions of the United States during the nineteenth century. In the last chapter of this book, I will return to general historical themes and cases, including movements in the twentieth century, underscoring the differences that these processes exhibit under different conditions.

Traditional Institutions: Authority and Exchange

Feudal, tribal, and other stateless societies can be categorized as low in instrumental rationalization. Authority is embedded in kinship groupings that have quasi-religious significance.[6] There are several overlapping spheres of authority in family, clan, tribe, and religious office. For example, in feudalism the emperor, or overlord, has no direct sovereignty over the population, but only indirect authority through the personal oaths of allegiance taken by vassals, who alone have direct authority over the local population (e.g., Bloch 1961; Poggi 1978; Strayer 1970).

Authority relations are not abstract and legal in the sense of being standardized and universalistic (cf. Parsons 1951). The basis of authority is personal obligation: the allegiance of the subordinate and the patrimonial responsibility of the superordinate (Bloch 1961). Oaths of allegiance and responsibility are governed by one's position within a kin group and that kin group's position in the larger clan and tribe. Obligations define ties within and between families and groups, and they therefore maintain relations among social groupings. The unit of society in which value is immanent is the kin group; people are not individuals in terms of being sources of value but are agents of corporate, collective reality.[7]

Theorists have referred to exchange in such collectives as social exchange, in contrast with competitive economic exchange (e.g., Blau 1964; Levi-Strauss 1969; Polanyi 1944). There is no autonomous economic system because exchange relations are governed by moral rules and communal authority. For example, fair prices, reciprocity obligations, limitations on usury, and prohibitions against the buying and selling of land and labor as commodities are taken for granted within

41

the moral community. Individuals have personal obligations deriving from status identities within the community, and the object of personal pursuit is status honor rather than competitive gain.

Rationalization of Authority: The State and the Individual

Historically, centralizing states emerged in Europe with the successful undermining of empire and of local feudal authorities by the territorial overlords—princes and monarchs (e.g., Anderson 1974; Strayer 1970; Poggi 1978). States emerged in Europe for many reasons, the analysis of which goes beyond our purposes. One relevant aspect was that through the investiture conflict, by the beginning of the thirteenth century, Christendom defined peace and justice as collective goals of secular authority. Strayer refers to this as the creation of external sovereignty deriving from Christendom. With the sovereign authority to pursue the collective goals of peace and justice, princes and monarchs gradually incorporated and mobilized society within central structures. The latter included taxation, a military, a judicial system, a unified monetary system, and national markets. The long-term consequence was that society became organized around one center as means to a collective purpose, broadly defined as progress, and equated in practice with military strength, economic growth, justice, and material and cultural rationalization (Meyer, Boli, and Thomas 1987).

The rise of the state therefore meant not merely the construction of rational bureaucracy, but more fundamentally, the reconstitution of the polity. The expansion of royal courts did not establish efficient central control, but it located local decisions in a broader (national) sovereign authority. Moreover, not only was there economic growth, but the monetarization of society, a standardized currency, and national markets rationalized exchange within the political-economic authority of the central sovereign. On the one hand, local authority of community, church, family groups, and feudal arrangements were undermined. But on the other hand, society, including these institutions, was incorporated into central authority structures and was reconstituted as a national polity.

This reconstitution is characterized by the rise of the <u>individual</u>. Personal identities embedded in kin groupings are defined as irrelevant to power and authority. The fundamental unit of social organization—the primordial quasi-sacred entity that replaces the group—is the individual. This development is defined as the "freeing" of the individual, and progress rhetorically is defined as individual welfare, happiness, and liberty. Social organization is the means to these abstract ends.

We see then that national authority structures—the state—and the individual emerge together (Boli 1987b; Durkheim 1958, 1972). Progress entails nationalism and individualism. This dual aspect is manifested in the institutions of citizenship and "the people" (Bendix 1964, 1978; Thomas et al. 1987). Individuals are directly linked to the central sovereign, at the expense of local authorities, through definitions and rights of citizenship that are both universalistic (Parsons 1966) and abstract (Marx 1963). The citizen is the abstract Individual that is the subject of progress. Moreover, the Individual is collectivized as "the people" or nation. Thus, progress and the abstract goals of society are rooted in the people; real flesh and blood individuals might have to be sacrificed for the good of the abstract Individual.

Rationalization of Exchange: The Market and the Individual

The expansion of individual liberty, even when pursued by the central sovereign for political purposes, initially occurred by the extension of economic liberties to the bourgeoisie. Understanding the dynamics of this symbiotic relation between the state and market over and against traditional authority is complicated but important to our task. A key factor is that just as sovereign state authority is opposed to local communal authorities, so rational exchange within monetarized markets is antithetical to social exchange and the authority structures that govern it. Open, competitive pursuit of private interest, profit, or gain, "filthy lucre" in the language of King James, is viewed as illicit greed that depersonalizes and oppresses. Weber (1961) points out that the depersonalizing aspects of rational exchange constitute the main reason for traditional resistance to it. Not only does it oppress people, but in making impersonal calculation the ground of action, it removes exchange relations from the realm of traditional authority based on personal obligation. Individual motives of gain organized and legitimated in a rational market undermine the fabric of personal ties within local groups and communities. Generally, capitalist markets are in conflict with and undermine local moral authority.

This tension is illustrated in the contradictory nature of the feudal commercial towns. From the Middle Ages through the sixteenth century, economic growth centered in imperial towns. On the one hand because of their profit motive the towns were at odds with the moral prohibitions of traditional society, and they continually strained at these limitations. On the other hand, towns were conservative. They attempted to maintain monopolistic control relative to feudal authorities, against competitive encroachments from other regions, towns, and independent wholesalers, and against the centralizing authorities (Braudel 1981; Polanyi 1944). Moreover, their authority derived from feudal arrangements, and they were quite sensitive to the traditional moral universe that cast the pure unrestrained profit motive as illicit (Poggi 1978). It was for these political-economic and moral reasons that long-distance profit markets were isolated from local social exchange (Polanyi 1944).

Through the fifteenth century, economic growth and the expansion of long-distance profit markets coincided with the consolidation of monarchal authority. The state forced many towns to submit to its authority; other towns were pushed naturally into the alliance because of a common interest in expanding rational markets (Poggi 1978; Polanyi 1944). Whether through military force or interest, economic growth coincided with the incorporation of exchange and economic enterprise into a national polity and market. Social exchange and the local regulating authority structures from guild to bishop were undermined and penetrated by impersonal market and state. For example, national guilds replaced town guilds.

As with the rationalization of authority, market incorporation depersonalizes exchange relations, but it also reconstitutes society. Exchange becomes based on the autonomous activity of individuals who act as agents of their selves independent of group memberships and the interrelations of groups within society (e.g., Durkheim 1933; Marx 1973). Individual action takes place in markets governed by rules of rational calculation, which level individuals relative to kinship status and personal obligation. Rights again play a crucial role. The bourgoisie no longer claim economic liberties as rights due to citizens of the town, but rather as deriving from the centralized state. Thus, rights greatly aided in centralization and rationalization by locating authority in and orienting demands and conflict toward a central national sovereign, at the expense of traditional moral regulators of social exchange.[8] The general point is that state and market incorporate local communities into national institutions that are mutually reinforcing.

Summary

The sketch of feudalism puts into bold relief the tension between traditional community and rational authority and exchange. Feudal authority and social exchange are less rationalized than the moral communities that flourished in the early United States. The latter already were capitalistic and embedded in a nation state. However, tensions and processes were similar to those in a feudal society. Compared to the rationalizing forces of their respective periods (rather than to each other), both societies exhibited patterns of personal relations, moral obligations, and the dominance of the community. Incorporation into national authority structures and markets undermines personal authority, communal morality, and family ties. But this is not so much a breakdown as a reconstitution of social organization. A new order is simultaneously being generated. Sovereignty is located external to the community, or as in the case of nineteenth-century United States, national authority is expanded. The resulting individualism is an outline of nationalism, and this co-emergence of national state authority and the individual is a fundamental dialectic of rationalization.[9]

The transformation of rationalization is by no means a rigid evolutionary single-track process. There are profound differences between the historical European cases and nineteenth-century United States. In the European cases, incorporation into national markets and authority was accomplished largely by a centralizing bureaucratic monarchy that had to deal directly with corporate towns within the context of resisting the feudal authorities of aristocracy and church. Consequently, the nation, individual, and sovereignty were explicitly defined in corporate bureaucratic organization. Generally, when rationalization of the polity primarily originates in the state against corporate societal interests, state formation movements occur that result in bureaucratized centers, France and Prussia being classic examples (Badie and Birnbaum 1983).

In the absence of strong corporate groups resisting change and in the context of a weak central sovereign, incorporation is pushed primarily by market forces. This leads to a more diffuse nationalism and style of nation building: Citizenship and sovereignty are not tightly managed by a bureaucratic state nor mediated by corporate interests but are defined broadly in terms of nation, people, and individual action. It is this case that I have termed market penetration and that characterizes change in nineteenth-century United States.[10]

Individuation as Concept and Variable

All forms of incorporation to some extent locate rationality and efficacy in individual decisions rather than corporate group processes.

I emphasize this general characteristic and underscore the extreme individualistic nature of market penetration in the U.S. case by referring to this change as individuation. I can explain this concept by briefly describing systems at different levels of individuation. An exchange system very low in individuation is a traditional, feudal system, as already described. Other examples of non individuated systems are found in the classical ethnographic literature.

In contrast, in individuated systems, traditional constraints on exchange have been stripped away, and individuals act as agents of self regardless of their relation to the means of production or status group. Owners in both the agrarian and industrial sectors are motivated by private gain, unrestrained by communal obligations. Laborers sell their labor on the market for wages and are not constrained by either law or interpersonal commitment to a particular position or lifestyle. If an individual is restricted to a work situation, it is the result of his or her rational calculation of alternatives with respect to particular market and power conditions. Examples of highly individuated markets are found in the early, petty capitalism of seventeenth-century England and nineteenth-century United States.

Agricultural production is dominated by smallholders and family farms. In such enterprises the family operates the farm and deals directly on the market. Given the small size of the farms and the presence of family labor, little wage or slave labor exists in such systems. Thus, notwithstanding the high risks due to the variability of nature, production within the small-holding agrarian enterprise is centered around the activity of the individual farmer. The farmer may identify with the land, but it is in a very different manner from the aristocrat or plantation owner. Unity with the land results from the work put into it and the produce returned. It is a unity based on rational choice . . . technique, is relatively transferable from farm to farm, and therefore does not result in the binding of a particular family to a particular tract.

A highly individuated industrial sector is characterized by small-scale entrepreneurs. Propertyless laborers sell labor for wages and are "freed" from paternalistic masters and guilds. The owner heads a small shop or business and organizes activity by rational means to attain the best profit. Within a highly commercialized system these enterprises are, of course, interdependent, but each business or shop survives or not according to its ability to meet the requirements of the competitive environment. This "ability" to produce competitively is attributed to the rational activity of the entrepreneur.

As with the reconstitution of the polity resulting from a centralized authority, traditional corporate authority is undermined and society is reduced to the rational action of individuals in the context of new corporate conceptions. Individuals are institutionally defined as abstractly equal with the same motives and the same rational decision-making capabilities. The integration of the market and the universality of rational calculation are attributed to abstract, universal individuals who comprise a nation or people. On the one hand, the nation is composed of individuals, but on the other hand the individual has value only as a member of the polity and realizes that value by actively participating in market and polity. This concept of the individual stimulates nationalism and provides an impetus toward nation building.

There are many examples of rationalized societies lower on the individuation variable than these petty capitalist systems. One is European corporatism as just described: Increased individuation over that of traditional systems is incorporated into rational organizations from state bureaucracies to national guilds to Estates.

A second example, one pivotal in interpreting national development and social movements in the twentieth-century Third World, is when new corporate structures shut off further rationalization: Rationalization is thus increased relative to a traditional system, but only to certain limits. For example, a region may be incorporated into a larger market but only as a peripheral actor (Wallerstein 1974a). Peripheral regions within the modern world system often have agrarian economies based on the exporting of labor-intensive produce. Plantations or other systems with slave or cheap wage labor usually dominate these economies. These systems are capitalist and not feudal (Wallerstein 1974a) and are more individuated than a traditional system in that the owners are carrying on capitalistic enterprise and the laborers may be paid a wage (Paige 1975). Nevertheless they are still dominated by corporate social groupings that lock the system against further rationalization and individuation. Laborers are often subordinate ethnic groups forced into labor in the process of colonization. Capitalist owners themselves are as much dependent on the plantation as an economic unit as the feudal aristocracy is dependent on its land. This similarity is manifested in the aristocratic lifestyle of the plantation owners, their close identification with the land, and their antogonism to entrepreneurship (Lipset 1968).

We see then that gross historical comparisons can be made between market penetration with high individuation and more corporatist forms of rationalization: the United States versus England, the United States and England versus France and Prussia, the United States and Europe versus colonial and peripheral countries. We also can compare regions within one polity, such as the southern plantation system versus northern entrepreneurship in the United States. Moreover, we can make even more finely tuned comparisons within a region. For example, in the northern United States there were many ranches, lumber camps, mining towns, and large farms. All of these enterprises were characterized by a corporate capitalism that was low in individuation. A fine-tuned comparison lets us recognize that, while related to changing historical processes and conditions, individuation as a concept varies within any single historical case across regions, economic sectors, economic enterprise, counties or parishes, and communities. For example, for nineteenth-century northern United States, one could measure individuation as it varied from county to county. Measures might include farm ownership and rates of self-employment and inverse measures would include farm wage labor, size of industrial and farming enterprise, and capital required for establishing and operating an enterprise.

Transformation of the Ontology

Market penetration and individuation result in the transformation of the cultural order. Rationalized society is coinherent with a rationalized ontology. New movements embrace this change and articulate the new ontology. Content and claims are interpretable in the context of these cultural changes. Because of the radical transformation of ontology, movements are implicitly (and often explicitly) religious. Building toward an interpretation of these movements, in this section I describe the content and structure of rational ontology. What is the rationalized ontology of individuation? How does it shape, and how is it shaped by, new (religious) movements?

Dialectics of Rationalization

The content of rationalized ontology is shaped by the three dominant processes of national authority within a bureaucratic state apparatus, individualistic nationalism, and rational capitalism. These are three aspects of rationalization that are dialectically interrelated. I do not use "dialectical" to refer to some vague reciprocal relation. I mean it in its technical sense: They constitute contradictory forces; yet, they dynamically create and recreate each other. For example, the rational market depersonalizes exchange and alienates exchange partners (Marx 1963; Weber 1930); yet, the market also confers primordial value on the individual as an autonomous, rational decision-making entity (e.g., Zelizer 1981; Simmel 1978; Marx 1973; Weber 1968). Individualism frames the expansion of economic liberties crucial to the dominance of the bourgeois and rational markets, but it also is the source of market restrictions for the purpose of protecting the individual from inequalities and injustice.

The state also is often at odds with the "free market" in its attempt to consolidate political authority, to politically define members, and to control exchanges; yet, its rationalization of the polity as nation provides the source and basis of long-range competitive markets (Polanyi 1944). Similarly, the rational market tends toward the destruction of political control, but at the same time it includes standardized exchanges, undermines traditional local authority, and provides revenues for the central apparatus.

Statism and individualism also appear to be opposite forces; yet, the individual emerges only as the state breaks down traditional privileged groups and estates and expands conceptions of citizenship (Durkheim 1958; Strayer 1970; Gierke [1881] 1958; Bendix 1964). In turn, the expansion of human rights in the modern world system provides a ready-made account for justifying state expansion and the national mobilization of individuals (Boli 1987b; Ramirez and Weiss 1979).

The dialectical nature of these interrelations is a source of much conflict and violence. Different movements may mobilize around different poles of the dialectic and consequently be in violent conflict; yet, their ideologies will have much in common, being built on different aspects of the same underlying structure, and they tend to increase overall rationalization.

Problems with Crisis Interpretations

Conventional interpretations of this transformation assume that movements in general and religious ones in particular are functional reactions to the disorganizing aspects of change. There are fundamental problems in these lines of reasoning. I have already dealt with some of the more serious ones related to cultural dynamics (see also Ramirez 1987). The fundamental error of crisis theories in analyzing movements emerging out of market penetration is a misunderstanding of the dialectics involved. They point to the fact that movements appear to reject change, especially the impersonal aspects of rationalization. Because these theories view culture as a monolithic system of generalized values (resulting from functional integration or elite he-

*- this is an incredibly
apropos e.g. of what
Fields called the "cultural"
approach.*

gemony), they interpret this critical attitude as a rejection of or escape from breakdown, disorganization, or alienation.

The institutional model presents a different imagery. Political-economic expansion on the scale we are addressing is rooted in major transformations in the structure and organization of everyday life. Consequently, the old world is destroyed and a new structure of everyday activity gives rise to a new ontology. Geographic regions and institutional spheres undergo cultural change to the degree that they are penetrated by market processes. Social movements are the carriers of this new ontology; they attempt to construct a new order of things. Because the rationalized world is a dialectical one, movements might "reject" one particular pole of the dialectic, but do so by organizing the new order around an opposite pole. That these movements mobilize resources and organize claims around different dialectical poles results in conflict and gives the impression that they are rejecting the whole order.

The phrase "destroy the old and construct a new" is strong language that attempts to capture the scale and intensity of political-economic rationalization. It does not, however, imply a complete discontinuity. Any initial political-economic expansion is possible only given particular institutional prerequisites (Weber 1961; Collins 1986, 19–44). The resulting new ontology is shaped by and built out of elements of the old. Movements that emerge use traditional symbols to frame the change (e.g., Geertz 1968; Walton 1984). This helps account for the illusion that such movements are traditional reactions against change.

The Ontology of Rationalization: Individualistic Nationalism

The rationalization of society generates many changes in the content of the ontology. It is beyond the scope of this work to deal with these transformations in detail; nor do we have the luxury of addressing the institutional sources that led to these particular changes in the West in the first place (see Thomas et al. 1987). At this point I simply want to review the major trends in the conceptions of God, nature, society, and the individual, reiterating and summarizing points made previously. To underscore the nature of cultural change, I refer to the fairly extreme transformation from traditional structures. Then in chapter 4, I will discuss in detail the specific transformations that occurred in nineteenth-century United States. These changes are also dramatic, and proceed in the same direction of rationalization, but they are not as severe as the following contrasts because nineteenth-century U.S. culture already was quite rationalized.

To begin, the concepts of God and the sacred are systematized and simplified by the reduction of animistic spirits and a pantheon of gods to one god. There are very few independent sources of primordial value. As this reduction evolves, the one god becomes increasingly abstract, first as providence and then as an impersonal power, the force of the cosmos or "humanity" (Bellah 1964). Concomitantly, nature is desacralized and stripped of immanent value and ceases to be a source of primordial value (Weber 1968). It becomes defined as a uniform, mechanical system devoid of arbitrary animistic spirits. The uniformity of nature is symbolized in universal laws of cause and effect, and as these increasingly become quantified, nature itself is abstracted, either as mathematical equations or as direct transcendental experience (Marcuse 1964). Rational action and social organization manipulate and transform nature to produce progress.

As both the sacred (the cosmos) and nature are simplified and made abstract, society is desacralized. Social structure, exchange, and authority lose ultimate value and are no longer taken as ends in themselves, but rather as means to the attainment of value exogenous to them. Social organization becomes profane and is rationalized as a set of interrelated means-ends chains. With the transformation in the external cosmos and nature, the ends of these chains become located in the abstract individual, who is now the primordial entity that anchors this ontology. The ultimate source of value is located in individual human security and happiness along with the rights that inhere in individuals, thus, the appropriateness of the term "individualism" to summarize this system.

The individual is abstracted as citizen and rational civic actor. The abstract, primordial individual is defined corporately as the people or nation. Rationalized value is framed rhetorically at the level of the individual, but is reified in the social processes of state and market. Thus, individual needs, motives, and rights are elaborated along with demands of liberty, equality, and welfare, but these devolve from and are worked out at the corporate level of national interest, gross national product, aggregate standard of living indexes, and regime stability.

This ontology anchored in the abstract individual derives from and legitimates the rationalization of the polity: the nation as the people, the market (organized competitively or bureaucratically) as the organization of production, and the bureaucratic state as the conscious carrier of this rationalizing project.

Knowledge increasingly focuses on the personality as a unique and sacred object; each person takes on a more active and often a more sovereign role in relation to the now vague and abstract Holy. In this context corporate religious authority progressively weakens as do all traditional structures. The religious organization becomes either an associational body or a manager of rituals and ceremonies. For example, religious bodies in the United States are primarily voluntary associations (Lenski 1961), selling their worldview on a symbol market (Berger 1963) to individual consumers (see also the analysis of Japan in Davis 1977). On the other hand, churches in Europe tend to manage individual and collective rites of passage and ceremonies.

While religious authority and power decline, corporate reality is not dissolved. On the contrary, religious individuality is universalistic in nature and entails a moral nationalism. Each person is directly tied to the sacred cosmos and to the moral collectivity; this heightens the immediacy and the magnitude of the collective's sovereignty. In short, corporate ecclesiastical authority gives way not just to "personal sovereignty" but also to nation-state authority and power over social life.

In that fundamental cultural change deals with cosmology and ontology, political-economic movements are implicitly religious in the broad sense of the term. It thus is understandable that many movements are explicitly religious (Bendix 1964; Hobsbawm 1959). This means that we have to take seriously not just the power and status positions of the members of a movement, we also have to examine the content of the movement's claims in order to see how it articulates a new ontology as a frame for the new structures of everyday life. New religious movements are specifically concerned with this frame and the religious issues involved. Weber argues that point throughout his work (especially 1946). Other observers have shown that movements such as cargo cults and millenarianism use traditional symbols to embrace, restructure, interpret, and control the new system (Smith 1976; Thrupp 1970). A new order is being constructed, usually using elements of the old.

In summary, the rationalization of society, especially in the case of market penetration and nation building, can be viewed as individuation. The corresponding ontology can be conceptualized as individualism or individualistic nationalism. Where market penetration results in individuation, we would expect to find cultural transformations and social movements toward individualism and nationalism.

Variations in Individuation/Individualism: Efficacy

In the historical discussion of market penetration I noted that European forms of individuation were more corporatist, and colonial/

peripheral development less rationalized overall. There also is variation over time. Petty capitalism and individuation evolve according to rational market processes toward the centralization and concentration of capital and the dominance of the market by large corporate enterprises (Marx 1963, 1967). These changes began to occur in the United States during the latter part of the nineteenth century.

The nature of individualism is fundamentally transformed when everyday life moves from an individuated petty capitalism to corporate capitalism. It is not my purpose here to formally articulate different types of individualisms, although this is an important theoretical task in the long run. For present purposes, it is helpful to address the different form individualism takes in corporatist capitalism in order to (1) assess the maintenance of revivalism as an individualistic religion through the latter part of the nineteenth century and (2) discuss the implications for religious movements within different forms of economic growth in the contemporary world. First, let us examine the extent to which corporate capitalism emerged in the United States.

Corporate Capitalism in Nineteenth-Century United States

As industry expanded, technological innovations in both production and transportation caused factors of scale to become increasingly important. Textiles were the first industry to experience the impact from this change. By midcentury, the iron and steel industry, fueled by the demands of increasing railroad construction, expanded rapidly and became characterized by large corporations and wage labor.[11] Concentrated capital and economic incorporations prevailed in industry by the 1880s and 1890s. Because of the railroad, western manufacturing came into more direct competition with eastern establishments, resulting in greater regional specialization and an increase in urban industrial centers.

Unionization first emerged in the corporate-dominated railroad and steel industries. Yet, until the mid-eighties most unions were general responses to social conditions, and they usually incorporated social reform issues. Not until the Knights of Labor and the more successful American Federation of Labor under Gompers did wage earners organize around specifically economic issues. Moreover, major growth did not occur until the turn of the century when union memberships increased from 440,000 in 1897 to over a million in 1901 (U.S. Bureau of the Census, 1970, pt. 1, 178, Series D 946–51). Before this surge, "from 89 to 99 percent of non-agricultural labor was always outside the union ranks, shifting for itself, fighting its own battles on

53

a single shop basis, depending upon employers, savings banks, private insurance companies, or fraternal orders for security" (Cochran and Miller 1961, 235; Bendix 1956).

Mechanization and factors of scale became more important in agriculture, but were not major factors as in industry. The capital needed for the initial purchase of land and machinery increased, but there was no significant rise in the value of implements and machinery before the nineties.[12] Individual, propertied farmers operating modest tracts of land continued to be the rule—although they were somewhat more dependent on urban financial interests (Hays 1957, 11; Cochran and Miller 1961). In the central states, especially in wheat areas, an increase in mechanization made large tracts of land profitable, leading to larger farms and a centralization of capital and land. Yet, these effects of mechanization were only beginning to develop, lagging far behind those in the industrial sector.[13]

The lack of political-economic power of the yeomanry, geographic isolation of farms, and individualism did not produce successful corporate organization. The agrarian movements of this period often were engineered by merchants, editors, and politicians who attempted to mobilize agrarian discontent for support of their own interests (Hays 1957; Stinchcombe 1961; Paige 1975).[14] Thus, farmers continued to rely on their own resources; "Up to 1933, at least, the farmer remained one of the few competitors in a business society that steadily was becoming less and less competitive. Hence, he almost alone was subject to the classic laws of the *laissez-faire* market" (Cochran and Miller 1961, 213).

In summary, corporate economic organization began to emerge in the last quarter of the century. It prevailed in many industries while in agriculture only the initial effects were felt. Concomitant social movements that could be characterized as more corporatist than individualistic (such as unions and cooperatives) began to be seen, but not to any great extent.

Corporate Capitalism and Individual Efficacy

The development of corporate capitalism does not affect the centrality of the individual in everyday activity, and each person still is constituted as a responsible rational agent of self. This change does, however, affect the nature of the individual. In particular, as the centralization of capital and power increases, the individual becomes more problematic and individual action increasingly lacks efficacy and productivity. Productivity is attributed to the collective enterprise, not to individuals. The self becomes viewed as soft, malleable and ever changing (Swidler, 1981). Rather than being an originator, the personality is considered to be the product of external causal processes or of "deep" internal mechanisms. Thus, corporate dominance within late capitalism is structured by an ontology anchored in a problematic ineffectual individual in contrast to the rugged individual of earlier times.

There are several variables related to the concept of efficacy and corporate dominance. Ownership of land is a basic social distinction within an agrarian system (Stinchcombe 1961; Paige 1975) and may affect the degree of efficacy. If people own their farms, they may have a greater sense of control, attributing production to their own activity. However, related variables of scale of the enterprise are important. The ownership of a farm may require large amounts of capital, resulting in large mortgages, a reliance on banks, a rise in tenancy, and the forcing of many farmers into the laboring class. The capital and social organization needed to market the produce also may be great. If so, the individual farmer cannot perform this task and must rely on middlemen or on a farmers' marketing association. Another variable also related to the importance of scale is the size of the average farm. As scale of operations increase in importance for the economic survival of the farming unit, the size of the farm increases. This results in a decrease in the number of individual farmers and an increase in wage labor. Therefore, factors of scale such as required capital, corporate dependence, size of farm, and need for wage laborers may be more important than mere ownership in determining efficacy.

In the industrial sector, factors of scale have similar effects. The advantages of larger concerns increase with the amount of capital and size of labor force needed for the minimal operation of a business. No matter what one's position in the market, individual efficacy is reduced. For both laborer and owner, success centers more on corporate economic groupings, whether they be industrial organizations or labor unions, rather than on the autonomous activity of the individual.

In general, within systems of exchange dominated by a centralization of value, a person's rational activity remains the focal point, but the individual is problematic and less able to ensure success. Success and production are a function of corporate organization and suprain-dividual factors. Practical strategies are developed concerning the prerequisites of success. The acting out of these institutionalized strategies in everyday action (or, more accurately, the everyday experience of the sanctionable aspect of these strategies—the negative consequences of being an autonomous individual and the positive ones of being in an organizational context) establishes a cultural definition of a problematic, ineffectual person. The reification of this individual results in nationalistic movements that locate the sovereignty of the people within the bureaucratic state or the party, tending more toward state-formation movements.

Individuation and the efficacy of the individual are two different concepts, but they are not totally independent of each other. When a society has a low degree of individuation, there is little individual efficacy. For example, in lumber camps, plantations, or mining towns individuals are not unique, autonomous, and effectual entities. As individuation increases, perceived efficacy also tends to increase. However, individuation may be high and the individual may have little autonomy as in corporatist societies and corporate capitalism.[15] "Effectual individuation" refers to the degree to which a social structure is characterized by high levels of individuation and individual efficacy. It is distinguished from both precommercial organization and corporate capitalism.

The empricial study of revivalism deals specifically with social movements arising out of effectual individuation for this is the system that arose with early market penetration and dominated the northern United States during the nineteenth century. With the rise of big business, distinguishing between effectual and ineffectual individuation—between entrepreneurship and corporate capitalism—will be important for the analysis of revivalism in the last quarter of the century.

Causal Analysis of Specific Transformations

The rationalization of exchange and authority goes hand in hand with the rationalization of ontology. As a general accounting structure, rationalized culture (individualistic nationalism) is rooted in the rational market and the nation-state, but it also forms the institutional frame and preconditions for the rationalization of market and polity. The specific direction of causality from one institution to another will depend on the historical context and the particulars of the situation. Building inferentially from our comparative historical discussion, general propositions concerning the nature of political-economic change can be made. I delineate several which, taken together, form a framework for concretely interpreting nineteenth-century change and revivalism.

1. The rationalization of authority and exchange is possible only when in the first place culture defines the individual as a relatively autonomous entity acting rationally in a relatively disenchanted cosmos (Weber, 1930; Collins 1986, 19–44).[16] In the case of nineteenth-century United States, the extreme individualistic and nationalistic form of rationalization largely was shaped by the already high levels of these cultural elements. For example, the rational individualism of Puritanism, the Enlightenment, and the First Great Awakening laid the groundwork for initial expansion within the early republic and the intensification of revivalism in the nineteenth century.

2. When a rationalized market and polity increase in value and individuate social life, each person becomes accountable as the primary unit of action. Because the individual dominates everyday life, the "personality" as a social concept is placed in a primary position in the emergent cultural knowledge. In general, any entity that is the focal point of activity and attention becomes the primary element around which the cultural order is organized.

Efficacy within everyday life, as a related quality of individuation, affects the nature of the resultant individualism. When persons are routinely confronted with practical rules and strategies that support them as effectual, autonomous entities, the personality within cultural knowledge is seen as an autonomous causal agent, acting on, manipulating, and to a degree producing its environment. Thus, effectual individualism depicts the personality as oriented to direct control of the external environment—rational action.

3. When rational exchange and authority are institutionalized and dominate social experience, cultural accounts are rationalized and radically centered on the individual, and individualism is institutionalized as an underlying interpretive structure. As a guiding myth and metaphor, individualism comprises a cultural environment for institutions and institutional sphere. It thereby affects knowledge in all social spheres resulting in isomorphism.

4. The specific form the rational ontology takes is in part a function of relatively autonomous cultural dynamics and in part a function of the driving forces of political-economic expansion. When the latter is driven largely by market forces, the individual is defined in terms of nation and people—nation building. When political-economic expansion is rooted largely in the state, the individual is defined by state membership—state formation. The particular version of the ontology is also affected by the content of the world system as a whole and by the location of the particular country within that system.

5. Social movements emerge as carriers of change by specifying the cultural order. The institutional model views this in two complementary ways. First, it can be said that the underlying cultural structure is used to restructure the rules and organization of an institution. But the given institution is an integral part of the larger order and is itself part of the frame for other institutional spheres of action. Thus, a second view is that such movements construct the new cultural order by specifying it within a particular institution. For example, religious movements use the new cultural order of individualism to rework religious symbols and organization. In the very act of doing this, they use religious symbols, including traditional ones, to specify, fill in, and in general construct a particular version of rationalized ontology.[17]

6. If a specific institution such as religion frames change, that institution may become the "manager" of the new cultural order and therefore directly affect change and social movements in other spheres. For example, any given religious specification of the cultural order will narrow the range of possible political movements and ideologies. Competition among institutions may result. As a political movement gains in strength and its ideology is institutionalized, the movement may challenge the privileged status of the managing religious institution. If it is successful in ousting the religious management of the polity, the result might appear as secularization, although overall religiosity might diminish only subsequently as a result.

7. Political-economic expansion does not develop uniformly across geographic regions or institutions. Those most dominated by this expansion will experience the greatest change in cultural ontology and resulting social movements. In short, where we find the effectual individuation of everyday exchange, interaction, and authority, we expect to find that the cultural order is characterized by effectual individualism. Additionally, the framing of the change by an institution, for example, religion, will also vary across regions and institutions. The degree to which a particular (religious) articulation occurs within a region or institution will affect the support for corresponding, isomorphic (political) movements. The following three implications relate isomorphism to empirical patterns of institutional change and social movements and thereby capture important dynamics of nineteenth-century United States:

Implication 1: The more exchange is characterized by effectual individuation, the greater the legitimacy of an effectually individualistic religion, and the greater the growth in adherents of such a religion.

Implication 2: The more exchange is characterized by effectual individuation, the greater the legitimacy of an effectually individualistic political ideology (individualistic nationalism), and the greater the growth in adherents to that ideology.

Implication 3: The more a religion of a population is characterized by effectual individualism, the greater the legitimacy of an effectually individualistic political ideology (individualistic nationalism), and the greater the growth in adherents to that ideology.

8. There are important conditions which must be considered in applying these implications. First, central, sometimes coercive, apparatuses of state and established church might manage material and cultural change. Also, classes and status groups often resist change. The exercise of influence and especially of power and coercion by such groups will affect the manifestation of these relationships. The processes behind these relationships will still be at work, but in order analytically to expose them one must take into account coercion and power. Second, when inefficacy is built into an individuated system, the individual personality still remains autonomous and the focal point of knowledge, but it and its activity are seen as ineffectual and problematic.

In summary, we have moved in a spiral from a fairly abstract model of change and social movements through a "middle-range" theory of market penetration to three specific implications. These implications, along with the other generalizations, form an interpretive framework that specifies and conditionalizes the abstract model developed so far. The general model, of course, has many implications; these particular ones have been drawn because of their relevance to nineteenth-century United States. Applying them to revivalism in the United State simultaneously tests the theory and provides a novel approach to revivalism. I develop this in the next section by elaborating the three implications, which can be summarized in the following argument:

Political-economic expansion in nineteenth-century United States was driven by market forces. This market penetration, coupled with the low level of statist organization within the new republic and with the nature of the world system during the nineteenth-century, resulted in petty capitalism in the North and West. High both in individuation and individual efficacy, this change resulted in an ontology fundamentally rooted in the rugged individual. The lack of a dominant coercive center in either state or established church allowed social movements grounded in individualistic nationalism to flourish. Those regions most penetrated by market forces and dominated by effectual individuation moved toward and maintained an ontology of individualistic nationalism. This to a great extent was accomplished through revival religion.

Market, Polity, and Ontology in Nineteenth-Century United States
The National Polity within the World System

The American Revolution left three major factions vying for political control. The first, as represented by the Articles of Confederation, visualized the collective as a set of distinct nation-states loosely bound together for the interests of common defense. The second, the Federalists, pushed for a relatively strong federal administration that would actively support American political-economic endeavors in competition with Europe. In between these factions lay the Democratic-Republicans or Jeffersonians. They argued for the importance of the nation and the federal government, but the nation was to be realized through individual action, not through the construction of a strong central regime (Lipset 1963). Immediately after the war, the Federalists dominated the polity; yet, there was a gradual movement toward the Jeffersonian ideal of a strong nation built on individual action and a weak central administration.

The causes of this movement are many—I will review them only briefly here. One causal factor is that the religious-cultural elements of Puritanism and the Enlightenment and events such as the First Great Awakening articulated aspects of rational individualism and a democratic republic. Additional causes are found in the nature of the world system and the position of the United States in it. The world polity was dominated by the British laissez-faire model which delegitimated strong bureaucracies. There was no long-term military or economic threat to the United States. The only interested and capable power, England, was too preoccupied with conflicts in Europe to continue military expeditions or to complete ones started, as in the War of 1812. Also, the United States was a dependent peripheral region, shipping raw materials to Europe in return for manufactured goods. Consequently, there was no direct economic competition with European industry and therefore no economic or political interest on the part of Europe to threaten American political independence. Internally, the Federalists were not entrenched in either a privileged economic stratum or in a strong bureaucratic state. The lack of such corporatist structures meant that change did not depend on controlling and expanding state policy (Lipset 1963). Thus, because of these factors, and in contrast to Europe, the new nation was organized more by individualistic nation building than by a central bureaucratic state. The expansion of the American polity was effected largely by the growth of the rational market: the penetration of local communal markets by national, largely worldwide processes.

Nevertheless market growth was stimulated by federal support, even after the decline of the Federalist influence, and also by flows of capital from abroad, especially from England (Lipset 1963; Hobsbawm 1968).[18] Federal support, the influx of foreign capital, the resulting construction of an efficient internal transportation system, and an increase in world trade all dramatically increased the rate and extent to which local communal markets were incorporated into the larger world system, as described earlier in the chapter.

Viewing markets as institutions underscores the fact that the political-cultural aspects of market penetration do not form a superstructural order that functions to legitimate a particular interest, but constitute an integral accounting frame of the market.[19] The shift from social exchange relations and kin obligations to rational calculation shifted the accounting frame of action from communal and family authority to that of nation and citizenship (Ryan 1981). Social identities and accounts became located in the nation; individual economic action was oriented to private profit, but in the context of national growth. In the United States, the constitutive aspects of the country were "carried" by the market. To be incorporated into and to act within the national market was to take part in the constituting of the polity. Conflicting interests manipulate, restructure, and ignore various aspects of this order in pursuing private or class ends, but the accounting order is itself relatively autonomous, having important effects on behavior and polity.

Two seminal works on these issues in general, and on the American polity in particular, are by Lipset (1963) and Moore (1966). While divergent in interpretation and theoretical framework, both emphasize the political-cultural nature of economic growth and of the emergence of democratic polities. Lipset views as crucial to the stability of any modern state the construction of a legitimating rational order that institutes national unity, membership in terms of equal citizenship, and broad rules of pluralism and tolerance. These requisites were attained in the United States by the extension of democratic values such as individual autonomy and responsibility, equality of opportunity, and personal achievement. These general values were supported by a successful petty capitalism and by the unique individualism of American voluntary religion.

Lipset's analysis is couched within a consensual model so that the construction of the legitimating order is viewed as the gradual emergence, through various levels of conflict, of a consensus on the rules of the game. In this manner, conflicts do not emerge over basic institutions but are restricted to particular issues within the polity. The consensual model leaves problematic the origin and content of specific political frames. The concern is how consensus is forged and that it in fact is forged, often with an overemphasis on an intellectual elite coupled with a mass internalization of general values (Bendix, 1978). Yet, whatever the shortcomings of the approach, it does point importantly to the role of a legitimating order in framing conflict.

Moore also takes as critical the political—used in a broad sense— aspects of political-economic dynamics, but parts from a consensual conception. "Consensus by itself means little; it depends what the consensus is about" (1966, 139). Moore argues, as does the present study, that important developments in nineteenth-century United States cannot be explained by reference to material interest. Rather, the expansion of the market as a social institution organizes life in particular ways and therefore not only structures interest, but also constitutes and is constituted by political, cultural, and moral structures. For example, Moore argues that the difference between the North and the South was not simple economic interest, but also concerned issues over the very nature of society: "the ultimate causes of the [civil] war are to be found in the growth of different economic systems leading to different (but still capitalist) civilizations with incompatible stands on slavery" (p. 141). In particular, both nationalism and revivalism were initially similar for the North and South, but evolved in divergent directions. It therefore is crucial to understand the context of political-cultural frames that are associated with political-economic expansion.

Ontology, Revivalism, and Republicanism

With the American polity already showing high levels of individualism, market penetration in the North and Midwest resulted in an intensification of individualistic nationalism. The individual became the center of cultural order and social organization. Individual freedom, security, and happiness became core collective goals. This change was celebrated as the progressive freeing of the individual, and "values" of autonomy, responsibility, achievement, and the like were all attributed to the "rugged individual." Rationalization undermined local communal obligations, and rational authority was located diffusely in the nation and national institutions such as law and elections. Individualism and rationality were directly coded into the conception of the people, primarily through the categories of citizenship, progress, and civilization. Thus, as in other such systems, the concept of the individual was abstract and collectivized as the people and nation, and individual happiness entered social accounting as the collective good or economic growth. The yeoman farmer and entrepreneur were the living expression of the underlying ontology, but economic growth was the fundamental criterion of national success.

Despite the somewhat secular nature of these changes, to a great extent they were brought about by religious movements, and revivalism was one of the most successful. Revival religion embraced the new ontology, articulating it within already individualistic categories, but modifying the symbols to fit the new myth of individualistic nationalism. In some respects, revivalism manifested secularization. Deism in many ways was built into mainstream Christianity (see McLoughlin 1978) by revivalism's viewing God as the creator of a mechanical universe. Nature was reified as "natural resources" which individuals were to use to produce the Kingdom of God through rational action.

Within this system, the individual was autonomous, even with respect to God's sovereign grace in that people chose to accept or reject salvation. Mechanical nature was extended to include rational human choices: Decision making, including spiritual decisions, was governed by mechanical laws that were to be manipulated for the sake of evangelism. All of these aspects led to the possible perfecting not only of the individual before death, but also of the collective before the return of Jesus. The meaning of history centered on the work of Christ and looked toward the millennium, but this history became more closely linked to the progress of civilization than to a mysterious divine plan.

Four elements of revivalism summarize the transformation not only in theology but in ontology generally: (1) free will and individual conversion experience, (2) rational methods of evangelism and sanctification, (3) perfectionism, and (4) collective optimism or postmillennialism.

Revivalism as it evolved in the North and West led to moral crusades that had the goal of morally defining citizenship and the nation: The Kingdom of God would be established by the moral actions of citizens. The moralistic link between revivalism and American civilization led naturally to the emergence of and support for various political movements. Antislavery and temperance grew directly out of revivalism. Republicanism, and later various third-party movements such as the Prohibition party and the Greenback party, were political movements that attempted to specify the new order in a theory of authority and society and to a great extent were framed in revivalism. The category of "citizen" was a key symbol used throughout to define abstractly equal individuals and to link them to the sovereignty of the nation. These movements were still suspicious of centralized bureaucratic authority, but they were relatively willing to expand that authority to insure the collective goals of a moral citizenry, economic growth, and the sovereign rule of the people.

Theoretical Interpretation and Hypotheses

The interpretation of political-economic change in the nineteenth-century United States is a straightforward application of the theory and already has been alluded to in several places. Because of internal cultural and economic characteristics, and external world-system factors, the American polity was not organized around a strong central bureaucratic state. Rationalization via political-economic expansion was carried by market penetration as evidenced by the rapid economic growth between 1830 and 1850. In the North and Midwest this took the form of a petty capitalism, and within the frame of the new democratic republic this led to a transformation in the sociocultural order to individualistic nationalism. A large number of social movements emerged, each attempting to articulate the new order.

Just before the economic takeoff, the revivalism of the Second Great Awakening marked a shift in American religion; it marked the emergence of an individualistic religion that structured the early polity. With the rapid increase in rationalization, a political process carried by the rational market, revivalism concomitantly grew into a dramatic movement in the late twenties. In articulating a more extreme individualistic religion, revivalism simultaneously specified the expanding ontology of individualistic nationalism and framed that change within a religious morality geared toward establishing the Kingdom of God.

Thus, with the absence of a bureaucratic state and an established church, revival religion became an important institutional manager of the American project. It by no means had a monopoly (official or informal), and there were many secular versions, but revival religion dominated the cultural order. A broadly accepted civil religion and the Kingdom of God ideal were specified and expressed by it.

Subsequent political movements arose in an attempt to specify politically the nature of authority and society within individualistic nationalism. These movements ranged from antislavery to temperance to the Republican party. Some grew directly out of revivalism; all, including the Republican and Prohibition parties, were framed within the revivalistic ontology. As the Republican party itself became institutionalized, it competed for dominance and control of the core political metaphors. It finally purged direct revivalistic control by 1892, although revivalism still greatly influenced it.

This interpretation of revivalism can be summarized in three statements, corresponding to the three implications for market penetration, for the North and Midwest:[20]

1. The more a population was organized within effectually individuated exchange, the more it embraced revival religion.

2. The more a population was organized within effectually individuated exchange, the more it supported the Republican and Prohibition parties.

3. The greater the prevalence of revival religion within a population, the greater the support for the Republican and Prohibition parties within that population.

The adequacy of the interpretation depends on the existence of structural isomorphism among the three institutions; all three are viewed as being characterized by individualistic nationalism. In chapter 4, I describe the content and structure of revivalism and Republicanism. I demonstrate the individualistic and nationalistic aspects of revivalism and why it should be viewed as a frame of a new rationalized order. I then show that this causal argument runs counter to major interpretations found in the literature on revivalism. The same process then is carried out for Republicanism, although here there is much agreement with the literature. The adequacy of the interpretation depends also on the three institutions occurring concomitantly. Given isomorphism of content, the interpretation hypothesizes a pattern of causal interrelations as described in the three statements. Chapter 5 builds on the phenomenological and structural analyses of chapter 4 by formally testing the three hypotheses relating market individuation, revivalism, and Republicanism.

FOUR

The Social Meaning of
Revivalism and Republicanism

In this chapter my primary purpose is to document that revival religion and Republicanism are individualistic and nationalistic in structure and content, and to explore their relationship to changes carried by the market. In so doing, I also hope to convey the optimism and goals of the revivalists. I briefly sketch the early context of the American polity with respect to each institution and then describe the new content of revivalism and Republicanism. I relate their content to the evolution of market penetration, and conclude with an institutionalist interpretation. Finally, I compare this interpretation with those found in the literature. The interpretation of Republicanism is largely congruent with that in the literature, while that of revivalism departs in most respects from previous studies.

I contrast each institution with eighteenth-century religion and polity in order to show the radical change that was occurring. For my purposes a detailed account of the earlier period is not necessary, and it would be a distraction from my primary interest in nineteenth-century change. For similar reasons, the chapter does not explicate the effects on revivalism of divergent sectional development and issues; it simply notes how early southern revivalism, sharing much of the content described here, became institutionalized within an evangelicalism that had importantly different emphases and political-economic linkages. Finally, this chapter is not an historical narrative; events are recounted only to document larger trends and the development of institutional content and structure.

Revival Religion
Early Context

Christianity in the United States was always more individualistic and pietistic than in Europe (Sweet 1948). During the colonial period, this individualism remained within the framework of Puritan Reformation theology and was integrated into a strong community (e.g., Berthoff 1982). The eighteenth-century revivals of the First Great Awakening under Jonathan Edwards and George Whitefield coupled with the failure of Wesley's sojourn to the colonies exemplify the continued dominance of Reformation beliefs: the total depravity of fallen humanity, the bondage of the will, the sovereignty of God, election, and the irresistibility of grace. Excesses of emotionalism and antinomianism existed, but did not prevail (e.g., Hofstadter 1962). Nevertheless, during this period, and especially after independence, there was an increase in Arminian theology, which emphasized free will and the sovereignty of the individual, and also a growth of secularization and deism.[1]

The Second Great Awakening at the turn of the nineteenth century focused on individual conversion experience. It thereby reinforced the individualism of petty capitalism and of democratic rationalist theory. The revivals of this period showed significant changes in religious content and structure. These changes were intensified with the wave of revivals that swept the country, and especially the North, in the twenties and thirties. What was beginning gradually to appear throughout the country in the Second Great Awakening accelerated and intensified in subsequent northern revivals.

The nineteenth-century revival was a complex institution. Two predominant characteristics were individualism, as reflected in Arminian theology, and emotionalism, as seen in the methods of the revivalist and in the nature of the camp meeting (Weisberger 1958, 19). The latter has been emphasized over the former in a literature which hypothesizes that revivalism was escapist. However, the nature of its individualism and the resulting effects on the secular and political behavior of the revivalists have been acknowledged (e.g., Smith 1957; Hammond 1979; Ryan 1981), and it is this which I view as crucial.

Revivalists varied in their orthodoxy, but the common thread was that they defined the individual as the unit that approaches God and chooses to be saved or not. A central belief was that an emotional, life-changing experience marked salvation, and one maintained religiosity and salvation through continued experiences, inward piety, and right moral behavior. Therefore, while the individual's relation to God was a unique one, it had to conform to the definitions of a true salvation experience and a subsequent moral lifestyle.

Much of this approach was shared with the European pietistic tradition and was built on Protestant themes. For example, "revival" is a Protestant and especially a Puritan concept. The First Great Awakening developed a focus on an "experimental religion" which was fully integrated into the Puritan system. The focus on revival during the First Great Awakening certainly laid the groundwork for the rationalism and individualism of the revolutionary period and articulated elements that would be elaborated by nineteenth-century revivalists. However, nineteenth-century revivalism was centered on rational self-determination within a mechanical universe. It shifted its base from the action of a sovereign God and from the moral authority of community to autonomous rational human action in nature. These revivalists parted company with most of European and American Reformed theology including mainstream eighteenth-century revivalism. For example, Berthoff (1982) and Bellah (1975, 16–20) describe the nineteenth-century transformation of the communal nature of Puritan individualism. Hofstadter (1962), who takes great care in pointing to continuities with the First Great Awakening (e.g., pp. 58, 64), describes the Evangelicalism and revivalism of the nineteenth century as "a new and distinctive Christianity" (p. 81).

This "new Christianity" built on earlier religion and Puritan revivalism; but is also syncretized Arminiamism and deism (McLoughlin 1978). In doing so, it departed radically from eighteenth-century religion. The revivals of the 1820s were a quantum jump in the institutionalization of this radically different religion. This is reflected in the splintering of almost all denominations over the revivalism issue (Ahlstrom 1972; Gaustad 1966; Mayer 1956; Mead 1965; Pritchard 1976).

Four components illustrate the distinctive individualistic nationalism of nineteenth-century revivalism. They are free will, rational methods of evangelism, perfectionism, and postmillennialism.

Free Will

Freedom of choice was basic to nineteenth-century revivalism. God was viewed as a somewhat passive actor whose will was accomplished only through the free activity of individuals. Tyler (1944, 23) takes as the central issue the question, "Is the will of man completely free or is it wholly subject to the 'stable' will of God?" Methodism, the earliest and purist denominational organization of revivalistic piety, emphasized "the gospel of free will and free grace, the belief that men are equal before the Lord, and the tenet that each must obtain his own salvation through conversion" (Tyler 1944, 34). Charles Finney, the leading revivalist of this period and a name synonymous with revivalism, asserted that regeneration itself, the creation of a new, pure heart, was the result of the will of the individual. To say that regeneration is the work of God is misleading for, emphasized Finney, "*Conversion or regeneration is the work of man;* . . . God commands you to make you a new heart, expects you to do it; and, if ever it is done, you must do it" (1835, 197). The freewilled response of the individual was built into the revival meeting. A person sat on the "anxious bench" away from kin and friends as an individual. A person that did sit with saved kin (parent, spouse, aunt, or uncle, who might have cajoled the person into attending) went forward alone as a public display.

By constructing a system based on free will, people rejected the belief that human nature was corrupted with the fall (e.g., Bellah 1975, 75–76). Human nature was still good, and an individual chose to do good or evil. "Finney did not in fact affirm the existence of . . . a fallen nature and argued that humankind was fallen in its dispositions, not in its nature" (Smith 1980, 26).

> Sin then is not any part of our physical or mental consti-
> tution. It is no part or principle of nature itself but a voluntary
> state of mind, that is, an action or choice of the mind, a
> preferring our own interest, because it is our own, to other
> and higher interests. (Finney 1980, 117)

These same ideas are found in the New Divinity of Nathaniel Taylor and Lyman Beecher. Divine influence never "contravenes the freedom of the subject" (Smith 1980, 12)![2]

Free will and individual autonomy led to a decline in the role of a corporate church, not only in conversion, but also in sanctification (the growth in spirituality and holiness) (Sweet 1948). Revivalists valued subjective religious experience and direct revelation as sources of wisdom and knowledge more than systematic church instruction. They relied more on the personal leading of the Spirit than they did on certified theologies and doctrine (see Sweet 1944; Smith 1957, 139). They deemphasized the importance of doctrine and focused on the emotional and ethical responses of individuals. For example, Methodism was labeled the "creedless religion of the heart" (e.g., Tyler 1944, 34). Yet, extreme antinomianism was not embraced widely because creedless religion was expected to lead to well-defined experiences. For example, the emotional display of a person at a revival, while starkly individualistic, closely conformed to an expected model. Moreover, such experience was to lead to a pious and moral life.

This emphasis on piety and morality over doctrine had special appeal within the pluralistic context of the new republic (Lipset 1963; Handy 1984). In making this connection, Lipset discusses the descrip-

tions of religion in the United States by several contemporary observers. "In 1860 Anthony Trollope was struck by the fact that 'everybody
is bound to have a religion, but it does not much matter what it is' "
(Lipset 1963, 176–77; Trollope, [1860] 1951). Tocqueville (1945, 314)
observed that each denomination worships in its own way, "but all sects
preach the same moral law in the name of God . . . and provided the
citizen professes a religion, the peculiar tenets of that religion are of
little importance." After a visit around the turn of the twentieth century to various churches in North America, Weber stated that generally
"congregations refused entirely to listen to the preaching of 'dogma'
and to confessional distinctions. 'Ethics' alone could be offered" (1946,
307). William Miller, in characterizing American religion as individualist, freewilled, and pragmatic asserts, "The penumbra of beyondness,
absoluteness, and mastery fades away, and leaves—as the core of what
Americans think religion to be—the moral" (1961, 94).

Revivalist doctrine tended to be broad enough that few were excluded. If revivalists engaged in "divisive disputes" it was over revivalism itself, and they quite frequently did just that. In this sense,
revivalistic doctrine legitimated the "new measures" and their Arminian foundations. For example, the *New-York Evangelist*, an inter-
denominational revivalist paper in the first half of the century,
contained two front-page headings: revivals and doctrine. The latter
concentrated on issues specific to revivals. For instance, the 26 January
and 2 February 1833 issues contained a continuing editorial on "Cause
and Effect Within Revivals" and a two-part reprint of a sermon by
Lyman Beecher on "Dependency and Free Agency." The section on
revivals gave accounts of events throughout the country. Reports of
conversions hardly ever stated that people came to see the truth of
Christian doctrine. Rather they described the number that expressed
anxiety about their salvation with tears and emotional effects, and the
number who showed signs of inward piety as displayed in outward
morality. The authenticity of conversions was not judged by doctrine
as was insisted upon in the eighteenth-century, but by the intensity
and quality of the experience. Thus, the increase in individual autonomy and rationality coincided with emphases on morality and,
counterintuitively, subjectivity.

Rational Methods of Evangelism

The second element which emerged within revival religion was what
some have described as voluntarism or persuasion. Because of dises-

tablishment, one was both free and required to recruit individuals and establish collective goals through persuasion (Handy 1984; Lipset 1963; P. Miller 1961). Yet, revivalism went beyond a mere voluntarism; it proposed a rational unity of the natural and supernatural that allowed Christians to attain spiritual results through the manipulation of the laws of nature. The revivalists coupled radical free will and self-determination with a mechanical nature, requiring systematic strategies of evangelism and sanctification.[3] For example, a writer reporting the labors that went into a revival stated, "The exertions were reduced to system. A regularly organized plan was adopted" *The New-York Evangelist*, 12 January 1833).

Women, who constituted a large majority of church memberships before the revivals, constructed the infrastructural organization of revivals. The systematic work theorized by male revivalists was carried out, and often initiated, by women in prayer groups, maternal associations, missionary societies, and fund-raising boards, and who in the end brought unsaved husband, children, and boarders to the meeting (Ryan 1981).

The most well-known and representative articulation of the new measures is found in Charles Finney's *Lectures on Revivals*.

> There is nothing in religion beyond the ordinary powers of nature. It consists entirely in the *right exercise* of the powers of nature. . . . [A revival] is not a miracle, or dependent on a miracle, in any sense. It is a purely philosophical result of the right use of the constituted means—as much so as any other effect produced by the application of means. . . . There is no *natural* event in which His own agency is not concerned. (1835, 13, 21)

Within this view, each person is capable of choosing good or bad and this choice is governed by mechanistic laws of the mind. The will and decision making are governed by laws of "excitement" wherein the will is controlled by the focusing and raising of attention through excitement. Again, we see emotionalism as an integral aspect of rational individualism.

> The great political and other worldly excitements that agitate Christendom, are all unfriendly to religion, and divert the mind from the interests of the soul. Now, these excitements can only be counteracted by *religious* excitements. . . . (Finney 1835, 11)

"Excitement" is necessary because of humanity's fallen dispositions and "if the Church were far enough advanced in knowledge, and had stability of principle enough to *keep awake*," this would not be so. But,

> there are so many counteracting causes, that the Church will not go steadily to work without a special excitement. As the millennium advances, it is probable that these periodical excitements will be unknown. . . . But so long as the laws of mind remain what they are. . . . There must be excitement sufficient to wake up the dormant moral powers, and roll back the tide of degradation and sin. (Finney 1835, 11–12)

The Christian was responsible for developing strategies and manipulating laws of the mind to bring about conversion decisions. Thus, conversion itself is as much attributable to the evangelist and his measures as to God. "If, therefore, one [church] is visited with a revival, and another not, the fact must be attributed to the use of means in the one case, which are wanting in another."[4] The primary criterion of the proper evangelistic technique was success—the number of converts (McLoughlin 1959).

> The amount of a minister's success in winning souls (*other things being equal*) invariably decides the amount of wisdom he has exercised . . . the amount of wisdom is to be decided, "other things being equal," by the *number* of cases in which he is successful in converting souls. (Finney, 1835, 183)

It therefore was necessary to adopt "new measures" in order to effect large numbers of converts. Finney goes so far in his vision of an ordered set of mechanical laws governing human will as to say, "Perhaps it is not too much to say, that it is impossible for God Himself to bring about reformations but by new measures" (1835, 269–270); and, "God has found it necessary to take advantage of the excitability there is in mankind, to produce powerful excitements among them, before He can lead them to obey" (p. 9).

The importance of using proper means is highly developed within Puritanism and comprises the prior institutional context of the "new" methods. Yet, the Puritans drew a sharp distinction between what they saw as futile effort or manipulation and God-ordained means. In contrast to a mechanical universe to which even God must adapt, the Puritans saw no efficacy inherent within means apart from what God sovereignly bestowed. Compare the preceeding quotations with these from the seventeenth-century English Puritan, John Owen: "Now, there is nothing in religion that hath any efficacy for compassing an end, but it hath it from God's appointment of it to that purpose" ([1658] 1967, 17). In discussing how mortifying evil deeds leads to spiritual vitality and peace, he states that mortification, like any means, does not necessarily produce the desired results: "I do not say they proceed from it, as though they were *necessarily* tied to it. . . . 'I will do that work,' says God, . . . 'I create it.' The *use of means* for the obtaining of peace is ours; the *bestowing* of it is God's prerogative" (p. 21; emphasis in the original).

This view is maintained throughout the First Great Awakening. For example, it is in this vein that Edwards, in his "Some thoughts concerning the present revival of religion in New England," first describes the "surprising," "unexpected," and "uncommon" "overturning of things" ([1742] 1974, 379), and then discusses what should be done to promote and advance, not create or produce, this work of God. He introduces this section on the work of promoting revival by appealing to the obvious sovereign work of God as evidence against the Arminian notion of free will. Things that do promote revival, such as prayer, fasting, increased frequency of the Lord's Supper, and increased acts of charity, are themselves produced by and part of the work of God. For example, God produces revival by "pouring out a Spirit of prayer and supplication" (p. 423). This relation of human and divine action is captured concisely in a phrase at the close of this section (p. 429): "One thing more I would mention, which, if God should still carry on this work, would tend much to promote it. . . . " The revival is from God, and human action can *promote* and be a part of only what God has willed.

Thus, an important controversy with respect to revivals was over their rationalized methods, which struck some as manipulation and therefore unworthy of the gospel.[5] It was also argued that these measures "worked-up" faith and conversions, faith created by humans and not the truly regenerating faith that is a gift from God. The revivalists defended their activity by arguing that anything that effected conversion was appropriate and required; they thereby were the early developers of American pragmatism (Hofstadter 1962). Opponents flatly rejected the autonomous mechanics of means coupled with free will, in the tradition of Edwards ([1742] 1974, 407) who had explicitly condemned such pragmatism as an "erroneous principle."

That individuals make decisions autonomously and freely within this rational cosmos in practice resulted in the exclusion of the Holy Spirit from the everyday mechanics of evangelism and from the organization of activity around techniques of effecting conversion (Cross 1950; Weisberger 1958). Most observers have ignored the subtlety of this element of revivalism, many quoting out of context, making it appear that revivalists made the Holy Spirit totally irrelevant. Many did do just that, but revivalism as an institution cannot be that simply categorized, and the ambiguity in these issues is found throughout revivalist discussions. For example, all revivalists attributed success to the Holy Spirit, at least in partnership with the church and preacher. For instance, the writer who stressed the systematic work of the believers in a revival stated in the same article, "God chose to dispense the gifts of eternal life through the instrumentality of his children, yet the efficacy was entirely his" (*The New-York Evangelist,* 5 January 1833). Yet at other times, as previous quotations illustrate, efficacy is located in the systematic work of church and preacher. Moreover, in the face of failure it never was considered that the Spirit did not desire a revival (such a thing was unthinkable): "On account of various unpropitious circumstances, this meeting resulted in the conversion of but few persons. . . . " (*Christian Advocate and Journal,* 9 September 1840, p. 40). Contrast this with Edwards's narrative of the decline of a revival, "The Spirit of God not long after this time appeared sensibly withdrawing from all parts of this country" ([1736] 1974, 364).

Thus, while revivalism cannot be categorized as totally denying the work of God, it did radically shift the locus of action from a sovereign God to the autonomous individual as exemplified in the demand for new rational methods. This demand was rooted in the assertion that individual decisions arise out of subjectivity governed by natural laws and that the rational manipulation of those laws (means) *will* produce the desired subjective ends—conversions and revival.

Perfectionism

The third element of revivalism is perfectionism. It was argued that the Holy Spirit wants to give a full and abundant life to everyone. It is only the individual's refusal that leads to a mediocre Christian life, in a way parallel to the non-Christian's rejection of the Gospel as leading to his or her damnation. The call to full obedience and the Spirit's desire to bless were core elements in Puritanism and the Reformed churches, but within Arminianism they led to the idea that if the individual wills it, the Spirit will perfectly sanctify the believer in this life.

Perfectionism, rooted in Weslyanism, was given impetus by Finney and his Oberlin school through a series of lectures printed in *The New-York Evangelist* in 1836 (see Smith 1957, 103). While there were many versions of this belief, holiness came to be institutionalized in revivalism as "entire sanctification" or "true holiness." It came by faith and was a gift of the Holy Spirit—a second blessing which brought the Christian to a "higher life." The old carnal dispositions and desires were swept away, which left the believer "gloriously liberated" from the cares and excitements of the world and from the effects of the fall.[6] Smith quotes a minister who received the blessing in 1854 as saying, "I united with the M. E. [Methodist Episcopal] Church February 24th 1819, and thought once or twice I tasted the perfect love of God. But I desire now to say it, to the praise of God: on Wednesday night, 12 P.M., God sanctified my soul in the Rusville tent" (1957, 118).

The Christian's duty was to seek after this second blessing of entire sanctification in order to be led and empowered by the Spirit. The perfecting and purifying of the individual's subjective core was the secret to a powerful Christian life. In one letter of 1840, Finney states that

> pains enough are not taken to lead the convert to seek earnestly the "baptism of the Holy Ghost, after that he hath believed. . . . " [T]he baptism of the Holy Ghost is the secret of the stability of Christian character. . . . Converts should therefore have their attention definitely directed to what this blessing is—its nature, how it is to be obtained. . . . (1980, 262)

In another letter of the same year concerning unfruitful ministers, he states "Now the thing which they need and must have, before they will have power with God or man, is the baptism of the Holy Ghost" (1980, 263). The Methodist Church, the chief proponent of holiness, required its ministers upon ordination to answer in the affirmative, "Do you expect to be made perfect in love in this life? Are you earnestly striving after it?" By the revivals of 1858, holiness was accepted to such a degree that it was almost equated with the revivalistic movement (Smith 1957, 138–42).[7]

The individual held onto salvation and either strove for or continued in a state of holiness through piety expressed in outward morality. This along with the ethical emphasis gave special impetus toward moral reform, but while moral reform sprang from inward piety it was necessary in its own right; the nation and the earth must be perfected. Thus, perfectionism led naturally to the quest for the millennium.

Postmillennialism and Moral Citizenship

Indeed, all elements of revivalism came together around the postmillennial ideal of establishing the Kingdom of God in America

(Moorhead 1984). Revivalism specified and described the dynamics of the millennium in a new and unique way. There were continuities with previous views, but the revivals of the late twenties marked the beginning of a particular millennial vision, one that paralleled the increase in nationalism.

Eschatology in general and the millennium in particular have played a vital role in Christian thinking. There are three main eschatologies, two of which are relevant to our discussion. *Pre*millennialism emphasizes the inadequacy of even regenerate persons to establish a perfect order and therefore asserts that things will get progressively worse in the world until Jesus returns to save the elect, banish the condemned, and rule the now regenerate creation for a thousand years. Thus, Jesus must return physically to the earth *before* the millennium can be established. *Post*millennialism emerged after the Reformation and constituted a dramatic departure in its view of history. Instead of the world sinking further into depravity until ultimate defeat is averted only at the last minute by Christ's return, history is seen as a progressive unfolding of victory. It is not a peaceful evolution. The battles become fiercer as the end draws near, but each battle ends in victory for Christ and the church. The new age then would be established (Tuveson 1968) and *afterwards* Christ would return.[8]

The millennial ideal of the Kingdom of God was the common bond of North American Christianity (Niebuhr 1937; Handy 1984). From the time of the earliest settlements, the New World was viewed as the idyllic garden in which the millennium would be nurtured (Tuveson 1968). The Kingdom of God ideal formed the broadly defined common faith of all religious denominations and provided the basis for civil religion (Bellah 1970, 1975). It thus is important to distinguish revivalistic piety from civil religion. Revivalism was a particular specification or version of civil religion and the ideal of the Kingdom of God. Revivalism from the late 1820s became the institutional manager of civil religion. It was the interpreter of the Kingdom of God throughout the nineteenth century and its particular vision prevailed. But there were other versions, and the millennial ideal existed prior to revivalism and also outlived it (Moorhead 1984).

Revivalism shifted the responsibility of bringing about the millennium from a sovereign God of history to the individual and the people. It previously was thought that individuals merely prepared for the Kingdom of God through virtue and benevolence (Tuveson 1968, 60). According to revivalism, through inward piety manifested in outward moral lives, individuals would establish the millennium (Tuveson 1968, 84–89). Revivalists emphasized a steady progressive movement. If, as

Edwards and the other reformed millennialists claimed, history was a progressive victory over Satan and over the effects of original sin, then how great a victory and what tremendous progress now that individual Christians were voluntarily becoming moral and perfected.

Optimistic postmillennialism paralleled secular theories of evolutionary progress. The millennial order was linked to secular progress.[9] Increasingly throughout the century the Kingdom of God in America was equated with a Christian "civilization" (Handy 1984; Marsden 1980). The millennium would be the final sacralization of a faithful society. Handy points out that the revivalists "saw the millennium coming as the climax of the Christianization of civilization, fulfilling history" (p. 30). The millennium and the goals of civilization were coterminus. For revivalists, "the millennial expectancy provided a goal for civilization as well as for religion; . . . For them, the religious quest and the civil process, though clearly distinct, moved toward the same happy climax" (p. 31). Smith describes the common dream of a Christian society as "one in which evangelism, education, social reform, economic progress and advancing democracy were all heralds of the approaching rule of Christ on earth" (1980, 10).

Revivalists intensified and sharpened the early emphasis on morality as the pivotal element of their system. Perfectable evangelical piety became generalized as morality and was the guarantor that a voluntary, freewilled Christianity would progressively establish a Christian civilization. Morality inexorably led to the progress of civilization— and the revivalists did not always feel compelled to make "Christian" an explicit modifier. Handy (1984, 31–32) states that "there was virtually universal and consistent emphasis among Protestants on a basic and familiar theme—morality as the all-important link between religion and civilization." " 'Morality' was considered to be an indispensible accompaniment of true religion, both of which were essential to the progress of the best civilization" (p. 34). Revivalists in preaching perfectionism "affirmed that the ethical renewal of persons was prerequisite to social righteousness" (Smith 1980, 10). In 1835 Edward Beecher encouraged Christians to produce personal holiness "as God requires, and the present exigencies of the world demand."[10] As stated by Smith (1957, 105), "On its success, he believed, depended all hopes for the early inauguration of the Kingdom of God on earth." Some went so far as to state that the Christian ministry was the agency of a "high and pure civilization" (Loveland 1980, 31; Handy 1984, 29).

A moral people creating civilization meant the construction of moral national institutions and a moral citizenry. The most effective and important way of establishing a moral citizenry was, of course, through evangelism and conversion. Interestingly, revivalistic methods—the very institution of the revival as a collective event—manifested the universalism of national citizenship. Revivals were often planned by one church, or sometimes a few denominations sharing one building. When a revival reached its peak, the church members systematically made arrangements with other churches in the town and surrounding areas. This frequently was facilitated by women's intercongregational prayer groups and missionary associations. Whole regions would come under the influence of a revival in which individuals from sometimes a large area would gather together and share common circumstances, problems, and hopes. Thus, the universalism of conversion extended beyond the local congregation and community. This universalism extended to the national level, for the rational methods which worked in one's own church would unfailingly work in other churches throughout the nation. Religious newspaper reports of revivals across the country emphasized the universality of method and result, and regional missionary societies put those methods to use.

Christians were not to evangelize only. They were to build moral institutions and legal order. The United States, it appeared, was blessed by God to lead the advance in the progress of moral civilization. This view was rooted in the early conception of the New World as God's provision for a fresh beginning (Tuveson 1968; Niebuhr 1937). Moreover, the decline of the colonial theocracies was not interpreted as a setback; it was God freeing "America" from the deadness of state churches to voluntarily choose true obedience and moral reform and thereby establish a sanctified community. The millennium would be the natural result for a people who voluntarily chose to pursue perfection. The separation of *church* and *state* was the basis for the unity of *Christianity* and *nation* while moral persuasion was the unifying link (see Handy 1984, 27; W. L. Miller, 1961, 90–91; Mead 1954; Hudson 1953; Perry Miller 1961, 360).[11]

In this context, sacred qualities were attributed to the Declaration of Independence and the Constitution. They were believed to be God-given because they adhered to His principles of free agency and rationalism, and under their influence a nation—both citizens and institutions—could be nurtured on the moral principles of piety (Niebuhr 1937).[12]

Again, revivalism radicalized this mainstream Protestantism: A moral citizenry must actively construct the Kingdom of God. Viewing themselves blessed by God with foundational documents of democracy, Christians were to push forward and directly transform the nation. This led to an emphasis on social reform movements that had as their goal the defining of citizenship by building moral categories into the legal order, education, and work. These reforms included temperance, abolition, observation of the Christian Sabbath, and public schools (e.g., Tyack 1974).

In describing the social reform of the early revivalists as exemplified by Finney, Hammond (1979, 60) states, "The distinction between religious and secular reform, and likewise that between personal conversion and creation of a new social order, had no meaning in the world in which Finney and his converts lived." The revivalistic impetus toward moral social reform is the main theme of Timothy Smith's now classic *Revivalism and Social Reform*, and, as Handy (1984, 42) describes, "The evangelical vision of Christian civilization was of a free, literate, industrious, honest, law-abiding, religious population . . . [and] such goals as an effective educational system, a sound legal order, and a widespread network of religious institutions."

Summary

From early in colonial times, North American religion was more individualistic than European Christianity. By the early 1800s a new revivalism grounded in Arminianism appeared, burgeoning in the twenties and thirties. It articulated a rational, individualistic cosmos based on free will, rational methods of evangelism, perfectionism, and postmillennialism. These elements were integrated into an individualistic nationalism which envisioned a moral people and their institutions driven by individual piety.

Maintenance of the Order

By mid-century, this complex cultural order of revivalistic piety was a dominant force in American religion. There was by no means a complete consensus. Nevertheless, revival religion was firmly institutionalized as a manager and interpreter of the Kingdom of God, and if the latter had not yet arrived, the revivalistic cosmos, at least, had been fully constructed.

Toward the latter part of the century the tone of revivalism changed. It was still optimistic, but the later revivalists were clearly maintaining an institution, not creating one. Within the rhetoric of institution building, early attacks on revivalism and lack of interest in pietism were viewed as relics of an older order. Within the rhetoric of institution maintenance, later antagonistic positions and apathy were interpreted as shifts away from the wisdom and advancements in knowledge that the revivalists had established. For example, in the

1880s one Methodist wrote that the church should actively use "certain tried methods which, faithfully applied, inevitably secure a revival." Another, reflecting the tone of the day, demanded, "The imperfect perfection scaffolding that has been and is being so persistently built ought to be torn down, and Arminian theology" of perfectionism restored.[13]

While the rhetorical tone of revivalism changed, all evidence indicates that revivalism was successfully maintained in the face of formalization and countervailing trends until at least the 1890s. Free will and rational evangelical techniques remained at the core of the institution. Weisberger (1958) and many others have also documented the continuity of revivalism in the latter part of the century, showing that Dwight L. Moody and other urban revivalists of the later period used essentially the same rational technique that dominated the antebellum revival. Hofstadter (1962, 109) argues that it is under Moody that the "new methods" were fully mechanized and depersonalized through the application of business organization and method. Marsden (1980, 7) claims that even in the divergent views of fundamentalism, "Revivalism and pietism were at the center."

There was more mention of perfection and total sanctification in revivalist newspapers than any other topic (except for revivals themselves and possibly the threat of the Roman Church). For example, the *New York Christian Advocate* printed a series of articles and letters in 1887 and 1888 that laid out with force the full doctrine of holiness, including some letters against it. The major objection to the doctrine of perfect sanctification was the antinomianism that it spawned. As previously noted, revivalists never accepted extreme antinomianism, and in the then established churches in the latter part of the century they were even more intolerant of it, as part of a greater formalization of denominational authority and creeds.

The millennial ideal (and the moral reform tendency in general) became increasingly specified and focused on the nation in and of itself as the carrier of Christian civilization. Previously, civilization was defined and derived value to the extent that it conformed to Christian morality. By the end of the nineteenth century,

> in most cases unconsciously, much of the real focus had shifted to the civilization itself, with Christianity and the churches finding their significance in relation to it. Civilization itself was given increasingly positive assessment, chiefly because it was understood to have absorbed much of the spirit of Christianity. (Handy 1984, 95)[14]

The progress of the nation within the wider world *was* Christian progress.

The institution of revivalism was maintained even in the face of new developments in the latter part of the century, some directly in the revivalistic tradition and others antithetical to it, but none of them gripped the popular culture until the late nineties and after.

One important movement was the social gospel. It detached the moral reform element of revivalism from the roots and goals of salvation and the millennium. The more radical versions did not gain support even among the seminaries and the clergy until the turn of the century (McLoughlin 1967) and were not widely accepted at the congregational level before World War I (Weisberger 1958, 168; McLoughlin 1959).[15] Holiness and Pentecostal groups rose in the nineties. They rejected the increasingly conservative codification of holiness by the established evangelical churches, and founded themselves on more extreme conceptions of the second blessing and the higher life. *- maybe revivalism liberated religion for newly lower auth. tier*

Liberalism and premillennial fundamentalism were more distinct from the basic propositions of revivalistic piety. These systems were articulated to varying degrees by individuals and small followings as early as the seventies; yet, liberalism did not make major inroads among the clergy until the nineties, and the fundamentalist groups did not grow to any large degree until the turn of the century (Ahlstrom 1972; McLoughlin 1967; Marsden 1980; Handy 1984).

These new movements are traceable not so much to the problems of modernity but more to the structuring of modernity as ineffectual individuation and to the decline of revivalism's cultural monopoly. Interpretations of these movements are dealt with in chapter 6 where I compare the effectual individualism of revivalistic pietism with other types of systems.

Thus, movements that were antithetical to revival religion arose in the last quarter of the nineteenth century, but they did not take hold of the seminaries and clergy until the late nineties nor did they spread at the congregational level until the 1900s. In short, the institutionalization of revivalism kept intact its key components, and revival religion remained an influential manager and interpreter of U.S. religion and individualistic nationalism throughout the century.[16]

Causal Interpretation of Revival Religion

The early American polity was characterized by petty capitalism and rational individualistic political organization. As the American polity expanded gradually through economic growth, local communal populations were incorporated into national political-economic organizations. Effectual individuation and corresponding political institutions were framed within individualistic religion in the postrevolutionary period as exemplified by the revivals of the Second Great Awakening.

Market penetration accelerated in the 1820s and caused an intensification of individualistic nationalism as the core myth of the cultural order. As the plausibility structures of revivalism, this nexus of cultural-political-economic structures not only expanded the appeal of revivalism, it also intensified its individualistic nationalism. The revivalism of the late 1820s and 1830s was a religious movement that specified and framed the expanding U.S. polity and its institutions. It grounded and legitimated the identities and rational activity of the petty capitalist and citizen. Revivalists were out to transform civilization into the Kingdom of God. Because of its dynamic isomorphism with the new rational ontology, revivalism gained in legitimacy and was both cognitively credible and morally imperative.

The structural isomorphism of revivalism with the culture of individualistic nationalism has been described by delineating interrelated elements. By defining and creating a rational, self-determining, perfectable individual, it constituted the effectual autonomous "rugged individual" of petty capitalism and the enlightened citizen of the new democratic republic. Rational evangelism defined the individual as one who autonomously makes decisions and acts according to rational laws within a mechanical universe. This both supported and was supported by the impersonal rational calculation and authority of market and polity. Moreover, revivalism elaborated and integrated the subjective emotional core of the individual as the dynamic behind rationality, morality, and progress.

All of these elements were integrated into the ideal of the millennial order. The autonomy of the individual, the rational cosmos, and the infinite possibilities of perfectionism made the Kingdom of God something to be built here and now. Increasingly the Kingdom was identified with the particular development of "Christian America." Personal and national moral reform would infuse technological, economic, and political development with the Kingdom. Moreover, the progress of the United States was to be the progress of humanity. Just as participation in the world market was experienced as participation in national markets and the U.S. polity, so the remaking of the world was to be accomplished through the reform of the nation.

As the dominant ontology, individualistic nationalism provided a plausibility structure for revival religion; it made revivalism credible and seem vastly superior to traditional Reformation theology. Recall the example I gave, in the first chapter, of the Calvinist and Methodist sermons. The Calvinist minister might sermonize that his congregation could not control their own destiny and were totally dependent on God's sovereign grace. A traveling revivalist would preach to the same people that they were dependent on no one and would exhort them to take control of their salvation. The revivalist message was cognitively compelling because it corresponded to their everyday experience as shaped by the dominant cultural myth of individualism.[17]

Moreover, isomorphism has in addition to a cognitive component, a moral one as well. The Calvinist minister would be viewed, especially during and after the revival, not only as speaking nonsense, but also as being bad. Reformed theology went against nineteenth-century conceptions of liberty, rugged individualism, and the sovereignty of the people. It was thought that it bred fatalism in economic rationality, political participation, and morality. People would use it as an excuse to escape their responsibility of choice, thereby creating spiritually dead churches, a morally bankrupt nation, and a stagnant economy.

Market penetration did not spread uniformly throughout the country, nor did it always take the form of effectual individuation. The theory implies that those areas most penetrated by market processes resulting in the dominance of effectual individuation were the most dominated by myths of rationality, individualism, and nationalism. Thus, yeoman farmers, small-scale entrepreneurs, and shopkeepers would be most supportive of those myths. Those regions less penetrated by these market forces or ones incorporated within dependent or corporatist forms would be less organized by the new ontology. Because of its isomorphism with myths of individualistic nationalism, revival religion gained its greatest support in those populations whose everyday lifestyle was characterized by effectual individuation and concomitant cultural structures. The theoretical implication, then, is that those populations most dominated by effectual individuation would accept effectual individualism as the guiding cultural myth and would more likely subscribe to revivalistic pietism.[18]

During the last quarter of the century, increases in scale in industry and the greater importance of state action within the world system caused the cultural order to define an ineffectual individual. These changes began to erode the plausibility and legitimacy of revival religion. New movements of fundamentalism, premillennialism, liberalism, and the social gospel emerged late in this period. These systems tended to define the inadequacy and limitations of the individual. Just as ineffectual individualism did not reach sizable proportions, so these movements did not gain mass support until the turn of the century. Nevertheless, I argue that those areas most affected by corporate organization, and therefore by the myth of ineffectual individualism, were the most likely to abandon nineteenth-century revivalistic pietism and embrace one of the new divergent movements. In short, throughout the century, the more that social life was organized as effectual individuation, the greater the prevalence of individualistic nationalism (effectual individualism), the greater the population's acceptance of revival religion as part, and frame, of the project of creating and maintaining the cultural order.

The Institutional Thesis and American Religion Literature

This interpretation of revivalism runs counter to most of the literature which is dominated by various versions of a crisis theory perspective. One set of explanations argues that revivalism resulted from the relative deprivation that accompanies rapid economic growth: With growth, expectations increase and are disappointed when the economy levels off. Case studies such as the now classic work of Cross (1950) do in fact show that revivals occur in areas undergoing rapid economic growth, but inferences of relative deprivation are tenuous. For example, a close reading of Cross's study of upstate New York in the 1820s reveals that a planned canal through a town generated expectations of growth and resulted in a boom before the canal was ever started. In situations where the plans were abandoned, there were raised expectations and disappointment; yet, there were no revivals. It would seem that the crucial factor is not the leveling of raised expectations but the sustained incorporation into a larger market.

A cultural version of the crisis argument is that loss of status results in symbolic crusades of revivalism and moral reform in order to reassert privileged position. These interpretations do not hold up under close scrutiny; for example, Hammond's (1979) analyses of quantitative data in the first part of the century show no support for this interpretation of the abolitionist movement.

The most popular interpretation of revivals is that rapid change causes disorganization, anomie, and anxiety. Individuals aggregate into movements attempting to revitalize a traditional order to alleviate anxiety and uncertainty. Some scholars emphasize breakdowns in the American consensus while others consider material disorganization to be crucial. For example, McLoughlin argues, "Awakenings begin in periods of cultural distortion and grave personal stress, when we lose faith in the legitimacy of our norms, the viability of our institu-

84

tions, and the authority of our leaders in church and state" (1978, 2). He maintains that the conflict between the Jeffersonians and the Federalists "brought doubt, division, and confusion to the young nation" (p. 98). This was compounded by "the philosophical conflict between the world view of the Calvinists and the new enlightenment rationalists" (p. 99). This crisis of disorganization was the precondition for revitalization through revivals.

Was the postrevolutionary period through the 1820s really a continuous period of major crisis and disorganization? Critics of McLoughlin's work tend to attack the idea of cultural consensus (e.g., Neitz 1981). The crisis dynamic itself is rarely questioned. One critic (Pritchard 1979), argues that McLoughlin's emphasis on consensus and values does not adequately take into account material disorganization—the "wrenching social transformations" and the "jarring impact" of rapid economic growth.[19]

In a recent study of the Rochester, New York, revivals of 1830–31, Paul Johnson (1978) rejects explanations that attribute revivalism to broad social strain. Using detailed occupational and demographic information he presents evidence that revivals were not the result of "rootlessness, isolation, and anomie" (p. 36). However, he remains committed to a crisis theory approach. He argues that rapid industrialization resulted in a larger number of wage earners no longer living in the households of their employers. This created a crisis of labor control.

> Evangelicalism was a middle-class solution to problems of class, legitimacy, and order generated in the early stages of manufacturing. Revivals provided entrepreneurs with a means of imposing new standards of work discipline and personal comportment upon themselves and the men who worked for them, and thus they functioned as powerful social controls. . . . (P. 138)[20]

The data are striking: Those people involved in occupations most incorporated into the growing rational market seem to make up a large proportion of the converts. Of proprietors in these occupations there is an increase after the revivals in the proportion who are church members. The interpretation that labor control is the crucial explanatory variable is more tenuous. Johnson's data show that professionals, and especially lawyers, who have no labor problems, also constitute a large proportion of converts, and there is a large increase after the revivals in the proportion of lawyers who participate in the churches. Johnson attributes this to Finney's being a lawyer and to lawyers also being politicians, sensitive to middle-class issues. This ignores the fact that lawyers as a profession stood at the center of a system increasingly rationalized within a formal legal order. To the extent that the new order was framed by religious symbols, it is understandable that lawyers showed high levels of revivalism: "The pre–Civil War American political system lay in the hands of preachers and lawyers" (Meyer 1984, 1267; see also Ryan 1981). Thus, the appeal of revivalism appears broader than interests in labor control.

Locating the origins and the essential social nature of revivals within some such crisis is made even more problematic when the Rochester revival is placed in the context of revivals throughout New York and the nation. Clearly, Rochester elites did not create revivalism; Finney himself had been leading successful revivals since 1825. In many ways his Rochester revival was unique. First of all, Rochester was an urban center relative to western towns, and Hammond (1979) has shown evidence that revivals were to some degree located in areas low in population density. Hammond also points out that it was the first time that Finney consciously courted the upper classes and the first time that temperance became an integral part of the revivalistic message.

All of this might support Johnson's insight that the upper classes attempted to use the Rochester revival to construct labor control structures; but the strength of this evidence simultaneously undermines the more general point that this issue constituted the essential social nature of revivalism. The evidence that indicates elite manipulation also suggests its uniqueness; at the same time it underscores the origin and power of revivals apart from those elites.

The evidence raises the crucial question of why was revival religion, as an event and as an institution, so powerful in mobilizing and convincing populations of the reality and moral superiority of individual autonomy, discipline, and impersonal relations? Why was revivalism able so totally to delegitimate traditional paternalistic structures and build new rationalized ones? Johnson presents images of workers flocking to revivals. But if so, why? Were they really herded through the imposition of false consciousness? If so, the question remains as to why this particular (false) consciousness was so effective and imposed so easily.[21]

Revivalism had power to delegitimate traditional organization and authority because that is what revivalists were in the business of doing: They were constructing a new rational order that produced moral individuals and promoted rational action. This project was defined in terms of individual freedom and progress. Small-scale merchant-manufacturers, shopkeepers, and farmers were freed from local communal constraints and could pursue profit and enter into impersonal relationships to that end. Laborers, no longer controlled by a reactionary master's household, gained greater autonomy, rights, and the prospect of upward mobility (Hackett 1988). Petty capitalists, yeoman farmers, and laborers all flocked to a revival, notwithstanding their conflicting interests, because it articulated new freedoms from local paternalistic institutions. Lawyers and doctors went because their professions were central to the emerging order.

Ryan (1981) makes a complementary argument in her analysis of revivalism's role in transforming the patriarchal family. Ryan's rich study of Oneida county portrays the effects the expanding market had on family relations. Revivals and missionary societies were innovations in public participation, recasting intergenerational family ties in voluntaristic, individualistic terms: Children were to be influenced through persuasion and affection rather than obligation and (partiarchal) authority. Revivals often were attacked as a threat to traditional authority. Converts were those who faced the commercial market: young adults and especially women, but also some "unsaved" husbands. Youths were anxious, but they explored enthusiastic, exuberant, and independent forms of religion (p. 100). The sizeable conversion of males, mostly young single merchants, professionals, and clerks, resulted in a slightly larger proportion of males in churches than before the revivals. Women in revivalistic and moralistic activity were married to lawyers and other professionals, merchant-manufacturers, and (increasingly) clerks, and to a lesser extent (depending on the association) shopkeepers and artisans. In rejecting a class analysis, but affirming revivalism's ties to the market, Ryan describes revivalism as actually linking classes. For example, the Female Missionary Society

> extended its influence horizontally as well as vertically, out through the agricultural hinterland and down through the middle ranks of the urban population. Both these directions led through the essential links of the regional marketplace where the husbands of female missionaries made their fortunes. (P. 103)[22]

Revivalism presented a unified order, but one within which old and new conflicts were fought out and ideologically framed. For example, Hackett (1988) in his study of Albany, New York, argues that the revivals of this period helped consolidate national identity around goals of economic growth and rights. National identity framed conflicting class positions on these goals. An interest—economic or political, elite or otherwise—that framed its claims within the larger order would gain in legitimacy. In this way many interests found themselves supporting and manipulating the new order. Thus, Johnson's particular point remains insightful and important: The Rochester revival's emphasis on temperance can be interpreted as the influence of elites attempting to solve problems of labor, but they did so by tapping into an emerging religious-cultural order which was broader than their interests in using it.[23]

Generally, the empirical evidence, when stripped of crisis imagery, supports the interpretation of revivals and the rationalization of market and polity proposed here, as seen by the data already cited in developing the historical description. Impressionistic evidence suggests that revivals took place in those areas experiencing rapid economic growth (Cross 1950; Pritchard 1976) and were supported by the more capitalistic sectors of the country (Weisberger 1958). The composition of revivals, and especially the high rates of participation by lawyers and doctors, is particularly supportive of the institutionalist interpretation.

The correspondence in content between revivalism and effectual individualism (individualistic nationalism) is also supported. Again, Johnson's insight that revivalism framed an impersonal authority structure, McLoughlin's suggestion that it defined national citizenship, and Ryan's argument that it constructed individualistic intergenerational relations are all complementary to the present interpretation. Other observers more explicitly argue that everyday experience within petty capitalism and a democratic republic influenced people to find Arminian revivalistic piety more compelling then Reformation theology. For example, Tyler (1944, 23) states, "The idea of progress and of the importance of the individual undermined the old doctrines of election and predestination." Also Niebuhr (1929, 84) argues that historically predestination "derived by Calvin from purely religious sources was hard to reconcile with the native interests of the bourgeois mind and suffered an early eclipse wherever the trading class was dominant." This bourgeois mind was characterized by "the high development of individual self-consciousness and the prevalence of an activist attitude toward life" largely because of the "character of their employment which places responsibility for success or failure almost entirely upon their own shoulders" (pp. 80–81). Lipset (1963) argues that

American Protestantism, with its emphasis on the personal achievement of grace, reinforced the stress on personal achievement which was dominant in the secular value system. Both sets of values stressed individual responsibility, both rejected hereditary status. . . . The Arminian emphasis on the personal attainment of grace . . . served as a religious parallel to the secular emphasis on equality of opportunity and achievement. . . . (Pp. 183, 185)

Bellah's (1975) historically rich work on religion in the United States provides a concise summary:

. . . social institutions had not merely to be established but uplifted and improved. . . . The increasingly elaborated techniques of the revivalists for reaching into the deepest level of unconscious motivation in the common man were to be used not only as an aid to open him to the infusion of divine grace, but to make him a citizen. . . . [T]he great engine for maintaining the effectiveness of religion in national life was not dogma at all but revivalism, intense, immediate, and personal. . . . Evangelical religion contributed to the growth of a national consciousness. (Pp. 47–49)

Republicanism

The interpretation of Republicanism as individualistic and nationalistic is less controversial, and thus less space is required to document its content and development. There is, however, a growing literature on the revivalism-Republicanism linkage that requires more detailed attention. As is common practice, I refer to the *ideology* of Republican and other political parties. I use the term interchangeably with cultural theory of society or polity as it is used to define and justify political organization and policy. Again, I focus on the ontology—the assertions about the nature of things (citizens, classes, states, nation, goods, money)—that underlies any ideology.

Early Context

The newly independent United States was characterized by a fairly limited federal government. The sovereign people were organized primarily as citizens of the states. In this context, conflict and debate were dominated by that between the Federalists and Democrat-Republicans. The Federalists were committed to an internationally competitive commercial society supported by the federal state (e.g., Benson 1961). The Jeffersonians articulated the "republican ideal" of a productive agrarian gentry (Kasson 1976). Despite their differences, they held theories of society that were based on the privilege of the propertied and wealthy. Moreover, as they came to dominate, the Jeffersonians in fact used the federal government to support internal improvements and national growth.

Various egalitarian, populist movements emerged in the 1820s, pushing for the implementation of universal suffrage and the popular election of officials (e.g., Benson 1961, 7). This was initially resisted by the dominant Democratic-Republicans, but by the 1830s, egalitarianism was firmly in place as the guiding political myth for the new two-party system.

The Jacksonian Democrats essentially maintained a reworked Jeffersonianism, but legitimated states' rights policy in terms of the equality of the people. The success of this policy accounts for the somewhat false notion of Jacksonian Democracy as the avant-garde of egalitarianism (Benson 1961). The Democrats, however, remained firmly behind states' rights, laissez-faire relative to market and society, and a federal government that governed only the states.

The Whigs, on the other hand, departed more radically from the Democrats and previous theories of society. Their vision was not of an international mercantile power nor of an agrarian gentry. The new republic was to be a nation of free and equal farmers and petty manufacturers who formed a strong agrarian-industrial base for aggressive international competition. A classical liberal state was to stimulate this base through policies from financial support for internal transportation to tariffs.

The Democratic-Whig conflict was therefore over the basic nature of society and state. The differences were not over whether there should or should not be growth or "modernization" (as phrased by Jensen 1978), but over the form that it would take. Would it take a gentrified, somewhat idyllic agrarian form characterized by economic dependence (the selling of raw agrarian produce to Europe in return for manufactured goods)? Or, would it take the form of industrialization based on a productive agriculture, characterized by an aggressive competition in world markets. Benson (1961) describes these differences as an extreme laissez-faire state versus a positive liberal state. Kleppner (1973, 60) summarizes the debate:

> The Whig-Democratic polarity of the second electoral era revolved around a fundamental value conflict over the nature of man, of society, and of government's role. The party of moral order and positive government (the Whigs) pitted itself against that of laissez-faire ethics and passive government (the Democrats).[24]

The Whig coalition was short-lived and marked by a host of other competing versions, from populism to antimasonism to temperance to abolitionism. In the early 1850s, the Republican party emerged as a new synthesis of these concerns. It constituted a particularly powerful ideological integration of the various elements that composed the ontology of an individualistic nation and a liberal state. As such, it stood in even starker contrast with the Democrats than did the Whigs. It also marked a shift from (female-dominated) intense moralistic reform to (male-dominated) calculating political organization (Ginzberg 1986).

The Rugged Individual

Republican ideology as an ontology was anchored in the concept of an abstract individual and in ideas of freedom and egalitarianism (Benson 1961; Kleppner 1973; Foner 1975). The Republicans claimed that the union was a nation comprising individuals pursuing their interests in an international market. These individuals, they argued, were not divided into conflicting classes but were bound together by a harmony of interests in a self-made, secure life. The autonomous pursuit of self-interest was not to be a blind greed, for the fully enlightened individual would also show self-control, restraint, and virtue through moral discipline (e.g., Foner 1970, 25).

A quasi-sacred dignity was ascribed to human labor (Foner 1970, 11). All value, social and material, was produced by or flowed from human labor. To illustrate this point, Foner quotes William Evarts from 1856, "Labor, gentlemen, we of the free States acknowledge to be the source of all our wealth, of all our progress, of all our dignity and value." Later in the century, the phrase "honest money" would be used to attack inflationary policies; it tacitly assumed that value and profits were to be derived from labor, not from artificial mechanisms such as currency policy.

Within Republicanism, the dignity and productivity of labor was considered maximized when it was free. Freedom was the ability to base decisions on shrewd but honest rational calculation and to leave the wage-earning class by means of hard work.

> For Republicans, "free labor" meant labor with economic choices, with the opportunity to quit the wage-earning class. . . . The aspirations of the free-labor ideology were thus thoroughly middle-class, for the successful laborer was one who achieved self-employment, and owned his own capital—a business, farm, or shop. (Foner 1970, 16–17)

Thus, the belief in the existence of social mobility—the acquisition of property—was crucial to the Republican system. Inequality and poverty consequently were attributed to faults in the individual (Bendix 1956). The lack of social mobility often was blamed on either the interference of a reactionary state or on corporate monopolies. As long as mobility was not hindered by such things as "feudal" plantations and banks, hard-working individuals could, it was argued, move out of the wage-earning class.[25]

Moral Citizenship and National Economic Growth

As with other individualistic systems, the abstract, equal individuals of Republican ideology were reified as the nation. It was not just that the union was composed of individuals rather than states or classes, although this was an important aspect. Rather, it was also that the nation embodied the people and existed as a corporate reality. The first aspect resulted in an emphasis on federal citizenship over state memberships; the second made a moral national citizenry the basis of all national progress. The concept of citizen legitimated national goals and mobilized the population as individuals around them.

The value of labor was therefore collectivized as progress which included economic growth and democratic institutions (see Thomas 1987a). Foner (1970, 38) refers to the North in describing this aspect of Republicanism: "To the self-confident society of the North, economic development, increasing social mobility, and the spread of democratic institutions were all interrelated parts of nineteenth-century 'progress.'" That is, the goals of the nation were located within a history in which the United States, as the first democratic and now industrializing nation, would lead the advance in both material and moral progress.

> The important point was that material and moral developments were but two sides of the same coin. "Good roads and bridges," wrote the New York *Tribune*, "are as necessary an ingredient to the spread of intelligence, social intercourse, and improvement in population, as schools and churches."
> (Foner 1970, 38–39)

Economic growth was based on "internal improvements," but it required competitive power in the world system. World economic power meant confrontation with already existing powers—England in particular. Consequently, the sovereignty of the people and nationalism were linked to economic growth precisely as international competition increased and collective value became managed by the central state.

Federal authority over both society and the economy was expanded, at the expense of local authority. Relative to society, the central state was to establish law and institutions that would create an enlightened moral citizenry and thereby insure the progress and stability of American democratic civilization. Relative to the economy, it was to stimulate industry and protect it and labor from cheap foreign "slave labor," by a tariff if necessary; provide free homesteading land in the West; establish and protect free labor markets; and, in general, promote national economic growth in the larger world economy. To the degree that social equality and democratic principles were adhered to, the active role of the state would bring about industrial prosperity, social mobility, self-employment, and a highly developed moral civilization.

Republican ideals of citizenship and free labor coalesced on the issue of slavery. Previous groups and parties opposed to slavery did not develop a coherent theoretical critique of it nor muster the economic and political autonomy to attack it. The reason, Foner argues, is that

> [o]nly a movement that viewed society as a collection of individuals, that viewed freedom as the property of every man, that believed every individual had the right to seek advancement as a unit in competitive society, could condemn slavery as utterly and completely as, in their own ways, abolitionists and Republicans did.[26]

Class and Sectionalism

Discussions of Republicanism tend to center on opposition to slavery in the context of sectionalism and the causes of the Civil War. While this in some ways is necessary, it also is unfortunate. A focus on sectionalism tends to overlook the fact that the North was not uniformly taken up by the Republican vision of the polity. These discussions are also organized around the polemical issue of whether or not economic interest was the real force behind abolitionism and Republicanism. While not essential to the development of the present interpretation, it would be helpful to sketch the class argument and some of its empirical problems, and show how the institutionalist approach differs from it.

The class argument is that Northern industrialists along with the rich and propertied (including wealthy farmers) were the source of

Republicanism and the core support for the party. These classes were motivated solely by self-interest in promoting such policies as national industrialization, a tariff, and the maintenance of free labor markets. These policies contradicted the interests of Southern elites and were legitimated by abolitionism. Northern commercial enterprises stood between the extreme positions of southern landowners and northern industrialists. They were interested in dependent development as they were the distributors of southern cotton, but they also stood to gain from industrialization.

There are several problems with this argument. Evidence suggests that Republican popular support was not primarily from the rich propertied classes (e.g., Kleppner 1970, 1979; Jensen 1971). More fundamentally, there appears to be no inherent conflict of interest between northern industrialization and the southern plantation system. For example, Moore (1966, 114) points out that industrial capital can be quite tolerant of purchasing raw materials produced by slave labor.

The nature of western agriculture soon emerges as the crucial factor in the interpretation of interest and movements, and this is the weakest link in the argument. The key question is why western farmers were actively committed to a Republican (northern) organization of the polity and of economic growth despite their opposition to policies such as the tariff. Rubinson (1978) argues that the cultivation of new land was essentially a zero-sum game, and the resulting conflict between western wheat and southern cotton pushed the West away from the South, thus by default toward the North. Yet, there is no necessary reason within the logic of economic interest for land to be zero-sum. There was an enormous amount of available land and as the farming of wheat became mechanized, the expansion of land under cultivation was not the most efficient route for growth. Moreover there was no real reason why a free labor market could not coexist with slave labor when the markets and general economics of the two crops were so distinct (e.g., Moore 1966, 129, 133).

What made the cultivation of cotton and wheat zero-sum were political factors, the same factors that created a natural link between West and North. Western agriculture was organized as petty capitalism and was characterized by extreme individualism (Stinchcombe 1961). Consequently, the yeoman farmer did not have to be convinced by northern industrialists of individualistic nationalism and Republicanism. Town versus county conflicts took place within a common political frame and a common goal of national economic development. The South, on the other hand, as a result of the plantation system, was organized dramatically differently with a set of quasi-feudal myths and a political order based on local, family authority structures. "With the West, the North created a society and culture whose values increasingly conflicted with those of the South" (Moore, 1966, 136).

The issue of slavery revealed these differences at both economic and moral-political levels. The independent farm and free labor of western wheat were incompatible with the corporate plantation and slave labor of cotton, not because of a conflict in economic interest, but because each carried a different set of political arrangements—a different organization and theory of society. Moore (1966, 141) states that the fundamental difference was "found in the growth of different economic systems leading to different (but still capitalist) civilizations with incompatible stands on slavery." Relative to the causes of the Civil War, "The fundamental issue became more and more whether the machinery of the federal government should be used to support one society or the other (p. 136)." Consequently, issues such as slavery must be located in the larger theories of society (ontologies) in order to understand both their economic and moral-political aspects. Slavery itself was an intensely moral issue but at the same time one that was grounded in the different organizations of everyday life (Moore, 1966, 123).

Party and Ideological Conflict in the Postbellum United States

A party's stance on a particular political-economic or moral issue must be interpreted in light of its broad theory of the polity—its ideology. Additionally, the appeal of its stance to a particular population is affected by how similar that population's cultural structure is to the party's ideology. Consequently, in order to examine the economic and religious context of political participation and issues in the last quarter of the nineteenth century, I compare the dominant ideologies of the U.S. polity, how their differences were worked out in electoral competition and conflict, and their differing levels of isomorphism with revivalism. The two dominant parties—Republican and Democratic—represent two divergent ideologies, each giving rise to splinter third parties.

The northern victory ensured the institutionalization of the Republican vision of the central nation-state, and the military mobilization of the war with the subsequent construction of a standing army added a strong impetus to centralized authority. The individual's relationship to the center, defined in terms of national citizenship, became relatively autonomous from the states. As the direct link between individual and national center was elaborated in the rights of citizenship, state authority expanded as the manager of these rights.[27] With each new set of responsibilities, the state was faced with implementing policy, if only to ceremonially affirm its authority. Within this nation-building context, state bureaucracy was constructed during this period in a series of attempts at developing administrative structures (Skowronek 1982).

Republicans maintained the primacy of the individual and denied the existence of disadvantaged subgroups. Their attacks on monopolies became somewhat rhetorical and the ideology of individual liberties was manipulated to justify "big business." The Republicans increasingly rejected a strict laissez-faire attitude by espousing the principle that government was to promote national growth and prosperity as the fundamental national goal. However, they argued that the state was not to interfere beyond a general encouragement; arguments ensued over what that meant, all couched in terms of the inviolable principles of rugged individualism and progress.

Beginning in the 1870s but more notable in the 1880s, social reformers, largely from the Republican party, organized around moral reform within the Prohibition party. They argued that national strength could be established and maintained if and only if individuals held to various moral rules—temperance being the focal one. The rules were to be formally built into the definition of citizen by national law. Thus, Republicanism and Prohibitionism were two different versions of the same underlying cultural structure, belonging to the same "family" of movements. The Republican party was the more dominant one and to some degree came to be defined as *the* carrier of individualistic nationalism, while the Prohibition party had dropped in popularity by the 1896 election.

The Democratic party's national machinery still espoused states' rights and laissez-faire. Yet, the growing authority, administrative capacities, and ideological base of the central state were difficult to resist. In this context, movements attempted to redirect that authority. Rejecting Republican individualism, they maintained that the market created economic and political inequalities and that the central government had the responsibility to protect disadvantaged occupations, classes, and ethnic groups. If the national regime was to have more authority, it must at least support individuals by recognizing the subgroupings into which the market and society organized them. In this vein the Populist party emerged in the early nineties focusing primarily on the economic problems of the farmer, and gaining most of its support in the central, western, and southern states. It was coopted by the Democrats in 1896. Thus, while these movements were not major contenders until 1896, under Bryan's candidacy—and then only temporarily—they did grow in size throughout this period.

The election battles from 1876 to 1896 were fought over complex concrete issues (see chapter 5), but they were framed in the more general issues of the different ideologies at stake. At one level, at issue was the role of the central state in the economic and local affairs of individuals, and, at a more basic level, at issue was the relation of the individual to the center by means of the concept of national citizen.

Causal Interpretation of Republicanism

The causal interpretation of Republicanism directly parallels that of revivalism. It was a political movement that espoused an ideology that was structurally isomorphic with individualistic nationalism. Republicans held as their model a strong industrial nation based on small-scale manufacturing and yeoman farming and capable of successfully competing in world markets. They saw themselves as creating a political-economic order that would continually transform nature into progress.

The isomorphism of Republicanism with individualistic nationalism is manifested in its emphasis on rugged individualism, free labor, economic liberalism, and the liberal state. These elements framed and legitimated rational action by locating primordial value in individuals and their labor. The institution of citizenship incorporated individuals into the polity and mobilized them around national goals of economic growth. Through rational decisions and a moral, restrained lifestyle, the people would come to enjoy unheard of prosperity. As a nation, the United States would lead the advance in progress, thereby legitimating aggressive political-economic action in the world system.

Petty capitalism and individualistic nationalism constituted the plausibility structure of Republican ideology. The organization of everyday life around myths of individual autonomy and rational decision making within an impersonal moral order made credible the Republican location of value in free human labor and the reification of that labor in a "moral citizenry." There were no valid accounts for recognizing subgroups. The moral overtones were even more pronounced than the cognitive dynamics. Republicanism was viewed as being morally superior to what was viewed as a reactionary, quasi-feudal ideology. All of this was reinforced by the larger world polity: The hegemony of British imperialism provided a relatively secure context for growth while supplying a laissez-faire model of a corporate nation managed by a diffuse state and a restricted bureaucracy.

I argue that those populations most penetrated by a rational market resulting in effectual individuation and myths of individualistic nationalism showed the greatest support for Republican ideology. Those populations in the South and various regions of the North that were less characterized by effectual individuation exhibited less support for individualistic nationalism and Republicanism. Thus, although popular among various interested classes, the core of the Republican popularity was with family farmers, small-scale entrepreneurs, and urban and rural laborers—those groups most tied to its plausibility structure.

The Republican party readily adapted to a corporate-dominated economy during the latter part of the century, as monopolies and large-scale production came to dominate more sectors of the economy and as the bureaucratic state expanded administrative authority into social life. Nevertheless, Republicanism lost a certain amount of credibility. New movements emerged that articulated the dependence of individual success and equality on corporate aspects of the polity—anticipating to varying degrees the New Deal. The implication is that those areas least affected by the development of large-scale production and ineffectual individuation would continue to support Republicanism. Thus, my general argument is that, throughout the century, where everyday life is marked by high levels of effectual individuation we will find support for the individualistic nationalism of the Republican party. The same argument applies to the entire "family" of social movements grounded in individualistic nationalism, and therefore the same hypothesis is made for the Prohibition party.

Because the ontology of individualistic nationalism were framed by revival religion, and because the latter can be viewed as an institutional manager of the cultural order during this period, Republicanism was to a great degree supported by it. Revivalism's emphasis on free will, morality, and nationalism made it a distinct institutional basis of plausibility. When applied to the political sphere, it favored strong democratic institutions that would guide the individual to sanctification and the nation to becoming a prosperous, moral community, and eventually to the millennium. Both Republicanism and Prohibitionism were built on just such a mythology, and, I argue, gained more adherents—more votes— in precisely those populations dominated by revivalism. This is not to say that revivalism and Republicanism were identical, but revivalism's ordering of a sacred moral cosmos was fundamentally similar in structure to the political moral universe of Republicanism.[28]

The tension between religious moral fervor and rational political calculation led to conflict and competition over the management of the cultural order. As Republicanism became institutionalized within the polity after the war and as the Republican party grew stronger, the party increasingly attempted to distance itself from direct control by revivalists and moral reform associations. It was successful in the early 1890s, although revivalistic influence remained. Despite this tension and competition, the structural isomorphism remained. Thus, the institutional model hypothesizes that throughout the century the greater the prevalence of revival religion within a population, the greater the support for Republicanism, including both the Republican and Prohibitionist parties.

The Institutional Thesis and Prior Studies

The literature is dominated by analyses of Republicanism from the point of view of economic interest, and there are few systematic studies relating economic *organization* to party vote. There are few quantitative studies relating voting to economic variables other than occupation, class, or the rural-urban dichotomy, all interpreted in some sort of crisis or conflict model. Nevertheless, there is some support for my interpretation. Based on impressionistic evidence, Benson hypothesizes that "a strong causal relationship existed between . . . the Transportation Revolution and the egalitarian movements . . . from 1825 to 1850. . . . In short, my hypothesis holds that the boom in transportation and the dynamic expansion of the economy acted as powerful stimulants to movements inspired by the egalitarian ideals of the Declaration of Independence" (1961, 12–23). And Moore's (1966) previously cited interpretation of the Civil War rests on the importance of the sociopolitical organization of the northern and southern economies.

Substantially more evidence is available on the relation of revivalism to Republicanism. Standard surveys of U.S. religious history (e.g., Ahlstrom 1972; Gaustad 1966), studies of revivalism in particular (e.g., McLoughlin 1959) and social and political histories (e.g., Lipset 1964; Key and Munger 1959) describe the support of revivalists for the Republican party. Additionally, several specific and some quantitative studies document this alignment (e.g., Sizer 1978; Kleppner 1970; Jensen 1971; Hammarberg 1974). Hammond (1979) in particular has demonstrated this relationship using quantitative data from throughout the Republican period. Revivalism had strong positive effects on the vote for anti-slavery parties and had similar effects on the Republican vote (e.g., pp. 130–57).

Interpreters, however, disagree on the meaning of the revivalism-Republicanism relationship. One dominant view attributes the behavioral support of the revivalists for the Republican party to a general Protestant consensus that included general civil religious values, nativism, and anti-Catholicism. While many of these elements were shared by both revivalism and Republicanism, they were derived from more basic structural affinities and were pushed by small factions within each movement. To argue that they constituted the essential link between the two greatly oversimplifies the particular force of revivalism and does not take into account the tension between revivalism and civil religion and that between Republicanism and nativism (Hammond 1979, 189; Foner 1970). Hammond (p. 106), for example, shows that revivalism had no effects on support for nativistic parties such as the Know-Nothings.

Another prevalent interpretation found in quantitative history views the polity as being composed of conflicting ethnocultural groups. Revivalistic pietism—or simply Protestant pietism—was associated with various groups that asserted a particular vision of the polity over and against that of other groups. Pietism therefore shaped attempts at morally defining citizenship and nation in reaction against liturgical ethnic groups such as ethnic Catholics and Lutherans.

A problem with the formation of the ethnocultural argument, pointed out by Hammond (1979, 189), is that it views pietism as not having a religious content but as a general impulse to define boundaries. The resulting tendency is to play down as insignificant the content and nature of the particular issues being contested. This leaves as problematic why the particular moral reform issues were important to the pietists. Hammond (p. 191), in emphasizing the disparate content of specific movements, goes to the other extreme by rejecting the notion that moral reform issues hung together as a coherent set. Jensen's (1971) formulation of the ethnocultural model lies in between. He emphasizes the coherent (although not necessarily consistent) moral ethos of the pietists, and he takes issue with other ethnoculturalists who do not adequately take into account the content of revivalistic pietism and how it might be related to the moral issues.

My institutional model lies closest to Jensen's formulation. It recognizes the content of an issue as significant in its own right, but considers any issue understandable only in the context of a movement's ontology. Moreover, movements composing a "family" and organized around different specific issues, while possibly having different constituents, are considered interpretable in reference to the broad ontology that they share. For example, any economic issue assumes a morality and structure of existence. Consequently, the cultural order within which a movement is organized will affect the movement's economic stance. In many cases the narrowest of issues is an affirmation and dramatization of the larger order. The irony of the pietistic-liturgical terminology of the ethnoculturalists is that the single issue on which pietistic groups focused often was a ritualistic symbol through which the group's entire worldview devolved into political action. Thus, many issues in the nineteenth-century United States, such as abolitionism, temperance, educational reform, and later currency, did work together as a unit, although Hammond is correct in asserting that this is open to empirical verification.

A final important interpretive issue concerns the institutionalization of revivalistic piety. Hammond emphasizes that religion affects political behavior through its ethos: Individuals undergo an eventful consciousness reformation and then are morally compelled to change the world. The implication is that revivalism's effects should decline with institutionalization in the latter part of the century.

I argue that revivalism's effects were strong even in institutionalized denominations. I have emphasized that, because all action implicitly carries a cultural accounting structure, this structure has direct effects on and is embedded in institutionalized practice. Moreover, the cultural order is coded in formal organization. Thus, a movement's or denomination's formal organization and practice concretize and reproduce the reality of the cultural order. For this reason, I have referred to revivalistic pietism as revival *religion* that spans the range of institutional forms, from emotional camp meeting to denominational organization. There are important changes with formalization, but there also is an ontology and moral structure institutionalized throughout.[29] The present study therefore examines moral-political issues in the context of a coherent worldview and thereby takes seriously the content of movement, denominational, and party claims.

Summary

This chapter has examined the content of revival religion and Republicanism in order to demonstrate their mutual isomorphism with individualistic nationalism especially as they appeared in the North and Midwest. Much more could be done in this line of research. Detailed analyses of sermons, liturgies, religious practice, newspapers, diaries, political speeches, party platforms, and the like would be able to shed further light on the linkages between political-economic-based cultural myths and metaphors and the content of these two systems. Analyses of newspapers and pastoral sermons would be especially fruitful not only because of the number available but also because they more than any other documents capture the folk tradition. For example, content analyses of metaphors used throughout the century could be used to map out thematic developments of underlying structures.

The present study moves in a different though complementary research direction. Having described isomorphism, it now is necessary to show that effectual individuation, revival religion, and Republicanism occurred together. I have focused on the dynamic interrelations of these three institutions and on the causal process by which revivalism and Republicanism came to be institutionalized to varying degrees within different populations. Quantitative analyses, over time, of indicators of popular support enable formal direct tests of the causal interpretation. To that end the three interpretive statements of chapter 3 can be recast as specific hypotheses that describe the causal ordering of change and expected patterns of support.

Hypothesis 1: The level of effectual individuation of a region positively affects the degree to which revival religion is embraced, as measured by, for example, the number of people espousing it.

Hypothesis 2: The greater the effectual individuation within a population, the more that population will exhibit popular support (e.g., votes) for the Republican and Prohibition parties.

Hypothesis 3: Revival religion formed a plausibility structure for individualist nationalism distinct from economic organization; thus, the level of acceptance or institutionalization of revivalism within a region, when controlling for effectual individuation, will positively affect that population's vote for the Republican and Prohibition parties.

The analyses in the next chapter attempt to add to the present literature by putting these three hypotheses to a formal quantitative test for northern and midwestern counties during the latter part of the century.

FIVE

Political-Economic Aspects of Revivalism: Quantitative Analyses, 1870–1896

Research Approach and Design[1]

In order to test the three hypotheses set forth in chapter 4, this study uses quantitative data on the 266 counties in Maine, New York, Ohio, and Iowa. These states represent various levels of industrialization in the North and Midwest. The analysis covers the period between 1870 and 1896. The first half of the century is the ideal period for studying the emergence and spread of effectual individualism, but quantitative data is scarce for this time period. By restricting attention to the latter part of the century, we can focus on the *maintenance* of effectual individualism as the dominant cultural structure in the face of increased concentration of capital.[2] Throughout this period, the American polity was characterized by low levels of coercion relative to adherence to a religious or political body. Conservative religious or political organizations were not capable of using or threatening force to suppress a movement and consequently affect the hypothesized relations. Informal pressures, of course, existed; however, even here there was relatively little systematic coercion that needs to be taken into account (regarding voting behavior, see Jensen 1971, chap. 2).

Aggregate data are appropriate because the theoretical argument is at the macro level. The variables of interest are cultural or social institutions that structure the nature of reality and that confront and shape with phenomenological force the experience of the "non-revivalist" as well as the "revivalist." Thus, the hypothesis is not that revivalists voted Republican to a greater degree than non-revivalists, but rather that a population of an area dominated by the institution of revivalism will manifest greater support for Republicanism. Similarly, in a highly individuated system, not only the successful entre-

103

preneur but also the wage earner is influenced to accept individualism. Likewise, the plantation owner is as much confronted with the corporate nature of the plantation system as is the laborer.

Therefore, populations dominated by effectual individuation adhere to the religious and political structure of effectual individualism to a greater extent than populations not dominated by this system of organization. One consequence of this is that I do not, as does Hammond (1979), distinguish between religious effects that are due to the mobilization of people through values and effects due to socioreligious organizations (cf. Lenski 1961).

A religion that is isomorphic with its cultural environment will grow more and faster than one that is less isomorphic. If at a particular time, say 1870, memberships in religious groups are identical, then the isomorphic religion will have more members by a second time point, say 1890. For many reasons, a less isomorphic religion might in 1870 have greater membership than a more isomorphic one, and by 1890 it might still have more, but the isomorphic religion will have closed the gap. Panel models allow us to analyze the relation of memberships in 1890 (the dependent variable) with independent variables indicating isomorphism in 1870, while controlling for initial memberships in 1870. For instance, in relation to hypothesis 1, which predicts a causal effect of effectual individuation on revivalism: the greater the dominance of effectual individuation in 1870, the greater the adherents to revivalism in 1890, controlling for revivalistic memberships in 1870.

An example of the type of equation used to test the hypotheses is given in equation (1). It shows that revival religion in 1890 (the dependent variable) is affected by the economic individuation (multiplied or weighted by population) of the county in 1880, the number of foreign-born persons in the county in 1890, the county's level of industrialization in 1890, and the previous level of revival religion measured in 1870.

$$
\begin{aligned}
\text{Revival Religion, } 1890 = {} & b_1 \text{ Economic Individuation} \\
& \times \quad \text{Population, } 1880 \\
& + b_2 \text{ Foreign Born, } 1890 \\
& + b_3 \text{ Industrialization, } 1890 \\
& + b_4 \text{ Revival Religion, } 1870
\end{aligned}
$$

The b's refer to a statistic (regression coefficient) that estimates the relation of the variable to revival religion in 1890. In this example, hypothesis 1 would be supported if b_1 were positive, that is, if economic individuation had a positive effect on revival religion.

Concepts and Measures
Effectual Individuation

This concept is concerned with the degree to which an individual acts autonomously and efficaciously in the market. Put another way, it is the degree to which production is attributed to and identified with the individual. An overall index might be constructed for the entire field of production, possibly composed of component scales for various sectors. However, because of differences among the sectors and specialization among regions, two separate measures are used. Two sets of equations will be estimated, one with a manufacturing index and the other with an agricultural one.

Manufacturing

Given the rise of corporate capitalism during this period, measurement of effectual individuation within industry can be based on the structural conditions that hinder self-employment: the degree to which the owner is dependent on external resources and organizations. This is a negative index in that high values would indicate low levels of efficacy. The primary factor is the amount of capital needed to start and maintain a business. The greater the requisite capital, the more dependent individuals are on external organizations such as banks, and on their own organizations including partners, financiers, and laborers. The greater the capital per manufacturing establishment the more that effectual activity is attributed to and identified with corporate organization rather than the individual entrepreneur. Thus, Capital Per Manufacturing Establishment is a good *inverse* index of effectual individuation during this period, and the theory predicts that it will have a negative effect on revivalism and Republicanism.[3]

This variable also allows us to test a social control hypothesis derivative from Johnson's work: The greater the relevance of scale of industrial enterprises, the larger the wage earning class, and the greater the problem of labor control. By this line of reasoning one would hypothesize a positive relation between Capital Per Manufacturing Establishment and revivalism. Johnson had in mind the initial industrialization of an agrarian community in which labor had not yet been organized within the corporate factory. Nevertheless, we can test a general argument that links a disciplined, moral, individualistic religion to the prevalence of wage labor.

Agriculture

Following the arguments of various sociologists (e.g., Stinchcombe 1961; Paige 1975), land is taken to be of primary social importance in agrarian systems. Therefore, ownership of land should positively affect farmers' identification with production and increase their perceived autonomy and efficacy. Sharecropping, renting, and ownership therefore would indicate in turn increasing efficacious individuation.

Considerations other than ownership are also important. If an agrarian system is based on the renting of land but is very productive and profitable the fact that the farms are rented may not decrease the centrality of the farmer as entrepreneur or the validity of effectual individualism. On the other hand, a system of operator-owned but unproductive farms would not constitute effectual individuation.

If it can be assumed that family farms still predominated during this period, then the production per farm can be used as a positive indicator. The assumption allows us to infer that the production of a farm is collectively defined as the result of the individual farmer's rational action. The previous historical description notes that the agrarian sector was not greatly influenced by scale of operations or by the size of the farms during this period, and this is supported by the historical literature and the statistical treatment in the Appendix.

Scale does not dominate this sector, but it was beginning to have some influence. Because of its relatively low relation to production, scale factors can be included in the equation as an explicit control. The best indicator available is the amount of wages paid per farm, available only for 1870. Production Per Farm, controlling for the amount due to hired labor, is a direct measure of efficacious individuation and would have positive effects on revivalism and Republicanism. Wages Per Farm is itself interpretable as an inverse indicator of effectual individuation and would therefore be negatively related to revival religion and voting for the Republican party. We can pursue the alternative argument that revival religion was rooted in problems of labor control. Other things being equal, if the presence of a large number of wage earners increases labor control problems, the competing hypothesis is that the variable of Wages Per Farm has positive effects on revivalism.

odd tension here is that of an agrarian system has more "individuation" that cap. system!

Summary of Effectual Individuation Indicators

Capital Per Manufacturing Establishment is an inverse index of effectual individuation in the industrial sector. Hypothesis 1a is that it has a negative effect on revivalism; hypothesis 2a is that it has a negative effect on Republicanism. In the agrarian sector two indexes are used:

also, both measures seem very distant from concept they are intended to measure

Production Per Farm is a direct measure, and hypotheses 1b and 2b are that it has a positive effect on revivalism and Republicanism, respectively. *Wages Per Farm* is an inverse measure of effectual individuation, and hypotheses 1c and 2c are that it has a negative effect on revivalism and Republicanism, respectively. Data are obtained from the U.S. censuses between 1870 and 1900.[4]

Revival Religion

I have conceptualized revival religion as a cultural order or knowledge structure and have described four key components: free will of the individual, a rational methodology for bringing about conversion and revival, perfect sanctification, and postmillennialism. These four points describe the underlying ontology of revival religion.

Denominations each held to their own worldviews, which varied in their similarity to revivalism. The membership of a given body may be taken as an indicator of the number of adherents to its particular religious ontology. This, of course, ignores internal variations and divisions within the denomination, but by this time the major issues with which we are concerned had created splits among the religious groups. Different internal factions fighting over the revivalism issue had already split into distinct denominations leaving each religious group more homogeneous relative to this dimension.

The number of members of a denomination indicates in two ways the predominance within a population of its corresponding ontology. It directly measures the "believers" or adherents who order their actions within this reality. It also measures the visibility and force of these cultural elements relative to the phenomenological experience of the "nonbelievers" in the population. Ontologies are institutionalized propositions about reality present in the cultural environment of everyone in the population, believers and nonbelievers alike. The force of these propositions on the individual and the degree of assimilation by the individual are functions of the perceived social support for or the collective taken-for-grantedness of the ontology which itself is partly a direct function of the number of adherents. This is distinct from but related to friendship networks. That is, it is not necessary for the nonbeliever to have a revivalistic friend or family member before he or she is confronted with revivalism as a cultural element. Yet, a higher number of adherents increases the likelihood of a friend or relative's being a member.

This means that if particular denominations closely subscribed to the ontology of revival religion, then the size of their memberships may be interpreted as a measure of the predominance of revivalism as a cultural institution. To this end, the denominations on which there are available data were rated on a five-point scale (0 to 4) according to their adherence to the four components of revivalism.

Several historians of religion in the United States rated the denominations on the various components noted above. Additionally, I abstracted two ratings from various histories of American religion and from the description of various bodies found in the United States census of 1890 (cf. Carroll 1912). I then combined these four ratings into one (see table A2). While the ratings of some denominations varied from state to state, this variation was small enough to ignore. For example, Maine Congregationalists were probably less revivalistic than their midwestern counterparts, but not by much. Thus, one rating is used for all four states.

County-level data on religious memberships and church facilities are available from the U.S. census for most denominations in 1870 and 1890.[5] Similar data were collected in 1880 but were never compiled. The 1890 census includes memberships, but the 1870 enumeration contains only the seating capacity of a denomination's church buildings. Denominational seating capacities are good indicators of relative memberships if and only if there is no great variation in the ratio of seatings to memberships across denominations. This appears to be reasonably correct in that the seating capacity is consistently from one-and-one half times to double the available membership figures across congregations, and this small variation is not related to denominations.[6] Moreover, being measured for 1870, this variable is used only as a control. For convenience all data, including the 1870 information, will be referred to as memberships, but it should be remembered that the 1870 data are only indirectly indicative of memberships.

Two different indexes are constructed from this information. The first measures only the most extremely revivalistic adherents. This is done by taking those denominations that are rated 4. Their memberships are summed and interpreted as the extent of radical revivalism within a county. This includes Methodists and "Christians" in 1870.[7] By 1890 the latter had given rise to the Christian Connection and the Disciples of Christ. Because of their common origin and similar beliefs (they are both rated 4), both of these bodies are used in the 1890 index. This index is based primarily on Methodism, by far the largest of the bodies rated 4.

This index provides a good first approximation of the predominance of the institution of revival religion within a county. It is conservative to the degree that it does not rely heavily on the subtle differentiations present in the rating. This has its advantages but it also does not make use of much rich information and ignores the number of adherents to less extreme forms of revival religion. Thus, a large group of Presbyterians in a county may not be as indicative of revivalism as the same number of Methodists, but its presence should be incorporated into any measure of revivalism as such a county would be more influenced by revivalism than a county dominated by Primitive Baptists or Lutherans.

In order to take full advantage of the information present in all of the ratings, and to be less dependent on Methodism, each denomination's membership is weighted by its rating, and the results for all denominations are summed. Substantively this index is interpretable as the interaction between the degree to which a denomination subscribes to revivalistic pietism and its visibility or social support. This provides a good indicator of the collective phenomenological influence of revivalism on an individual in the population and of the degree to which it as a cultural institution prevails within a county. This index may be interpreted literally as the number of revivalistic "unit persons" in a county. Although it is tenuous to push the equivalence too far, it may be said that one Methodist is equivalent to four "unit persons" or adherents to revivalism while one Baptist is equal to three adherents. The first index is referred to as the exclusive index and the second one is referred to as the inclusive index.

Summary of Revival Religion Indicators

Two Revivalism Indexes are used: The *Exclusive Index* is the total membership of denominations that are rated "4" on revivalism; the *Inclusive Index* is the sum of various denominational memberships, each weighted by its rating on revivalism. The Appendix describes the ratings in greater detail.

Political Ideology

Voting data at the county level for all parties are available from the Inter-University Consortium for Political and Social Research (ICPSR). The focus is on the presidential elections between 1880 and 1896.[8] Republican party vote is used as an indicator of individualistic ideology throughout the period. The Prohibition party emerged in the seventies and espoused a more moralistic version of the Republican ideology, and I view it as one version of individualistic nationalism. It gained notable support in 1884 and remained sizable until 1896 when it was swamped in the larger clash between the two major parties. Therefore I analyze it from 1884 through 1892. Within the states being studied, the populist parties and other groups did not have enough strength during this period to warrant longitudinal analysis.

Summary of Individualistic-Nationalistic Ideology Indicators
Republican Vote and *Prohibitionist Vote* are used to measure support for ideologies of individualistic nationalism during this period.

Control variables[9]
Number of Foreign Born

It could be argued that apart from political-economic factors revivalism and Republicanism resulted from threats to a homogeneous white "native" population. This would imply a positive relation between the percentage of a population that is *Foreign Born* and both Revivalism and Republicanism, and thus a spurious positive relation between the latter two. A different line of reasoning is that large numbers of immigrants were members of non-revivalistic denominations (e.g., Lutheran) and voted Democrat for ethnic reasons apart from political-economic structure. This would result in a negative relation of Foreign Born to both Revivalism and Republicanism and again a spurious positive relation between the latter two. The second line of reasoning seems more plausible given the literature already cited (see also Christiano 1988), but in either case it is necessary to control for the percentage of immigrants in assessing the hypotheses.

Industrialization

Industrialization is measured by the ratio of manufacturing production to the sum of manufacturing and agricultural production. Industrialization is in actuality a proxy variable for a myriad of different dimensions. It is negatively related to effectual individuation (see the Appendix). We thus can interpret it, in part, as the collectivization of the market under large corporate concerns. However, in that effectual individuation is measured independently, Industrialization is included as a distinct control variable. It is interpreted substantively as an indirect indicator of urbanization and also as a control for economic interest in urban-industrial versus rural-agrarian issues.

Relating Industrialization to Revivalism Indexes draws on the traditional idea that revivals were rural-agrarian events. Thus, Industrialization would be negatively related to them. Cross (1950) supports this contention; Hammond (1979) found little relation between the percentage of farms and revivalism in Ohio and New York in the early part of the century, although revivals seemed to thrive in less densely populated regions.

The parallel conventional argument is applied to voting: Rural areas were Republican and the labor-dominated cities were Democratic (e.g., Schlesinger 1933; Diamond 1941), at least until the Bryan era beginning in 1896. This is complicated by the fact that manufacturing interests were more in line with the Republican ideology of nurturing home industry within the international market. This linkage was especially salient in the 1896 election in which Bryan and the Democratic party mobilized anti-industry rhetoric. As noted in chapter 4, the empirical evidence is ambiguous. Hammarberg (1974) shows some town versus countryside effects while Kleppner (1970) and Jensen (1971) find no such effects on voting. At this point the working hypothesis is that Industrialization (the proportion of production in manufacturing) is negatively related to Republican and Prohibition Vote until the election of 1896 in which it has a positive relation to Republican support.

Population

Because raw values are used throughout the analyses, *Population* is entered as an explicit control.

Total Memberships

It could be argued that the independent variables are affecting religiosity in general and have nothing to do with different denominations. In order to control for this argument, *Total Memberships* in all denominations are included in some equations.

Total Vote

Party vote is at times affected by voter turnout. For this reason *Total Vote* is included in some equations. Its inclusion presents certain statistical problems that are discussed in the Appendix. Because this variable makes little difference in findings for 1880–92, the text reports the results of equations without Total Vote included. Any differences that were found when including this variable are noted either in footnotes or the Appendix. Total Vote plays an important role in the 1896 election, and therefore I include it in equations discussed in the text and describe it to a greater extent for that election.

Splitting the Sample and the Exclusion of Cases

It makes little sense to say that effectual individuation in manufacturing affects a population's cultural order when industry is only a small part of productive activity. The same, of course, is true of agriculture. Thus, in those equations using the manufacturing measure, the bottom 20 percent of counties on Industrialization are excluded; the top 20 percent are excluded for the equations with the agricultural index.[10]

Because the manufacturing index of individuation (Capital Per Manufacturing Establishment) and Industrialization are highly correlated, their effects cannot be estimated in the same equation. As detailed in the Appendix, we can estimate them simultaneously for those counties in the bottom half of Industrialization, for in those counties the two variables are not highly related. The results will be reported first for the entire sample and then for only those counties falling below the median.[11]

In the political models the correlation between Foreign Born and Revivalism is too high for both variables to be included. Excluding the counties with the highest proportion of Foreign Born greatly reduces this correlation. This methodological procedure is possible because this variable is a control and not of substantive interest at this point. By excluding these cases the actual effects of Foreign Born are not accurately measured, but while still controlling for this variable it provides a more accurate assessment of Revivalism's effects. As would be expected, this exclusion reduces the estimated effects of Foreign Born on voting patterns.[12]

The Socioeconomic Context of Revivalism, 1870–1890: Results

The core findings are summarized in table 1 for the Exclusive Index and in table 2 for the Inclusive Index. (Details are reported in the Appendix.) The results are substantively identical for both indexes. I examine first the control variables. Revivalism Indexes measured in 1870 have large effects, indicating stability of memberships over time (and noteworthy since they actually number church seatings). The number of Foreign Born in a county dominates the analysis with large negative effects on the Revivalism Indexes; this holds for both the whole sample and for the less industrialized counties. Industrialization (proportion of production in manufacturing) has a negative effect on Revivalism Indexes and supports the conventional lines of reasoning.

Table 1 Panel Analyses of Revivalism, 1870–1890: Exclusive Index[a]

Hypotheses and Independent Variables	Predicted Effect on Revivalism, '90	Estimated Effect on Revivalism, '90	N
Hypothesis 1a:			
Capital/Manufactur-		−.09[b]	201
ing Establishment, '80	−	−.18[c]	74
Hypothesis 1b:			
Production/Farm, '80	+	+.17	175[d]
Hypothesis 1c:			
Wages/Farm, '70	−	−.16	175[d]
Controls:			
Industrialization, '90	−	−.28	229
Foreign Born, '90	−	−.33	229
Revivalism, '70	+	+.43	229

[a]Summary of table A7. Estimations are standardized (beta) coefficients.

[b]Not controlling for Industrialization; excludes counties with less than 18% production in industry, 1880.

[c]Controlling for Industrialization; estimated for counties in bottom half of Industrialization, excluding counties with less than 18% production in industry, 1880.

[d]Excludes counties with more than 69% production in industry, 1880.

Table 2 Panel Analyses of Revivalism, 1870–1890: Inclusive Index[a]

Hypotheses and Independent Variables	Predicted Effect on Revivalism, '90	Estimated Effect on Revivalism, '90	N
Hypothesis 1a:			
Capital/Manufactur-		−.08[b]	194
ing Establishment, '80	−	−.21[c]	69
Hypothesis 1b:			
Production/Farm, '80	+	+.24	159[d]
Hypothesis 1c:			
Wages/Farm, '70	−	−.14	159[d]
Controls:			
Industrialization, '90	−	−.21	211
Foreign Born, '90	−	−.32	211
Revivalism, '70	+	+.45	211

[a]Summary of table A8. Estimations are standardized (beta) coefficients.

[b]Not controlling for Industrialization; excludes counties with less than 18% production in industry, 1880.

[c]Controlling for Industrialization; estimated for counties in bottom half of Industrialization, excluding counties with less than 18% production in industry, 1880.

[d]Excludes counties with more than 69% production in industry, 1880.

In support of hypothesis 1a, Capital Per Manufacturing Establishment (the inverse index of effectual individuation in manufacturing) has a significant negative effect on the Revivalism Indexes, as predicted. This holds for the whole sample and also when controlling for Industrialization. It therefore is reasonable to infer that effectual individuation as measured inversely by the average amount of capital invested in a manufacturing establishment is distinct from industrialization. These processes are intertwined historically and therefore have similar causal relations to revivalist memberships, but to the extent that the two dimensions can be separated, effectual individuation has a positive causal effect which is independent of industrialization.

The effects of effectual individuation within the agrarian sector are estimated separately. In support of hypothesis 1b, Production Per Farm has a positive effect on Revivalism Indexes. Wages Per Farm is included in order to partial out factors of scale that might be included in production, and is interpreted as an inverse index of effectual individuation. As predicted by hypothesis 1c, it has a negative effect on the Revivalism Indexes. Thus, in support of hypothesis 1, effectual individuation within the agrarian sector as measured by these two variables has a positive causal relation to the acceptance of revivalistic pietism.

Both Capital Per Manufacturing Establishment and Wages Per Farm reflect the size of the wage-earning class and indicate potential crises of labor control. According to the labor control argument, they would positively affect adherence to revivalism; yet, both variables negatively affect it. This holds even in the less industrialized counties that might more closely resemble early industrialization. Thus, the fact that both variables have negative effects on Revivalism Indexes not only supports the institutional model, but, with the qualifications noted, calls into question the labor control interpretation.

It could be argued that the various independent and control variables affect total religious membership or religiosity, thereby creating a spurious relation to revivalist memberships. This is not credible in relation to the Exclusive Index which includes only a small proportion of total members. Nevertheless, Total Religious Membership was included as a control in each of the reported equations. While it had a large positive relation to both measures of revivalism, it did not alter any other coefficient in the various models.

These analyses reveal several things about revivalism and its social context. Regarding the control variables, counties with larger numbers of foreign born have fewer revivalist memberships, independent of economic factors. This implies that revival religion was not a nativistic reaction to the local presence of immigrant groups. Industrialization has a negative relation to revivalism, independent of the concentration of capital and labor and of immigrant populations, all of which characterized industrial centers.

The statistical results relevant to hypothesis 1 can be summarized in four points. (1) Effectual individuation within manufacturing and agriculture is distinguishable from industrialization both conceptually and empirically. (2) The average amount of capital invested in a manufacturing establishment is an inverse measure of effectual individuation, and it has a negative causal relation to the number of revivalist memberships. (3) The average production of a farm is a direct indicator of this concept, and it has a positive causal effect on the adherence to revival religion. (4) The average amount of wages paid on a farm is an inverse index of effectual individuation, and it has a negative effect on adherence to revivalism.

Thus, at the level of statistical relations among measured variables, we have corroborated the predictions of hypothesis 1. We move from this level to the conceptual level and infer that by the latter part of the century, revival religion prevailed in those counties most organized in individuated production and exchange. Effectual individuation was associated with individualistic nationalism. Together they formed a plausibility structure for revival religion that found its greatest legitimacy and adherence in the areas they dominated. Because this hypothesis was derived from the institutional model, we further can infer support for the broader institutional interpretation. I belabor the steps of inference to caution the reader that while the statistical evidence is quite dramatic, more work is needed to better measure the concepts and specify the models. Thus, these analyses are only a modest step in testing the institutionalist interpretation. The qualitative demonstration in chapter 4 provides a deeper context for these inferences and thereby increases our confidence in them. With these cautions, we can infer that revival religion was legitimated by the cultural environment of individualistic nationalism, rooted in market penetration and effectual individuation. It articulated that sociocultural order within a unified ontology.

The Political Consequences of Revivalism, 1880–1896: Results

My present concern is the effect of revival religion and individuation on voting behavior. I am not interested in explaining why a particular party won a given election or in the details of the various issues. Nor do I wish to delineate elite class interests in the different policy positions. While these are all important for constructing a descriptive model of the polity, I want to show that any analysis must include cultural contexts of conflict and popular support for particular ideologies. Nevertheless each election during this period was characterized by certain issues, particular performances of the party in power, shifting economic conditions, and the like. These must be noted in order to place the analyses within the political and social context of the election, and therefore I give short descriptions of the elections. They are general summaries only, which concentrate on those points most relevant to the present hypotheses and are designed to highlight the distinctive institutionalist approach to issue politics.

1880–1888
Description

The nomination of James Garfield by the Republicans in 1880 marked a turning away from war issues. The Republican party was still the party of Lincoln which had saved the Union and "transformed 4,000,000 human beings from the likeness of *things* to the rank of *citizens*" (Republican National Platform of 1880; emphasis added). However, contemporary issues had to be addressed. The currency problem concerning the free coinage of silver and specie payment that dominated the national scene in the 1870s died down in the early eighties. The emerging economic issue of whether or not to protect industry by means of a tariff became the primary issue in 1884. The Democrats were against protection, but most of them were also against free trade. Indecisiveness within the Democratic party over this and other issues was in part due to the transition from their antebellum order. Grover Cleveland, still clinging to the old formulation, backed extreme laissez-faire. At the same time, however, the demand for federal action was continually present. This equivocation resulted in a tariff bill that was weak and easily interpreted as "irresponsible free trade." The Republicans, just before the 1888 election, drafted a strong protectionist bill that avoided extremes.

The national issues of currency and the tariff were not necessarily the primary focus at the local and state levels. Although often concerned with economic issues such as railroad regulation, elections at the state level usually were contested over different attitudes toward moral reform. The two primary issues were schools and prohibition. Both parties favored educational expansion. The Republicans, however, emphasized that the school system was intended to create national citizens and thus was partly a federal responsibility. The conflict over education was intensified with the growth of Roman Catholic schools. The Republicans maintained that the central government must insure that schools incorporate all individuals into the American nation. They therefore wanted to refuse any public aid to Catholic schools. The Democrats, relying on a large Catholic voting bloc, supported their school system. Public aid to parochial schools was the dominant issue in New York and several other states in 1880 and played a role in the elections throughout the decade.

By 1888, Prohibition had replaced the education problem as the number one issue although the latter still was important. The Republicans were firmly within the Prohibitionist camp, which hindered the Prohibition party throughout the eighties. However, the Republican national organization was split. The more moderate leaders, not wishing to antagonize the pivotal ethnic vote, did not want to push Prohibition and tried to distance the party from revivalist control. The more radical moral reform members desired full prohibition. In the face of this equivocation the Prohibition party grew. In the national convention of 1884 the Republicans snubbed the temperance leaders by excluding them from any central position (Hirsch 1971), and it was not coincidental that the Prohibition party made its largest gains in 1884.

The rise of Prohibitionism as a third party, coupled with the fact that it drew heavily from the Republican ranks, forced the Republicans to take a more moralistic stance. A Prohibitionist resolution was included in the 1888 national platform. Foraker, a national figure from Ohio and a radical Prohibitionist, had explicitly identified the Republican party with Prohibition in several state elections within Ohio (Kleppner 1970). In New York the Republicans espoused high license fees for saloons (Wesser 1971). Despite these trends, the Republican party still vacillated, and the Prohibition party grew steadily.

How are the moral and economic issues related? There is a debate over which set of issues was the most important. Quantitative historians (e.g., Benson 1961; Hays 1967; Kleppner 1970, 1979; Jensen 1971) have taken fellow historians to task for emphasizing national economic issues of tariff and currency over local social issues. Their criticism is correct to the degree that local party organizations and the voters were more concerned with social issues. Yet, both sides of the debate assume a sharp division of issues into distinct categories related to organizational levels and to social spheres.

Using an instructional approach, I argue that national economic issues and local social ones are in fact two sides of the same coin. Generally, to understand strongly focused issues, and especially "single-issue" movements, one must interpret how the issue fits into and comes to symbolize the broad ontology. The Republican demands for moral reform and a protective tariff flow out of the same institutionalized theory of society. On the one hand, the individual must be remade and morally transformed into a citizen if democracy is to be maintained and the nation is to progress. On the other hand, the central state must manage both the sovereignty and integrity of the nation in the international market and the autonomy of the citizen at home. While neither aspect is especially statist, nation building in the world-system context leads to bureaucratic state expansion.

For example Wesser (1971; cf. Kleppner 1970) emphasizes that the tariff question was a base from which the Republicans could reaffirm the American system—the radical unionism of the early party. The Democrats said the tariff was another example of Republican "paternalism," while the Republicans argued that Democrats supported "free trade" which would make the United States dependent on "British supremacy." Parallel to this point, Wesser argues that farmers in the eighties voted Republican and thereby supported protection, not because they calculated any direct benefit from a tariff, but rather because they were convinced that it would be unpatriotic to defeat the tariff and subvert America in the international market. This transformation of "national economic issues" into "local social rhetoric" illustrates their use as multifocal symbols reflecting the conflict over what theory of society was to reign.

At all levels, the Republicans were guided by the cultural myths of individualistic nationalism: the primacy of national citizenship linking the rights and needs of the individual to the central regime; moderate attempts to define that citizenship by the application of moral categories; policy that supported national economic growth in world markets. Because these issues were elements of individualistic nationalism, hypotheses 2 and 3 are that effectual individuation and revival religion causally affect Republican support.

For my analysis, it is first necessary to show that by 1880 there had developed a cross-sectional alignment between Republican voting and populations dominated by these structures. I then analyze change in voting between 1880 and 1888. Given an established alignment, it is doubtful that there were further shifts of revivalist and effectually individuated populations toward Republicanism. We know that the Prohibition party emerged and gained strength during this period. I therefore further hypothesize that any substantial change during this period would result from revivalist and effectually individuated populations shifting from the major parties toward Prohibitionism. Immigrant populations, as suggested by the literature, would show negative effects on the growth of the Prohibition party.

Results and Discussion[13]

1880. The results of the cross-sectional regression analysis of Republican Vote are summarized in table 3. Beginning with the control variables, Foreign Born shows a somewhat surprising positive relation to Republican Vote. Industrialization has small positive effects. Turning to the hypotheses, hypothesis 2a has mixed support: The inverse measure of effectual individuation in the manufacturing sector—Capital Per Manufacturing Establishment—is not related to Republican Vote, although we find the predicted negative effect when Industrialization is controlled. The effects of the agrarian indexes of effectual individuation also show mixed support for hypotheses 2b and c: Production Per Farm is positively related to Republican Vote but so is Wages Per Farm. Agrarian productivity, even with the presence of wage labor, is a strong basis for Republican Vote.[14]

Thus, scale in agriculture and industry has less of a relationship with Republican voting than expected during this period. Republican

[handwritten margin notes: "wealth", "this is ahead", "this measures not individ.)"]

Table 3 Cross-Sectional Analyses of Republican Vote, 1880[a]

Hypotheses and Independent Variables	Predicted Effect	Estimated Effect	N
Hypothesis 3:			
Revivalism	+	+.36	168
Hypothesis 2a:			
Capital/Manufactur-		+.00[b]	155
ing Establishment	−	−.15[c]	61
Hypothesis 2b:			
Production/Farm	+	+.17	137[d]
Hypothesis 2c:			
Wages/Farm, '70	−	+.28	137[d]
Controls:			
Industrialization,	−	+.08	168
Foreign Born	−	+.26	168

[a]Summary of table A10. Estimations are standardized (beta) coefficients. Counties in which more than 18% of the population are foreign born in 1880 are excluded.

[b]Not controlling for Industrialization; excludes counties with less than 18% production in industry, 1880.

[c]Controlling for Industrialization; estimated for counties in bottom half of Industrialization, excluding counties with less than 18% production in industry, 1880.

[d]Excludes counties with more than 69% production in industry, 1880.

flexibility in assimilating corporate capital into their ideology might be attenuating any delegitimating effects. Interestingly, the small negative effects of scale show up in counties low in industrialization, counties probably the most similar in economic organization to the petty capitalism earlier in the century. Nevertheless, the statistical relations between measures of effectual individuation and Republican Vote are ambiguous.

In contrast, there is a very strong positive relationship between the Revivalism Index and Republican Vote, as predicted in hypothesis 3. We find the predicted alignment between those populations that have a highly visible revival religion, as indicated by revivalist memberships, and Republican support.

1880–1888. The results of the panel regression analyses, 1880–1888, are summarized in table 4. For the two major parties the two four-year lags from 1880 to 1884 and from 1884 to 1888 show identical results. Therefore the overall effects from 1880 to 1888 are reported. The Prohibition Vote in 1880 was too small to analyze; therefore only the 1884 to 1888 lag is reported. The effects of Party Vote measured at time 1 for all parties is large, reflecting the high level of party loyalty. The number of Foreign Born has significant negative effects on subsequent Republican Vote and on the emergence of the Prohibition party as expected. Industrialization has small positive effects on subsequent Republican Vote and negative effects on Democratic change. This is the opposite of what was predicted by a literature that suggests that industrial counties would increasingly be dominated by the labor-Democratic alignment. While this association might in fact exist, given that the equations analyze the aggregate population, this finding lends weight to the arguments of historians who have emphasized the increasing affinity of industry with Republicanism. There is no effect of Industrialization on Prohibition Vote.

As with the cross-sectional findings for hypothesis 2, there is no statistical evidence that effectual individuation in the manufacturing sphere is causally related to voting behavior. Moreover, the agrarian indicators of this variable have the opposite effect from what was predicted and what was found in the cross-sectional equations: Production Per Farm has a negative effect on Republican Vote and a positive effect on Democratic Vote, while Wages Per Farm has the opposite relations.

The Revivalism Index performs as predicted by hypothesis 3: It has a negative effect on subsequent Republican Vote, a larger negative one on Democratic Vote, and a positive one on Prohibition Vote.

Table 4 Panel Analyses of Voting, 1880–1888[a]

Hypotheses and Independent Variables	Republican Vote, 1888		Democratic Vote, 1888		Prohibition Vote, 1888		N
	Predicted	Estimated	Predicted	Estimated	Predicted	Estimated	
Hypothesis 3: Revivalism[b]	±	−.15	−	−.25	+	+.13	169
Hypothesis 2a: Capital/Manufacturing Establishment[b]	−	+.01[c]	+	−.04[c]	−	+.02[c]	156/153[d]
		+.04[e]		−.09[e]		+.00[e]	60/ 57[d]
Hypothesis 2b: Production/Farm[b]	+	−.10	−	+.35	+	+.07	136/135[d,f]
Hypothesis 2c: Wages/Farm, '70	−	+.07	+	−.30	−	−.04	136/135[d,f]
Controls:							
Industrialization, '88	−	+.04	+	−.22	−	−.03	169
Foreign Born, '88	−	−.06	+	+.07	−	−.13	169
Party Vote[b]	+	+.95	+	+.89	+	+.79	169

[a]Summary of table A11. Estimations are standardized (beta) coefficients. Counties in which more than 19% of the population are foreign born in 1888 are excluded.

[b]Date of independent variable is 1880 for Republican and Democratic Vote, 1884 for Prohibition Vote.

[c]Not controlling for Industrialization; excludes counties with less than 18% production in industry, 1880.

[d]First N is for Republican and Democratic cases, the second is for Prohibition cases.

[e]Controlling for Industrialization; estimated for counties in bottom half of Industrialization; excluding counties with less than 18% production in industry, 1880.

[f]Excludes counties with more than 69% production in industry, 1880.

Summary. The cross-sectional analysis taken with the longitudinal results are suggestive. The Republican party began losing foreign-born populations during the eighties, but not industrialized counties. The manufacturing indicator of effectual individuation has no discernable statistical relation to the Republican Vote, although there is an indication of the predicted relation in the less industrialized counties. The agrarian indexes of effectual individuation show that by 1880 there is an alignment between agrarian productivity and the Republican Vote, possibly regardless of scale. Table 4, however, implies that such populations moved more toward the Democrats than toward the Prohibitionists. In short, the statistical relations predicted by hypothesis 2 are not found consistently, making inferences problematic.

The statistical relation of the Revival Index to electoral behavior is stronger and more consistent. It thus is reasonable to infer hypothesis 3: Revivalism supported Republican individualistic nationalism. So, by 1880 there had developed a major alignment between revivalism and Republicanism. With the rise of the more moralistic Prohibition party, revivalist-dominated populations shifted somewhat from both major parties resulting in a negative effect of revival religion on change in Republican support and an even larger one on Democratic change. These shifts occurred in the context of an already high interassociation between revivalism and Republicanism.

1888–1892
Description

After 1888 the currency problem reemerged. Because of the value placed on labor, Republicans were suspicious of inflation, but this at times was offset by an interest in using inflation to stimulate growth. The Republicans passed a moderate compromise bill, the Sherman Silver Purchase Act of 1890, which successfully avoided alienating anyone except the radical inflationists. The Democrats were split on the issue. Grover Cleveland and the national elites opposed inflationary policy while local organizations, especially in the West, came increasingly under the control of the silverites and favored inflation policies. In short, the two main parties continued their fence-walking on currency, albeit for different reasons.

The tariff issue also became more prevalent, but Kleppner (1970) demonstrates that, at least in the Midwest, it was still interpreted within the traditional social theories of the two parties: Protariff Republicans were paternalistic meddlers infringing on local rights; Democrats were unpatriotic and not willing to protect American laborers from foreign slave labor. As noted, these theories were grounded locally in cultural alignments and the social issues of education, Prohibition, and moral reform in general. Thus, as in the earlier elections, even the strictly economic issues oriented to world-system developments were rhetorically placed and interpreted within the ideology of each party.

After Benjamin Harrison's victory in 1888, the Republicans were defeated widely in local and state elections, largely because of the continued losses of the non-revivalistic ethnic groups and of other groups not supporting moral reform. Therefore, at the national level they redoubled their efforts to purge the revivalists, and by 1892, after waves of defeats, even state organizations attempted to distance themselves. However, before 1892 they merely skirted the problem by saying nothing. The result was that their identification with moralistic revivalism remained. It was not until 1893 and after that revivalists were driven from key positions in the party's national organization (see Jensen 1971).

Results and Discussion

Table 5 summarizes the analyses of electoral change for the three parties. Industrialization has a small positive effect on Democratic Vote which is a reversal of the trend in the eighties. The indicators of effectual individuation again show mixed support for hypothesis 2: Capital Per Manufacturing Establishment has the predicated negative effect on Republican Vote, but the agrarian indicators do not differentiate the major parties, having the same effects on each one.[15] We again are more confident in inferring hypothesis 3. The Inclusive Revivalism Index has a positive effect on subsequent Republican Vote during this period and to a lesser extent on Prohibition Vote, and no significant effect on Democratic Vote. Thus, shifts in voting for the 1892 election show patterns similar to that of the eighties: effectual individuation has mixed effects while there is strong support of revivalist counties for Republicanism and Prohibitionism.

The finding that counties high in revival religion moved toward Republicanism during this four-year period is slightly puzzling on the surface in light of the trend in the eighties. After the movement from the Republican party to Prohibitionism in the eighties, why is there a "return" of revivalist populations to Republicanism in 1892? The Republicans were not shifting toward a more radical stance behind Prohibition; if anything, they were moving away from an extreme position, and thus they were not coopting the purposes of the Prohibition party.

The institutional model provides two possible interpretations. The first is related to the perceived probability of successfully controlling the polity. Prior to 1889 Republican strength—and with it individu-

Table 5 Panel Analyses of Voting, 1888–1892[a]

Hypotheses and Independent Variables	Republican Vote, 1892		Democratic Vote, 1892		Prohibition Vote, 1892		N
	Predicted	Estimated	Predicted	Estimated	Predicted	Estimated	
Hypothesis 3:							
Revivalism, 90	±	+.17	−	+.04	+	+.08	184
Hypothesis 2a:							
Capital/Manufacturing Establishment, '88	−	−.05[b]	+	+.02[b]	+	+.03[b]	156
		−.03[c]		−.08[c]		−.04[c]	59
Hypothesis 2b:							
Production/Farm, '88	+	+.16	−	+.13	+	+.00	153[d]
Hypothesis 2c:							
Wages/Farm, '70	−	−.14	+	−.17	−	+.03	153[d]
Controls:							
Industrialization, '92	−	−.04	+	+.03	−	+.01	184
Foreign Born, '92	−	+.21	+	+.14	−	+.07	184
Party Vote, '88	+	+.85	+	+.98	+	+.90	184

[a]Summary of table A12. Estimations are standardized (beta) coefficients. Counties in which more than 17% of the population are foreign born in 1892 are excluded.

[b]Not controlling for Industrialization; excludes counties with less than 18% production in industry, 1888.

[c]Controlling for Industrialization; estimated for counties in bottom half of Industrialization; excluding counties with less than 18% production in industry, 1888.

[d]Excludes counties with more than 75% production in industry, 1888.

alistic political ideology—was never seriously threatened. While Cleveland won the presidency in 1884, the Republicans maintained predominance in the government. More extreme but less successful parties within the individualistic nationalism "family" could be entertained by revivalist populations. When the Democrats mounted a real challenge to Republican domination, as they did following the 1888 election and apparently because moral issues were causing the Republicans to lose the ethnic vote, pragmatic concerns came to the fore. The increasingly secularized Republican ideology may have been less consistent with revivalism than that of Prohibitionism, but it had a better chance of keeping the even less acceptable theory of the Democrats out of power. More generally, when there is a threat to a cultural order as carried by a family of movements, the internal differences of these movements are collapsed by mobilizing around the most politically powerful version. As noted in the theory, certain levels of incongruity between a given institution and its environment may be accepted for the sake of successfully controlling that institution and of preventing greater incongruence.

A second factor is that loyalties to the Republican party once established were relatively independent of Republican consistency or inconsistency with revivalism. The institutional model argues that once an organization is institutionalized—initially because it is congruent with its environmental myths—the primacy of the organization is established and the attainment of externally imposed goals is equated with the success of the organization. This is quite plausible relative to Republicanism: The Republican party by this time was institutionalized as *the* manager of individualistic nationalism and possibly was equated with it.

The second interpretation implies two things. First, when an organization and its corresponding knowledge system are threatened, there is an attempt to protect the organization per se and not solely as a carrier of the ideology. Second, even when there is no threat to the organization or its ideology, incongruities may still be tolerated. The assumed primacy of the social organization allows the population to tolerate this lack of isomorphism. When the primacy of the carrier organization is highly institutionalized, such "incongruities" may not even be perceived, being interpreted in light of the organization's now somewhat independent social base and ideology. Ritualized acknowledgement of religious themes and origins might be sufficient to allay any concerns and to "decouple" party policies from close scrutiny. Thus, under these conditions, a threat to the organization and its knowledge structure is not necessary for the toleration of incongruities.

Consequently, as the Republican party during this period pulled back from extreme moralistic issues, revivalistic groups might still show strong support because the Republican party was *the* party of the nation and the moral order. It should be emphasized that a priori this was only one possibility; revivalistic groups could have abandoned the party, morally outraged at a sellout. But given the institutionalization of the Republican party, and based on the results of this one analysis, this is the most plausible interpretation. This interpretation leads to unique implications for the 1896 election.

1892–1896
Description

The depression of 1893 was hard felt, and most of the country blamed the Democrats and President Cleveland. "Hard times" became the context in which the old issues of silver and the tariff were rehashed, again in the context of differing ideologies. Added to this was the concern for law and order that resulted from the outbreaks of labor violence. After the defeats between 1888 and 1892, the Republicans successfully purged pietistic control. They were no longer bound to radical moralism and Prohibition. Nevertheless, they still adhered to an, admittedly more secular, individualistic nationalism. William McKinley, the Republican candidate in 1896, stoutly refused to recognize either class or sectional interests: The government was to manage individuals as individuals for there were no larger aggregates or subgroups. A tariff was still needed to protect national interests and the laborer. Sound money was equated with honest men and honest work, whereas the inflationary policy of the free coinage of silver symbolized socialism and anarchy. Reflecting the dominance of individualistic nationalism, even Cleveland, before the silverite takeover, argued that the Democrats were not so "unpatriotic nor foolish" as to injure the country with the free coinage of silver (see Fite 1971).

The Democrats made a more dramatic shift in their position. The party had been split over the free coinage of silver and other economic issues since the eighties. The leadership in general argued that there should be no extension of federal power. Factions opposed to this weak conception of government grew throughout the period. Rejecting both antebellum "small government" and rugged individualism, they took the first steps toward articulating a basis for a stronger central apparatus. The center, in the face of corporate capitalism, was more extensively and directly to manage economy and society for goals of equality. When William Jennings Bryan and the silverites took control, the "new democracy" called for a stronger central regime that would reorganize the market and redistribute the wealth. The individual was oppressed by the system and it was necessary for the government to intervene. Silver, independent of its actual economic significance, symbolized an indictment of corporate dominance. This was an emotional, quasi-religious appeal, and Bryan made full use of revivalistic rhetoric and methodology.

The Populist party, previously centered on the silver issue, essentially was coopted by the Democrats; it in fact nominated Bryan as its presidential candidate. The Prohibition party had broadened its reform base to have much in common with both the Populists and Democrats. It was not made irrelevent in as direct a manner as the Populists, but it was abandoned in the heat of the larger battle.

Much attention has focused on this election (e.g., Key 1955; Hays 1967). Interpretations emphasize electoral shifts due to the Republican purge of revivalists coupled with Bryan's moral fervor and the use of revivalistic rhetoric. Previously Democratic ethnic groups, alienated by the new moralism, migrated to the now welcome arms of the Republican party. Revivalist populations made the opposite move, from the secularized Republicans to the moralistic Democrats, or at least Democratic revivalists did not flee Bryan as readily as others.

Jensen (1971, chap. 10) demonstrates these movements for midwestern groups. Kleppner (1970, chap. 8) states this more forcefully, amassing evidence that a major realignment occurred:

> This movement of pietists towards Bryan cut across categories of economic prosperity, place of residence, and size of place . . . everywhere the central tendency persisted: the groups most likely to respond favorably to Bryan were pietistic religious ones. (P. 317)

In subsequent work he tempered these statements. While still maintaining that this shift occurred, it evidently was not a permanent realignment (1978).[16] Hammond (1979, 157–60) replicates these findings using an index of revivalism based on the extent of revivalistic activity early in the century: Those areas that had a history of revivalism tended to move from their previous support for the Republican party to the Democratic party. He also notes that this was not a permanent realignment.

The institutional model put forth here entails a somewhat different argument. As suggested by the previous analyses, it could be argued that by this time the Republican party was accepted as *the* carrier of individualistic nationalism. It is true that it purged revivalistic control. However, I argue that the Republican organization changed only one aspect of its ideology related to religious definitions and symbols of citizenship. It still held the core of individualistic nationalism intact, and the latter was firmly institutionalized within the Republican party if not *equated* with it.

Following the discussion of the 1892 election, if this symbolic linkage existed, specific discrepancies between Republican policy and its cultural environment could be tolerated because of a decoupling; that is, the broad equating of the party organization with individualistic nationalism took precedence over specific discrepancies. The latter consequently could be played down, compartmentalized, or simply ignored. What the party did *was* individualistic nationalism. Discrepancies between the secularized Republican party and revivalism might be "tolerated" if not totally ignored by populations influenced by revivalism. Moreover, in 1896, the Democrats directly rejected the broad themes of individualistic nationalism and thus were even more incongruent with revivalistic pietism's view of the polity. Thus, the theory predicts that there was little electoral shift, if any, of revivalist populations from the Republicans to the Democrats.[17]

The only observer of American political and religious history who comes close to supporting this view is Lipset (1964). Lipset argues not only that there was no realignment in 1896, but also that very little movement of revivalistic groups occurred. Moreover, while not explicitly noted by Jensen, some of his analyses show that ethnic groups moved to the Republican camp independently of their religious affiliation (1971, 297).

In summary, previous arguments suggest that revivalism-dominated populations moved to the Democratic party resulting in a negative effect of revivalism on the Republican vote. Using the institutional model, I hypothesize that little movement took place: Revivalism had no effect on changes in the voting pattern. More extremely, as a reaction to Bryan's "misuse" of evangelistic symbols, revivalism had a positive effect on the Republican vote and a negative one on Democratic support.

Following the argument concerning revivalism, effectual individuation would be positively related to the Republican vote, although confidence in this hypothesis is weakened given the previously discussed ambiguous results. An important relation to examine is the effect of the agrarian measures. If economic interests dominate the process, then individual farmers should swing to the Democrats in the face of the unresponsive economic policy of the Republicans and Bryan's inflationary, agrarian stance. If the individualistic nationalism of agriculture is the major factor, then farmers should vote even more as "good citizens" for the "nation" and the Republican party.

It is hypothesized that industrialization positively affected Republican votes given Bryan's antimanufacturing position. That is, labor and owners were united against the antiurban, anti-industrial rhetoric of the Bryan campaign. Both the literature and the present theory imply a movement of the foreign born to the Republican camp. Independent of religious considerations, the nativism and antipluralism associated with moralistic issues were the primary reasons for immigrants not supporting the Republican party. With these stripped away, they were more than willing to express their patriotism by voting for the "party of the nation."

Results and Discussion

Table 6 summarizes the panel analyses of both Republican and Democratic Votes.[18] The counties with large numbers of Foreign Born, as predicted, show a greater Republican Vote, at the expense of the Democratic Vote. Industrialization has the same effects and also is in line with the predictions. Examining hypothesis 2a, we find a positive effect of Capital Per Manufacturing Establishment on Republican Vote. However, this is reversed when Industrialization is controlled for the less industrialized counties. Thus, the positive effect is a spurious result of the rather large positive relation of Industrialization to both Capital and Republican Vote. Capital Per Manufacturing Establishment in and of itself is negatively related to subsequent Republican Vote, as predicted by the hypothesis. In a similar manner, the negative relation of Capital with Democratic Vote is also spurious; no real relation is obtained when Industrialization is controlled.

While Wages Per Farm has similar effects on both parties, Production Per Farm shows positive effects on Republican Vote and small negative ones on the Democratic Vote. This is hypothesized and is especially noteworthy because an economic interest argument would predict the movement of farmers to Bryan. "False consciousness" or not, it seems that individual family farmers, dominated by individualistic nationalism, remained loyal to the concepts of nation and citizen and to a Republican party pushing for industrialization and a tariff.

Thus, the effects of effectual individuation measures on voting, independent of material interest, are as hypothesized. However, coupled with the previous analyses, the overall evaluation of hypothesis 2 remains ambiguous. Better controls for economic interest groups and voter turnout would allow a more precise test. The shift of more

Table 6 Panel Analyses of Voting, 1892–1896[a]

Hypotheses and Independent Variables	Republican Vote, 1896		Democratic Vote, 1896		
	Predicted	Estimated	Predicted	Estimated	N
Hypothesis 3:					
Revivalism, '92	0	–.00	0	–.12	171
Hypothesis 2a:					
Capital/Manufactur-	–	+.02[b]		–.07[b]	141
ing Establishment, '92		–.10[c]	+	+.04[c]	52
Hypothesis 2b:					
Production/Farm, '92	+	+.11	–	–.01	144[d]
Hypothesis 2c:					
Wages/Farm, '70	–	–.10	+	–.22	144[d]
Controls:					
Industrialization, '96	+	+.17	–	–.31	171
Foreign Born, '96	+	+.13	–	–.12	171
Party Vote, '92	+	+.92	+	+.53	171

[a]Summary of tables A13 and A14. Estimations are standardized (beta) coefficients. Counties in which more than 15% of the population are foreign born in 1896 are excluded.

[b]Not controlling for Industrialization; excludes counties with less than 18% production in industry, 1892.

[c]Controlling for Industrialization; estimated for counties in bottom half of Industrialization; excluding counties with less than 18% production in industry, 1892.

[d]Excludes counties with more than 77% production in industry, 1892.

industrial counties to Republican support does imply that economic interest is not always based on class lines, but also often is based on sectorial divisions. Sociocultural organization also has effects independent of material interest as seen in the Republican voting of farmers in this election.

Table 6 shows no effects of the Revivalism Index on the subsequent Republican Vote and a small negative relation to the Democratic Vote. This clearly goes against previous interpretations of the election but is what the institutional interpretation hypothesized and is consistent with Lipset's earlier assertions: There was no massive movement of revivalist populations toward Bryan's Democratic camp. It is reasonable to infer that Bryan's moralistic rhetoric could not hide the fact that the theory of society he was espousing was diametrically opposed to the power source of revivalist symbols—the moral individualism of revival religion and Republicanism. As such, his rhetoric profaned the sacred symbols and their context, causing a negative reaction. This again underscores the importance of interpreting issue politics in the context of ontologies. ??

To summarize, counties characterized by industrialization and a large foreign-born population show a significant shift toward voting Republican, supporting conventional lines of reasoning. Moving to the conceptual level, we can infer support for both hypotheses 2 and 3: Populations dominated by effectual individuation and by revivalism show continued adherence to Republicanism. This holds true even in agrarian populations which, it could be argued, voted against their interest in voting for Republicanism. Thus, based on this modest test of the theoretical implications, we can assert that the institutional model has better empirical support than previous interpretations of the 1896 election.

The Problem of Past Findings

A problem that arises out of these analyses and that requires an explanation is the dramatic difference in findings between the equations presented here and previous empirical studies of the election. Why do previous analyses show that revivalist populations shifted from the Republican to the Democratic camp (at least relative to the mass abandonment of Bryan), while the present analyses show no movement of revivalist populations from Republicanism but rather further movement from the Democratic party?

I argue that previous findings are primarily artifacts of the type of variables employed. (The Appendix presents the technical aspects of this argument more fully.) Most analyses measure party vote as a percentage of total vote—what are referred to as ratio variables. But Total Vote introduces a confounding factor. Revivalism has a high causal effect on voter turnout or Total Vote. In turn, for the 1896 election Total Vote has no relation to Republican Vote but a high positive relation to Democratic Vote. This means that a dependent variable calculated with Total Vote as the denominator will produce especially inaccurate results. Specifically, let REP/TOT equal Republican Vote divided by Total Vote and let DEM/TOT equal Democratic Vote divided by Total Vote. Estimates of Revivalism's effect on REP/TOT will be biased toward the negative because of its positive relation with Total Vote in the denominator. Estimates of its effects on DEM/TOT will be biased toward the positive because its positive relation with Total Vote in the denominator (a negative bias) is more than offset by Total Vote's positive relation to the numerator (a positive bias). If this is the case, revivalism's relations to both parties in previous works are artifactual.

If the difference in findings in fact is due to the different types of variables employed and misspecification of Total Vote and not to the data, we should be able to reproduce previous results by estimating similar ratio models. Then, if bias actually exists in this manner, controlling for Total Vote would reduce the bias, resulting in findings more similar to the present analyses. Including Total Vote as a control in an equation does not solve all of the problems introduced by ratio variables, but if it changes the results substantially—in the direction of the ones obtained with the models of the present study—then the interpretation that previous findings are artifactual is supported.

Table 7 presents a summary of ratio models. The first column of coefficients shows that the use of ratio variables replicates previous findings in the literature: The Revivalism Index is negatively related

Table 7   Effects of Revivalism on Party Vote, 1892–1986: Ratio Models[a]

Dependent Variables	Replication of Ratio Models[b]	Ratio Models Controlling for Total Vote [b,c]	Coefficients of Raw Equations[d]
Republican Vote	−.123	−.046	−.002
Democratic Vote	+.085	−.023	−.122

[a]Estimations are standardized (beta) coefficients. Counties in which more than 15% of the population are foreign born in 1896 are excluded. $N = 171$.

[b]From table A15. Dependent variables are percentages of Total Vote.

[c]Total Vote divided by Population, 1896.

[d]From tables 6, A13, and A14. Dependent variables are Party Vote divided by Population, 1896.

132

to Republican Vote and positively related to Democratic Vote. The second column reports the coefficients from ratio models that control for Total Vote. Revivalism's effect on Republican Vote is dramatically reduced while its relation to Democratic Vote becomes negative. The third column of coefficients reports the results of the equations from table 6 for comparison. Clearly results of the ratio models controlling for Total Vote are much more in line with the findings of the raw equations used in the present study; previous results appear to be artifactual.[19]

Summary: 1880–1896

The analyses show that counties with a large number of immigrants generally have high levels of Republican voting from 1880 to 1892. This could be due to nativistic reactions to local immigrant groups or to surprising immigrant support for Republicanism. The fact that the same counties strongly resist the rise of the Prohibition party during this period gives some credence to the latter. More industrialized counties, controlling for the number of foreign born, also tend to show greater Republican voting in the eighties and do not show significant shifts in 1892. In the 1896 election both foreign born and industry variables are sensitive to Bryan's moralistic, anti-industry campaign: Counties characterized by each shift greatly toward Republican voting and away from Democratic voting.

Hypothesis 2 predicts a positive statistical relation between measures of effectual individuation and Republican and Prohibition voting. The industrial measure has mixed effects for the whole sample with the strongest support for 1892 and 1896. There is more consistent support in the less industrialized counties. The agrarian production measure has strong positive effects in the cross-sectional analyses of 1880, possibly even in wage-dominated areas. During the eighties these effects are reversed counter to the hypothesis. The most telling evidence is from the 1896 election. Northern and midwestern farmers, largely individuated, voted Republican despite the agrarian appeals of Bryan. Overall, the support for hypothesis 2 is mixed.

Hypothesis 3 predicts a positive statistical relation between revivalist memberships and Republican and Prohibition voting. The results show a substantial alignment between Republican voting and counties with larger numbers of revivalist memberships. This association is maintained but attenuated during the eighties by a shift of revivalism-influenced populations toward the Prohibition party. This trend is modified in the election of 1892: Revivalism still is highly related to Prohibition party voting, but there is a substantial return to Republican voting. Thus, it is reasonable to infer that revivalism did form a plausibility base for Republicanism.

The institutional model was used to reinterpret the 1896 election. The dominance of the Republican party as the institutional manager of the polity linked the larger rational project of nationalism to the party's organizational success. The Democrat's attempts to use the religious symbols of revivalism failed—even as the Republican party had distanced itself from those same symbols. It was hypothesized that measures of effectual individuation and revival religion had no relation to electoral shifts or even positive effects on increasing the Republican vote. These statistical relations largely were found. Revivalist memberships have no relation to changes in Republican vote and a small negative effect on Democratic voting. The findings and interpretation of the 1896 election run counter to conventional studies which emphasize the shift of revivalist groups from the Republican to the Democratic camp, at least relative to the larger population which abandoned Bryan en masse. It was shown that previous findings are artifacts of the ratio variables employed in the analyses. When partially corrected for this bias, ratio equations yield results more similar to the findings of the models employed here.

General Inferences and Caveats

In this chapter I have used statistical analyses to test hypotheses relating quantitative variables. In discussing the results for the most part I remained at the level of statistical inference, simply describing the statistical relations found. At this level one need only accept the various assumptions of regression analysis and that the equations were properly specified. Even at this level, there is much more work to be done. It is necessary to explore the effect of having excluded cases for purely statistical reasons. Analyses should be extended to state and local levels. It is necessary to more adequately specify the important voter turnout variable and to develop indicators of class interest.

I also noted whether or not the statistical relations were what the hypotheses predicted. In summary, the analyses found relations that were predicted by hypotheses 1 and 3; the predictions of hypothesis 2 were found inconsistently.

But, I want to say much more than this. If the predictions are statistically obtained, we want to affirm the hypotheses at the conceptual level. Here, we must accept, although not without reservation nor without an eye for improvement, the measured variables as valid indicators of our concepts. First, because the statistical predictions of hypothesis 1 were obtained, I infer that a religion of effectual individualism (revivalism) was maintained to a greater extent in populations characterized by high levels of effectual individuation and low levels of corporate capitalism. Second, because the predictions of hypothesis 2 were not consistently found, inferences are problematic. Strictly speaking, we cannot infer that effectual individuation directly supported individualistic-nationalistic ideology. Yet, because we do find the predicted relations in some instances, one might want to pursue this hypothesis. For example, the inconsistency might be due to inadequately controlling for confounding variables such as material interest and industrialization. Moreover, the best evidence for the prediction is in fact a very dramatic one: farmers voting against proagrarian Bryan and for prourban and proindustry Republicanism. Third, because the revivalism index consistently had the predicted effects on Republican and Prohibition voting throughout the period, I infer that a religion of individualistic nationalism (revivalism) provided a plausibility structure for Republicanism.

The mixed support for hypothesis 2 in the context of the other hypotheses suggests that the individuation of everyday life might not have direct effects on electoral behavior. Any effects are mediated by cultural and ideological structures which in the case of the United States were constructed partly within the institution of revival religion. This raises a theoretical question requiring further comparative analysis: Under what conditions might there be direct effects, and when is there cultural mediation?

The three hypotheses for the latter part of the century were derived from the institutional model of market penetration and nation building. The description in chapter 4 of the isomorphism among individualistic nationalism, revivalism, and Republicanism adds an understanding of the meanings and moods that were being played out. The empirical support for the hypothesis in turn makes the institutional interpretation more credible. The three isomorphic institutions are found in the same populations. Thus, the interpretation of market penetration early in the century is plausible because the same theory is supported by empirical analyses for late in the century. Imagine if there were no statistical relations between the measures of individuation and revivalism for 1870 through 1890. There might be some post hoc explanation, but one would more readily reject the parallel interpretations of change earlier in the century. One would be forced to question the significance of institutional isomorphism. One would more readily reject the theory and not just the hypotheses.

Also, consider the ambiguous evidence for hypothesis 2. This mixed support, coupled with an acceptance of the other two hypotheses, suggests that earlier in the century Republicanism might have grown more out of the religious-political order of revivalism and individualistic nationalism than directly out of everyday experience in an individuated economy. After all, revivalism did flourish before the Republican party, and it took years to forge a lasting coalition around individualistic nationalism. Still, we cannot forget the 1896 election and the support of individuated agriculture for Republicanism—manifestly against its interest. Evidence that such patterns occurred in 1896 is significant. This makes more credible the claim that the antebellum West shifted toward the North and away from the South not over pure economic interest nor because of economic conflict with the South. Rather, the West-North alliance was forged because the economic organization of petty agrarian capitalism resulted in the same sociopolitical organization as that of the petty capitalism of the North, including the same cultural myths of individualistic nationalism and revival religion.

Readers must judge for themselves the feasibility of these inferences and their willingness to make the relevant assumptions, and more caveats could be added that would suggest necessary further work. The present analysis thus is only a modest attempt at assessing the interpretation of change in the nineteenth-century United States.

Yet, I push our inferences still further. The patterns of change, social movements, and electoral behavior in nineteenth-century United States and the demonstrated isomorphism of the institutions can be added to our comparative-historical base for the institutional model of change. The penetration of local communities by rationalizing processes dramatically changed social life. Identities and action were reoriented to impersonal national structures of market and state and to a rationalized ontology of autonomous individuals, rational calculation, mechanical nature, and abstract God. As these changes took place, people began using the underlying ontology to rethink and reshape particular institutions. Movements emerged to build new institutions and new ways of doing things.

It is a long way from regression coefficients relating variables constructed on census data to an abstract theory of market penetration and social movements. And I admittedly have drawn out this process rather tediously. However, the person who jumps immediately from one to the other needs to take the present qualifications seriously. On the other hand, the person who rejects such theory construction in principle must confront the reasoned, conditionalized (if somewhat tedious) logic of analytic comparisons that allows us to make such inferences. In the next chapter, I make some analytic comparisons and some suggestions for moving toward a general theory by placing nineteenth-century U.S. change in a comparative-historical perspective.

- Operationalization a major problem here. I like neither the measure of Rev. (too broad + vague), nor the measure of individualism (too abstract + distant), nor the assoc. of Repub. with reviv. (too arbitrary.)

- not to mention dropping into ecolo. fall. despite smooth maneuvering early on to sidestep it.

- whole cultural ontology is full of composition -- from lots of individuals doing something, can't infer cultural construct, esp. here where absolute #'s of members must have been quite low.

- ridiculous to put "word root" on the political conflicts of time when they didn't understand it such themselves. Classic e.g. of Field's "culturalist" approach, complete w/ all its failings -- ask our question instead of look at actual social relations + this makes for violent misinterpretation

(- I wonder if same crits he makes of TOT VOTE would apply to his measures of IND.)

SIX

Toward a General Theory of Religious Movements

A theory of sociocultural change and political-economic expansion has been developed based on studies ranging from Western Europe to the United States to the contemporary Third World. The institutional model of cultural change was used to analyze nineteenth-century United States, but its fruitfulness can be further demonstrated by placing this analysis within a comparative historical treatment of religious movements.

With the growth of historical sociology, much has been written on whether or not abstract theories of historical change are possible. It is now fashionable to celebrate historical uniqueness and to label as misguided any general theoretical enterprise. It is routinely repeated that an analysis of one historical case or set of cases cannot be "mechanically" applied to others. In developing the institutional model I have not explicitly discussed such metatheoretical issues, and a thorough treatment of them is not my present concern. However, I point out that an attempt to abstract general processes and then apply a theory of these processes to other historical situations does not necessarily assume a complete identity of processes across cases. Any theory comprises statements that while abstract are also conditional. The stipulation and understanding of the conditions under which such statements are true is a crucial aspect of theory construction. If conditions vary and relations do not hold, we are on our way to discovering the conditions under which different causal relations are operating.

In macrosociology the historical variation of conditions is a large part of our focus of study. Rather than making comparisons impossible, it makes them necessary. A common mistake in the construction of earlier grand theories or modernization theories is that they were constructed from one unique case or set of cases and then, unmodified, used unsuccessfully to interpret others. This failure illustrates not so much historical uniqueness, but the need for comparison in the ongoing process of theory construction. Consequently, within the comparative method, historical differences are as important as similarities not only in generating abstract propositions, but also in identifying the conditions under which they do and do not hold.

The institutional model developed in this book describes general processes, but ones that are manifested differently under different historical conditions. This chapter makes concrete empirical comparisons, not mechanically, but as a heuristic scheme to take initial steps toward a general theory. These comparisons and theoretical interpretations are necessarily exploratory, but important conditionalized hypotheses and interpretations are suggested. The hypotheses push to the extreme the underlying similarities within the context of historical differences in order to emphasize the complementary relationship between general theory and historical detail and to illustrate the fruitfulness of the institutional model in generating comparative-historical research.

I begin this chapter inductively with an historical classification of religious movements by Robert Wuthnow (1980). Various metatheoretical and empirical points are made concerning the changing world-cultural context of religious movements. These points are then used within the institutional model to examine briefly various historical movements as counterpoints to the case of nineteenth-century revivalism in the United States. Examining Reformation movements and Puritanism shows that religious movements that are linked to a form of political-economic expansion similar to that of the nineteenth-century United States are quite different in content, yet manifest similar tendencies. Later movements in the twentieth century are more distinctly statist in character. The institutional model provides, I think, the tools for comprehending both the differences and the similarities, and it has unique implications for understanding the dialectical nature of contemporary religious movements.

Empirical Issues and Trends
Cycles of the World System

Recent studies have attempted to couch the interpretation of religious movements in the context of large-scale, long-term historical change, not only at the nation-state level but also at the global level (e.g., Robertson 1985; Robertson and Chirico 1985; Hammond 1985; Lincoln 1985). The impetus for this direction partly is due to the inadequacies of conventional understandings and partly to the emergence of world-system theory within sociology. There is a growing realization that the interplay between the world system and the nation state is crucial in understanding change and social movements. Wuthnow (1980) presents a typological analysis of religious movements within the context of world economic cycles. His classification of religious movements, summarized in table 8, provides several insights for further work and can be used to discuss the issues at hand.

Wuthnow's typology is based on the description of three historical cycles of capitalistic development. Each cycle has three stages: (1) Political-economic expansion; this is characterized by economic growth and the extension of the rational market into new geographic regions and populations. (2) Polarization of rich core areas and poor peripheral areas; the former are organized within strong national states and dominated by merchant or industrial elites while the latter are characterized by a capitalist, usually agrarian, class emerging relative to traditional classes and groups. (3) Reconstitution of the world system; conflicts are neutralized by compromises and often the dominance of a new core power.

Each stage is characterized by particular types of religious movements carried out by particular classes: (1) Expansion is accompanied by revitalization movements within the periphery arising out of displaced groups reacting to their loss of traditional privilege and security. Expansion also witnesses reformation movements by capitalist elites within the periphery; this new class uses such movements to assert its newfound power and autonomy within the larger system and over its population. (2) Polarization leads to militant collective action by peripheral elites against core powers and to counterreformation or military repression by core elites. (3) Reconstitution and the reintegration of the system are carried out by movements accommodating the new system. Those groups that have gained power within the world structure tend toward liberalism or quasi secularization while those groups that have declined in power, status, or cultural centrality organize into sectarian often pessimistic groups.

This typology orders the historical record in such a way that certain empirical points become more apparent than otherwise. It is not my purpose to perfect this particular classification scheme or to debate the theoretical adequacy of cyclical theories. Rather, I use these empirical insights to go beyond the typology toward a general historical interpretation of the relation between religious movements and socio-political change.

Table 8 A Summary of Wuthnow's 1980 Typology

Expansion: Incorporation of new areas into the world market.	Polarization: Conflict between core and periphery.	Reconstitution: Reintegration
1. Revitalization movements by displaced traditional groups in the periphery.	1. Militant movements by elites in the periphery.	1. Accommodation.
2. Reformation movements by capitalist elites increasing in power in the periphery.	2. Counterreformation movements by elites in the core.	2. Sectarian movements.
1500–1550: 1. Anabaptists/ Radicals 2. Magisterial Reformation	1550–1600: 1. Dutch Calvinists 2. Counter-Reformation	1600–1650: 1. Arminianism/ English tolerance 2. Pietism
1700–1750: 1. Methodism in Scotland 2. Enlightenment in the U.S.	1750–1800: 1. Jacobins/ U.S. Revolution 2. Gallican Revival	1800–1850: 1. Liberalism/ U.S. revivals 2. Methodism
1875–1914: 1. Jehovah's Witnesses/ Pentecostal-Holiness 2. Marxism	1917–1945: 1. Bolsheviks 2. Fascism	1945–: 1. Liberal social reforms 2. Utopian cults

Trends of Religious Movements

While the typology is based on cycles, one thing emerges rather clearly:
The historical movement through each of the stages, across cycles, describes a trend toward greater individualism. The various branches of
the Reformation relative to Catholicism mark increases in individualism but they are less individualistic than seventeenth-century Arminianism. Individualism is further increased in the particular brand of
Arminianism defined by the rational methodical character of individual
activity found in Methodism. Rational activity of the individual and the
potential for perfection are increased even more within the revivals of
the nineteenth-century United States to the point that Reformation
Protestantism and Puritanism look almost as antithetical to individualism as medieval Catholicism. Secular versions beginning with the Enlightenment and extending through the French Revolution to the
revolutionary ideologies of the twentieth century all elaborate the qualities of the individual and the demand for liberty and equality.

We also know that each new wave of individualism was organized
within a more rationalized central state authority as exemplified by
the early Protestant states, the French state, and the twentieth-century
statist movements of Russia and Germany. Thus, while the cyclical
character of the change might be accurate in many important respects,
it appears that larger trends are operating throughout the cycles.
These trends can be characterized by the dialectical development of
both the individual and the nation state.

Another point that can be seen from the table is that this dialectic
takes on a particular quality during the late nineteenth and early
twentieth centuries. Movements such as those of various fundamentalist groups define the individual as ineffectual and powerless apart
from his or her relationship to impersonal supernatural forces. Other
factions link up similarly oppressed, powerless individuals to technological, nationalistic, and statist organizations. There are real differences between Pentecostalism and Marxism, and between
Bolshevism and Fascism, of course, but all share this linking of an
ineffectual individual to a larger source of power. This commonality
has been referred to as a gnostic impulse that becomes the dominant
structural dynamic in the last half of the twentieth century (e.g., Voegelin 1968).

Positing a World Culture

From these larger trends throughout the cycles I infer that during a
historical period, the world system is constituted by a particular cul-

tural scheme. This cultural order affects the structures of all countries. Put another way, the political dimension of the world system is not captured totally by the view that the system is a network of states. The world system is also a world culture—a world polity in the broad sense of the word. There is not necessarily a well-integrated culture on which there is consensus, but there is a world knowledge system to which corporate actors are oriented (Meyer 1987). 7

Movements in different historical periods may result from similar social change, but they will constitute these changes differently according to the current world culture. For example, sixteenth-century Europe and nineteenth-century United States both experienced political-economic expansion characterized by increases in individualism, nationalism, and state authority. In sixteenth-century Europe this partly was framed by the Reformation movements, and "nationalism," referring generally to the emergence of the principle of rational centralized authority, was more corporately organized in the state. In nineteenth-century United States, Arminian denominations grew dramatically at the expense of Reformation denominations in formulating a more extreme individualistic nationalism. By the nineteenth-century, political-economic expansion was centered more in the autonomous activity of individuals and in conceptions of a political nation. Increased individualism means an even greater articulation of the individual by Arminian theology.

Thus, a "nonmechanical" sociological understanding of nineteenth-century American Methodism must be based on examining both the similarities (increased individualism and nationalism) and differences (this individualism being more extreme and organized more within a diffuse nationalism) with parallel religious movements in earlier periods. Generally, cycles of expansion reproduce expansionistic movements centered on individualism and nationalism, but within each cycle the world system is more rationalized and therefore each successive set of movements is more radically individualistic and nationalistic.

The world culture also results in movements within each stage (each cell of the table) that, while often in conflict, might be surprisingly similar in worldview. Some conflicting movements are more similar with each other than with the same type of movement in a later cycle that is characterized by a somewhat different world-cultural order. The clearest example is that the revitalization and reformation movements of the sixteenth century (the two branches of the Protestant Reformation), despite their differences, had more in common in terms of ontology and worldview than each had with its counterpart in the eighteenth century (Methodism and the Enlightenment). The quasi-secularized Methodism of the nineteenth-century American revivals probably had more in common with European liberalism than with its Arminian predecessor of the seventeenth century. The common underlying structure of the twentieth-century movements, as already noted, is characterized by the ineffectual individual.

Conflicting versions of the World Culture

The presence of a world-cultural context that is tapped to varying degrees by contemporary groups does not preclude conflict or situations in which movements mobilize around basically different cultural conceptions. Certainly the historical tradition of a region shapes the unique characteristics of a movement. Also, Wuthnow forcefully argues that differences in movements within a given cyclical stage are due to their being rooted in different locations, positions, and classes within the world stratification system. Large-scale societal change in the form of the penetration and expansion of the international market causes the emergence of new groups that attempt to construct a new sociocultural order based on the rational cultural aspects of the world political-economic system. Other groups within the newly incorporated areas—possibly traditional elites, displaced groups, or those least affected by the world market (cf. Tilly 1964, 1978; Walton 1984)—attempt to resist the new order by developing their own more moderate conceptions. Thus, groups within the polarization stage, such as the Dutch Calvinists and the Counter-Reformation, are in conflict over their basic view of the world and society. It is not contradictory also to point out that these two movements have much in common, as becomes apparent when, for example, Calvinism is contrasted with Jacobin or Bolshevik ideology.

Another factor leading to different movement cosmologies within the same historical period is that different regions or countries will not necessarily go through the same cyclical stages simultaneously. For example, a given region might be experiencing incorporation into the international market and undergoing rapid economic growth and rationalization in a period in which the larger world-economic system is best characterized as being in the reconstitution stage. This appears to be the case of the United States during the early nineteenth century and much of the Third World during the post–World War II period.

Points of Comparison

Innumerable other insights and questions arise from this typology. There are four points relevant to the institutional model that can be used as a framework for comparisons: (1) The world system comprises a world cultural order. This order structures the culture and institutions of each society, and each movement within society, so there is a tendency toward isomorphic cultural organization. (2) Differences between countries and movements and accompanying conflict result from different national, regional, or class locations and experiences within the historical system coupled with the particular history of the country. (3) An analysis of a religious movement must look beyond factors internal to the society and time period; the content, goals, and organization of a movement must be placed in a comparative-historical context. (4) Religious movements attempt to construct a new sociocultural order grounded in the world-cultural context. Movement ideologies are shaped by the structures of everyday life and the underlying ontology of world culture, resulting in varying degrees of isomorphism.[1] They are not products of narrowly defined economic interests embedded within those structures nor of crises purported to occur at various structural levels.

These four points can be used to develop substantive implications of the institutional model for a broad range of religious movements as an initial step toward a general theory. In this chapter I first explore the general nature of religious and nation-building movements by putting American revivalism in the context of the historical line of Reformation movements and Puritanism, emphasizing the different world-cultural contexts and world locations of each. I then contrast these movements more sharply with statist ones. I develop the interpretation of the latter with a special application to new religious movements in the last half of the twentieth century. The contemporary order of technological society is dominated by the dialectics of state versus society, rationality versus irrationality, technology and bureaucracy versus personal value. These poles are dialectic in that while contradictory, they are mutually legitimating. Conflicting movements that arise out of such "structural contradictions" are isomorphic with and grounded in the same cultural order, but represent opposite dialectical poles. Many religious movements tend to formulate irrational subjective value as the means by which to transcend the rational technological or bureaucratic system. This model therefore suggests that we rethink new religious movements, not so much as negative

7 reactions to modern technological change and materialism, but as the cultural constituting value within a technological order.

Religion and Nation Building, Some Comparisons

The nineteenth century United States experienced political-economic expansion of market forces and the national polity, resulting in individualistic nation-building movements. As social life was stripped of traditional rules that maintained communal relations and group boundaries, everyday life became organized by new interpretative rules built on rational calculation, individualism, and nationalism. Revivalism institutionally framed these rules by locating them in a larger ontology. It built a sociopolitical universe within which individuals participated in a national market and a national polity. It above all was concerned with ontology, defining the nature of the individual, nation, and action. Revivalism was rooted in the rational organization of everyday life and had important political implications, which were expressed in moral reform, the abolitionist movement, and then later in the support of Republican nationalism.

Is this relationship between individualistic religion and nationalism unique to the civil religion of the United States? I think not. We may recall Geertz's (1968) study of literal, "back-to-the-Koran" Islamic nationalism of twentieth-century Indonesia or of the revolutionary Islam of the Middle East and Persia. Extending the institutional model to these cases is necessary in the long-term theoretical project, and would require dealing in great detail with the specifics of the different religious traditions.

Another example but one within the same religious tradition as U.S. revivalism is the emergence and development of Protestantism. Exploring the thread of continuity from Reformation movements to Puritanism to American revivalism allows us to focus on differences within a common religious tradition. The comparisons suggest that similar political-economic change produce similar movements, but dramatic differences also result from the different world-historic contexts and from the different locations within those contexts.

Reformation Movements

The institutional perspective calls into question the apparently accepted view that the Magisterial branch of the Reformation was a movement arising out of a capitalistic elite interest within the newly emerging world economic system, whereas the Radical branch was a negative, traditional reaction to change constituting an attempt to revitalize the precapitalist system of privilege and patrimonial authority. Instead, I suggest the following line of reasoning.

The Protestant Reformation, in addressing specifically religious issues raised by the nature of the feudal church, articulated a rationalized cosmos. The core of this cosmos was the autonomy and rational everyday activity of the individual. Nature lost its magical qualities and became the arena to which individuals oriented activity. Ecclesiastical bureaucracy was delegitimated at several levels, resulting in a transfer of authority to the secular state and local institutions. Expanded secular powers were to maintain peace, justice, and progress for the benefit of the people. The Protestant Reformation defined the requisites of capitalistic organization (Weber 1961; Collins 1986, 19–44), but it might be argued that its political-economic implications were not initially nor most importantly linked to the capitalist economy nor to the emerging economic elites. The Reformation found its first alliance with the territorial prince, partly because of a mutual interest in undermining imperial church authority, but basically because of a similar ontology based on rationalizing principles and a common acceptance of a rational central authority (Walzer 1965). The spread of the Reformation throughout the town councils must be interpreted in the larger political context of its isomorphism with the prince as well as with the town's increasing dependence on and incorporation into the central authority.

The Radical branch of the Reformation articulated a world similar to that of the Magisterial branch, but it did not conceive of authority as residing in a central secular apparatus. Various streams of radicalism emphasized the idea of people as those "called out" from such temporal and fallen structures. The concept of "people" was defined in part by an abstract universalism derived from scripture and the corporate towns rather than from newly introduced Roman law or a central state. The eschatological background for this critical stance toward the state was the full expectation of the imminent return of Jesus and the direct ruling by the people within the Kingdom of God. The construction of secular kings within the context of this expectation understandably was considered blasphemous. Thus, the antistate nature of the Radicals should not be interpreted as a particularistic feudal conception of authority. It in one sense expressed a more radical individualism than that of the Magisterial branch. Let me suggest that it was more purely a nation-building movement that resisted any connection with state formation, although its historical context makes it distinct from the individualistic nationalism of nine-teenth-century U.S. revivalism.

In coming to grips with the expanded interregional and eventually national frame of reference, many towns, often the most progressive ones, were open to the Radicals.[2] Throughout the reformation ter-ritories the Radicals gained strength in towns, articulating the larger national polity in terms of abstract universalism couched in terms of divine law. Because of the political-economic connections of the mag-istrates to the prince, and often because of direct pressure from the prince, town councils would recognize the "errors" of the Radicals and subsequently would force them to moderate or be expelled. In those cases in which a town resisted the prince, a radical town-peasant alliance would be violently suppressed. In those areas where the town-prince relation was weak or where the centralizing authority itself was weak, either Anabaptism became accepted or the Counter-Refor-mation eventually prevailed. This led to a peripheralization of the Radical branch.

Clasen (1972, see especially chap. 9) documents that in the early years of the movement, 1525–29, a large proportion of Anabaptists were craftsmen in the imperial cities and towns; nearly a third of its members were propertied. With persecution in the 1530s, the move-ment began losing these members, and after 1550 it increasingly be-came a movement of farmers, peasants, and laborers. Therefore, overall interpretations of the movement as emerging out of impov-erished marginal groups or traditionally well-off groups that were being displaced ignore the changing composition of Anabaptism. It appeared as a corporate radical form of "individualistic nationalism," both in composition and in theology, and it gradually took a more pessimistic (and nonviolent) stance as its nonstatist nationalism re-peatedly was suppressed.

Puritanism

Similar issues were hammered out a century later during the period of the English Civil War. English Puritans of the early seventeenth-century shared some of the separatist qualities of the sixteenth-century Radicals; yet there were important differences. Puritanism grew out of Calvinism which, as noted, linked the corporate polity to a relatively autonomous state. Moreover, English Puritanism occurred within a region undergoing political-economic growth in a world system that had a century of rationalization behind it. The latter point means that the concept of people was more closely tied to that of the nation state.

The location of the Puritans within England and within the larger world polity also greatly affected the movement. In his classic work on Calvinism, Michael Walzer (1965) detailed three different directions that the political theory of Calvinism took among three distinct intellectual groups: (1) English exiles in Geneva, (2) Huguenots among the French nobility, and (3) English Puritans. Any summary would not do justice to Walzer's work, but the relevant point is that the different groups led to different institutional developments. The "statelessness" of the exiles led to an almost Anabaptist spirituality and transcendence of political office. The French nobility transformed the radical individualism of Calvinism into a sacralization of status and honor. Through the local parish structure, English Puritans organized individualism and "the people" around what I have termed individualistic nationalism, oriented toward influencing state structure and policy.[3] Thus, similar elements of individualism and nation building took on different forms in different world-historical polities.

Early American Religion and Revivalism

Contemporary to the Puritans, New World colonization offered a political alternative to separatism versus conformity. It provided the possibility of establishing a theocratic "called out" collective in a peripheral region away from the direct authority of the nation state. The buffering from world-institutionalized conceptions of the nation state provided fertile ground for Anabaptism and later Unitarianism and Arminianism. Thus, the different world location of the colonies allowed room for individualistic communalism separate from both nation and state.

As the colonies developed common conceptions of a national polity, there was an overall trend toward isomorphism with the world model of the nation state by means of nation building. Thus, the revolution was couched in world-dominant themes of the Enlightenment and to a lesser extent Arminianism. By the nineteenth-century, revivalism in the new U.S. polity framed political-economic expansion by using "revived" religion to define the rational, moral citizenry and nation.

Religion and State Formation

The idea of "people" during the course of rationalization of the world polity becomes increasingly defined as a nation that is managed by the bureaucratic state. Even individualistic, nationalistic religious movements lead to state authority. Yet, we can contrast such movements with ones more distinctly concerned with state formation. A good example of this is found in revolutionary France. In France, the developments of capitalism and nationalism were dependent on the state because of the presence of a strong traditional aristocracy plus an external military threat (Skocpol 1979; Moore 1966). Political-economic growth centered in the state, and movements pushing for this expansion tended to be state-formation movements. Such groups emphasized impersonal abstract law and bureaucratic rule. This is all relatively individualistic, but the individual is defined bureaucratically as a unit of the state, and the nation is corporately embodied in state bureaucracy and policy.

State-formation movements are more likely to use secular symbols that can be viewed as religious only in the broad functional sense of being concerned with the cosmological foundations of everyday life. Thus, the French Revolution drew on and radicalized the Enlightenment and Gallicanism. The primary religious (in the narrow sense of the word) impact was in terms of legal principles from canon law and formal rights from liturgical modes of incorporation and ritualization of membership. This secularism was due at least in part to the fact that in France the state remained in direct competition with the church, for the failure of the Reformation in France and the inner, contemplative direction taken by Jansenism (and its subsequent repression) meant that there was no large-scale transfer of authority from the church to the state (Badie and Birnbaum 1983). Secularism also can be seen as an inherent quality of state organization. This can be grasped if we view the bureaucratic state as a technique of social organization (Ellul 1967). The basis of this technique, as of all technology, is the belief that power and the source of power reside in nature and are manipulable, rather than residing in an autonomous supernatural. This belief also implies that the conditions that lead to the mystification of technique will also lead to the mystification and sacralization of the state (cf. Ellul 1975).[4]

Cults of the State and the Individual

If eighteenth-century France was a particular case of political-economic expansion being dependent on the state, this type of case had become general by the turn of the twentieth century. This is so for several reasons. The world had become a denser, more competitive system. There was no new world in which nations could be newly constructed or markets extended without direct conflict with an already existing nation state (e.g., Chirot 1986). Capitalism was not only more firmly instituted, it was more fully evolved in terms of the centralization and concentration of capital. This meant that the core industrial countries had increased in their political-economic domination, and poor (peripheral) countries were poorer relative to them. Thus, maintenance of core status on the one hand, and any increased development of semi-peripheral and peripheral countries on the other, required strong state action in organizing society around goals of growth.

The individual was institutionalized within the world culture as a member of a state, while collective national identity and interest, specifically, economic growth, were also defined as the responsibility of the state. Individualism was more completely collectivized, and the rugged individualism of early classical capitalism had given way to a problematic, ineffectual individualism. At the personal level this meant individuals had to participate in large-scale organizations such as corporations, banks, unions, and political parties to create change and success. At the collective level, political power in general and the state in particular were necessary to overcome reactionary classes and extend competition in order to bring about autonomous economic growth.

Ideology and Gnosticism

The cult of the state and individual is open to different ideologies from fascism to communism to the liberal welfare state, all of which promise progress within the same ontology. Social scientific theories of statism/individualism in the twentieth century unfortunately are built on themes of the same ontology. Theories of authoritarianism accept the ideological assessments of the impersonal aspects of bureaucracy, technology, and state authority. For example, a charismatic leader or party organization might promise deliverence from these alienating structures. According to these theories, society follows because those structures really are alienating. Rapid change, economic depressions, and alienation, plus a mass society atomized before the central state, result in escapist movements. For many theorists, these movements are real deliverance and transcendence; for others, a mere escape. Few attempt to understand the dialectics and power of alienation-crisis and transcendence and how this nexus is rooted in rationalized structures.

A promising departure, but one with little impact in the social sciences, is to view ideological movements as parts of one structure, what has been referred to as gnosticism (e.g., Bell 1976; Jung 1933; Voegelin 1968). Put simply, gnosticism refers to movements of the first centuries A.D. that viewed material existence as evil and alien to the spirit. Salvation is a transcendence—an overthrowing of the order of existence—by means of esoteric knowledge and power. While pessimistic concerning the material everyday life, gnostics optimistically promised a liberation from this order, some speaking of pure rejection, others of transformation.

This dialectic of pessimism/optimism and the role of empowerment seem to be central dynamics of modernity, from small-scale movements to the world culture. On the pessimistic side, the world-cultural order defines the individual as ineffectual. Highly rationalized social organization is considered to be alien to the individual. Nature is no longer viewed even as a mechanical stage, but rather a set of misleading mathematical laws. In other words, fundamental reality—"the order of being"—is at odds with individual efficacy, success, fulfillment, and progress. These ideas are manifested in the prevalence of existentialism and subjectivity throughout the humanities in the first quarter of the twentieth century (Marcuse 1964; Zaretsky 1976).

The optimistic side to this argument holds that this negative order of being can be overcome by either rejecting or transforming it. This is performed by linking up to centers of power, and it is defined as self-transcendence over the alien world, where self is interpreted as both individual and collective. Education, economic rationality, and political participation all empower the individual and the people to achieve progress and prosperity. History is an especially powerful concept that infuses everyday economic and political action with meaning and value and allows a legitimating national mobilization. Citizenship incorporates individuals into the process, empowering them.

Gnostic elements are present in the two main ideologies of the early twentieth century. Marxism emerges at the beginning of late capitalism and flourishes in those states mobilizing for economic growth. The Marxist-communist linkage of society and individual to the power of the state is made meaningful in the context of a more abstract connection to the meaning of history—through the historical dialectic. The meaning of history is not found in the actual order of being, but it is created by humans who through labor (praxis) dialectically critique and overcome the order of being. Humanity,

> which is itself nature, also stands over against nature and assists it in its development by human labor—which in its highest form is technology and industry based on the natural sciences: "Nature as it develops in human history . . . as it develops through industry . . . is true *anthropological* nature."

> In the process of creating nature, however, man at the same time also creates himself to the fullness of his being; therefore, "*all of so-called world history* is nothing but the production of man by human labor." (Voegelin 1968, 23–24)[5]

These are secular symbols congruent with the materialism of technique and the state. Yet, there is great potential in harnessing particularly religious symbols to this framework as technique becomes more sacralized. This potential is actualized in the post–World War II period.

National socialism also links action and organization to the meaning of history, but its focus is on the role of a particular people within history. It is more directly influenced by existentialism which itself is a highly developed form of gnosticism (Jonas 1958). The meaning of history is created by the "will to power" of a people. This celebration of the people immanent in the state makes room for the use of religious symbols as demonstrated by, for example, Imperial Japan.

These analyses appear to be on the right track in examining the structure of ideologies and rationalized culture. Their assessments of social dynamics and why elitist gnosticism appeals to the mass of people, however, tend to fall back on questionable social-psychological assumptions and conventional crisis imagery. It is necessary to spell out the isomorphisms of everyday life, social organization, and world culture. I will attempt to show the fruitfulness of an institutional analysis of state cults and gnostic culture by outlining an interpretation of the political-technological order and the rise of new religious movements in the last half of the twentieth century.

The Dialectics of Political-Technological Order and Gnosticism
Political-Technological Order

The statist cults and a gnostic cosmos emerged during the early part of the century because of the evolution of the world political-economic system. This system has intensified throughout the century. In the post–World War II period cults of power proliferated dramatically in diverse and seemingly contradictory forms throughout the world, as can be seen in the emergence of new ideological and religious movements.[6]

Political-economic expansion after World War II is not strictly the expansion of markets, nor is it solely consistent economic growth. It also is the consolidation of political-technological organization and knowledge, as evidenced by several trends. First, all regions including colonies are redefined as states; previous increases in scale, state control over territories, density of the system, and overall competition are intensified. The environmental demands of the world polity for strong mobilizing states are felt throughout the world and result in a convergence of socio-political structures (e.g., Meyer, Boli, and Chase-Dunn 1975). Second, these institutionalized themes have been coded into and carried by a formal organization—the United Nations. While low in coercive power, the U.N., with its agencies and policies, expands and intensifies world culture. Third, there is an increase in techno-logical dominance of social organization and economy. Everyday ac-tion is embedded within an overarching theoretical knowledge and is dominated by specialized fields of expertise. The public sphere of work and authority are constituted by increasingly elaborated, for-mally rationalized rules and flows of information (Bell 1973). In core countries this transformation is manifested in an increase in high technology as well as in the techniques of social organization—re-search and development, strategic planning, and so on. In peripheral countries it is marked by the required importation of such technology and research. Fourth, as a technique of social organization, bureau-cracy continues to dominate the structures of economy and polity. The state in particular is technicalized and dominated by experts and technocrats (e.g., Ellul 1967). In general, technology and technological organization replace nature and even the machine as the immediate experiential environment of people. The existential environment therefore confronts the individual as an alien, antihuman system that is nevertheless the creation of humankind (Ellul 1975; Bell 1976; Berger, Berger, and Kellner 1973).

Technological, bureaucratic organization of everyday life, depicts the cosmos as an impersonal order governed by mechanistic laws and cycles (Weber 1946, 282–83). This impersonal order is a reification of the dominance of rationalized knowledge (Boli 1987a; Bell 1973). Individuals and collectives alike tap into this knowledge in order to "develop" in all of the individualistic and collectivistic, material and ideational nuances of the word. The knowledge and power required for meaning and progress must be created. Individuals must be en-lightened, empowered, and transformed, largely through education.

Resacralization and Gnosticism

Weber (1946) has described the disenchantment of the world that results from rationalization processes that make nature and society understandable and technical, pushing religion and mystery into in-creasingly narrower realms of irrationality. Yet, this desacralizing of traditional religious conceptions provides the basis for the mystification of technique and rationality. For example, Marcuse (1964) forcefully describes the one-dimensional nature of technical rationality as it both legitimates domination and embraces subjectivity.[7]

There are two distinct aspects of this resacralization. First, power and mystery do in fact remain within this technologically expanding order; but they are centered in human-made technology and organization, rather than residing in a nonrational, supernatural realm. These centers of power are themselves sacralized and mystified. For example, the state-science nexus is celebrated as the center of mystery and power and as the guarantor of progress, evolution, and history (Ellul 1978). A related factor is the inherent characteristic of sacred and profane that the thing or principle that is used to profane or desacralize is the very thing that replaces the sacred (Ellul 1975). The state and technology through pragmatic rationality desacralize traditional structures and then are sacralized as the sources of progress and power.

A second aspect of this resacralization is the dialectical nature of rationalization and (personal) value and meaning (Marcuse 1964; Simmel 1978; Weber 1946). Nonrational primordial value is not simply stripped away or pushed into marginal leftover cultural regions. Such value is transformed. As a greater part of social life is divested of *non*rational, traditional, substantive meaning through formal rationalization, new *ir*rational meanings are constructed as specific negations of rationality.[8] The movement toward the irrational increases

> the more denuded of irrationality the world appears to be. The unity of the primitive image of the world, in which everything was concrete magic, has tended to split into rational cognition and mastery of nature, on the one hand, and into 'mystic' experiences, on the other. The inexpressible contents of such experiences remain the only possible "beyond," added to the mechanism of a world robbed of gods. (Weber 1946, 282)

This dialectic of rationality and subjectivity is pervasive. For example, nature is technicalized and reduced to mathematical equations but is also romanticized as an ontological realm outside the boundaries of the rational project which individuals irrationally and mystically experience. We already have seen this dialectic elsewhere in market and polity. The rational market depersonalizes exchange and devalues persons while at the same time creates the primordial individual. Similarly, as people become increasingly defined and organized within an intensifying world market, technological psychologies, bureaucratic state institutions, schools, and positivistic evolution, the individual is reconstituted as primordial, irrational, antitechnological humanity. These are not traditional leftovers nor escapist reactions; they are a positive construction of primordial value.

Thus, as sociocultural structures are rationalized, a new type of individual emerges by means of a rebirth: the new socialist man, the born-again American. Weber (1946, 229) relates rebirth to the question, "For what should I be reborn?" In modern world culture, it is rebirth to the empowering of individuals and their action within a technological bureaucratic world system—their death to nature and their rebirth to the implicit meaning of technological advance, economic growth, and bureaucratic organization. It is also the experiencing and becoming one with nature, cosmic forces, true humanity, the unfolding meaning of history, and the inner self. Thus, I am suggesting that in order to interpret rational ontology, we must see that "rationality" produces "irrationality." Moreover, the "new irrationality" that is constructed is a mirror image of the rationality it claims to transcend.

This empowerment and transformation of self and everyday action is isomorphic with historical gnostic mysticism. Enlightenment and meaning are grasped by individuals and collectivities in order to transform or reject the mundane alien order and construct a new one. Knowledge and empowerment distinguish the initiated from the masses, the moderns from the traditionalists. As in the case of historical gnosticism, an elite share in the power of knowledge while the masses follow with faith.[9]

Linking rationalization to a gnostic mysticism is supported by Weber's (1946, 282–85) observation: Within any impersonal cosmology, individual "salvation" is pursued through mysticism, ritual, and the spirituality of an exemplary prophet—or class of elite experts or virtuosi. Ironically, whereas the origins of rationality are to be traced to an emissary prophet and his personal Holy God and ethical, active religion, increasing levels of rationality move toward the exemplary prophet, an impersonal god, and a contemplative mystical religion.

Thus, rationalized ontology is built on a split between rationality and irrationality, between objectivity and subjectivity, and on a promise of transcendence that dialectically integrates the two poles. This ontology is society-wide (Campbell 1982) and indeed worldwide (Thomas 1987b) and provides an underlying metaphor for collective and individual action. Out of this complex structure, a large number of diverse movements, often openly conflicting and in competition with the official version, emerge in an attempt to formulate their own vision of this cosmology. Parallel to the construction of material progress via technological, bureaucratic centers of power and the transformation of individuals through education, movements construct subjective meaning via cosmic power centers. These movements are antitechnique and anti-Western rationality and education. They rhetorically attack the depersonalization, alienation, and exploitation of these structures and promise transcendence. Yet, such movements toward subjectivity and mysticism in fact articulate the subjectivity/irrationality pole of an integrated dialectic of rationalization. Consequently, they tend to reflect and reproduce the very rationalized structures they rhetorically are rejecting. I illustrate this framework by using it to interpret new religious movements.

New Religious Trends and Movements

The key idea for understanding new religious movements during this period is that in their content and structure they attempt to construct a new order of things that is based on a rational ontology. Given the dialectical nature of the political-technological nexus, four structural aspects of contemporary religious movements, and contemporary movements in general, can be delineated:

1. *Pole of rejection.* Movements explicitly reject various aspects of the political-technological intensification and expansion, including science, technology, reason, discipline, materialism, and certified experts. This characteristic is the sole focus of most theoretical interpretations.

2. *Gnostic impulse.* Movements hold forth the possibility of both self and collective transcendence by linking self and society to centers of knowledge and power. Thus, there is an emphasis on subjective experiences. This transcendence is accomplished through subjective or esoteric knowledge.

3. *Dialectic embrace.* The gnostic impulse embraces the rejected pole in two general ways. First, the centers of transcendence are impersonal, often rationalized and mechanical in nature. Second, the knowledge required for transcendence is technical and "taught" by an expert. "Truth" is defined as process or movement upward; method and form dominate over content and substance.

4. *New corporateness.* The rules and techniques of transcendence define moral collective boundaries as well as distinctions within those boundaries between elites initiated into the gnosis and the masses who follow in faith. These rules often are coded into a bureaucratic hierarchy that parallels a spiritual one. The collective is oriented to a

new order that often is linked directly to world unity, to the nation state, or to a dissident political faction.

I use this four-point scheme to describe several sets of contemporary movements: antinomian/New Age movements, fundamentalism, Pentecostalism, and liberation theology. These movements display this structure to different degrees, and all are not essentially gnostic or mystical. Nevertheless, all show trends toward this structure. The descriptions are brief and do not include extensive citations in support of the argument. At this point I wish only to explore the implication that they share the same ontology. I therefore focus on the isomorphic structures of these diverse movements.[10]

Antinomian and New Age Movements

Examples include astrology, Eastern mysticism, transcendental meditation, and human potential movements such as Scientology, EST, Eckankar, and self-actualization psychologies. The components of these movements largely have been syncretized within the New Age Movement. (1) These movements reject the impersonality of the modern world and especially the bureaucratic and technological organization of individuals in education, work, medicine, and psychology. (2) They define the value of the individual as an irrational, primordial value that is actualized or attained through self-transcendence. The self is to be linked to or merged with a mechanical universe, a cosmic force, or deeper levels of the self. For example, reincarnation depicts the inner self as a transhistorical life force with many different historical-personal manifestations. (3) These "deep" levels of power, including the inner self, thus ultimately are mechanical and impersonal. They can be attained or experienced by consulting experts and guides and through the use of particular techniques of the mind. Both the "deep reality" and the techniques are couched in pseudoscientific and technological language. (4) Most antinomian movements are apolitical, but to varying degrees speak of world unity or a spiritual strengthening of the nation. Enlightened individuals are the knowledge-elite within the group which as a whole leads the way to world peace. Nevertheless, there are more authoritarian forms that combine personal commitment to a charismatic leader with modern mobilization.

We could also include in this category "mainline examples" of the middle-class. For example, impersonality of work is transcended through leisure ceremonies of irrational release and a lifestyle of absorbing into self symbols of "the good life" (Bell 1976; Lasch 1979;

Wolfe 1976). Yet, periods of release are methodically scheduled into the work week, symbols are linked to commodities, and lifestyles are managed to further one's career. Thus, the expression of the subjective is shaped by rationality and closely linked to consumerism, just as nineteenth-century romanticism laid the basis for modern consumerism (Campbell 1987). As another example, mainline liberal Protestant theology, notwithstanding its general stance of demystification, is grounded in an existential world that separates science (and the rational empirical world) from meaning and faith. The latter is attained through an existential self-actualization (Berger 1967).

Fundamentalism

(1) Contemporary fundamentalism rejects various aspects of modernity (rationality and science) and individualism; faith is viewed as non-rational and rooted in the emotions of the "heart" rather than in rationality or "head-knowledge." (2) Fundamentalism does not explicitly promise immediate transcendence and thus does not conform completely to the model. Ultimate transcendence is accomplished through the work of Christ at His return; one prepares for it first by conversion and then by keeping oneself separate from the world by adhering to moral rules. Yet, it does emphasize that morality guarantees finding one's true self and attaining an inner peace and happiness. Moreover, it emphasizes subjective experience. (3) Fundamentalism is based on a personal God; nevertheless, there are strong tendencies to abstract God as the source of power and blessings. It embraces modernity in that moral rules and inner leadings are couched in the language of self-esteem, popular psychology, and positive thinking, and they are taught through modern technological means (Hunter 1983). Inner peace leads to correct decisions and individual success and prosperity. (4) Fundamentalism usually defines the moral collective as a separated subgroup demarcated by moral rules, but often, the moral community is coterminous with the nation. Citizens are reborn moral agents and personal rebirth is associated with the rebirth and empowering of the nation within the world system. This creates the potential for the politicization of fundamentalist movements (Liebman and Wuthnow 1983). Some groups with a high growth rate, such as the Latter-day Saints, articulate a more explicitly gnostic cosmos. Individuals are emanations of God while the world is a realm of matter that is alien and opposed to the spirit. Salvation is a movement back to the source, a self-realization of deity, based on the subjective apprehension of these mysteries.

Chapter Six

Pentecostal and Charismatic Movements

(1) These movements are fundamentalist in nature and share a rejection of modernity and rationality. (2) They more extremely espouse a potentially immediate transcendence from the decaying world. Subsequent to salvation, one is to experience the Baptism of the Spirit which links the individual to a source of power manifested in signs, experiences, and a higher level of spirituality. (3) These movements in a way combine the gnostic forms of antinomianism with fundamentalism. The Holy Spirit in practice is described as an impersonal sourse of power, an empowering force, or as an energy source into which cne must be "plugged." There are techniques and steps by which one produces and maintains this power, which guarantees personal success, prosperity, self-esteem and health. (4) Because self-transcendence is here and now and subjective, there is a focus on intense solidarity in meetings of empowerment. There is a clear distinction between those members who have been empowered and those who have not. They are usually organized within a hierarchy of authority, and many hierarchical groups incorporate charismatic components. The extensive use of electronic media, including satellites, coupled with a centrist authority structure, lead to conceptions of world unity within a worldwide church. Yet, as in other fundamentalist movements, empowerment enables a people to be a strong moral nation and a leader in the world community. Politicization thus tends to legitimate state authority and policy.

Liberation Theologies

Politicized religion in core countries predominantly is a form of fundamentalism that supports the state. Politically conservative religion also occurs in the non-core, as evidenced by Pentecostalism's success in Latin America; yet, politicized religion in the Third World often is a liberation theology that supports the state's dialectical opposite—revolution (Ellul 1975). (1) Liberation theologies reject Western definitions of economic development, spiritualized ideology, and reason/truth. The exploitive aspects of the world system are interpreted by an existentialist view of the world as alien and impersonal. Economic dependence is a spiritual bondage. (2) The illusions and exploitation of the world are transcended by critical knowledge that unlocks the secret meaning of history—the historical dialectic. The "new critical man" uses this knowledge to create a new humanity and society through historical conquest or liberation. Thus, true salvation or liberation is an existential will to power that takes the form of

Marxist revolutionary praxis. (3) The rejected pole of Western development is dialectically embraced in several ways: (a) Liberation, while couched in religious symbols, is defined in terms of economic growth as an essential aspect of equality and well-being. (b) Revolutionary political action, as "salvic," is centered on control of the state. (c) The development of critical knowledge is accomplished through a technical hermeneutic method that views truth as process and form. (4) There is a division between those who possess critical knowledge and those who have only precritical faith. At times, the moral collective is the world poor, but ultimate world liberation is attained through national liberation. Thus, a dependent nation is identified as a poor people, thereby framing revolution as liberation/salvation.

Summary

couldn't anything fit this "structure"?

I have limited my discussion of these diverse movements to sketching their common structure. Some fit the gnostic model more precisely than others. Differences among the movements are due to different cultural traditions. For example, fundamentalism fits the model least well, but by relating it to its immediate historical frame—nineteenth-century revivalism—it can be interpreted as a rather dramatic departure toward the gnostic model, Pentecostal versions even more so. Thus, it is important to see worldwide trends in religion and religious movements and not simply "new movements" (Robertson 1985). Differences also are due to world-historical locations. For example, religions in core countries tend toward individualism and antinomianism with an emphasis on health and prosperity. When politicized they tend to support a conservative state regime. Similar movements are found in the Third World supporting state regimes or providing millenarian alternatives. Yet, the Third World (and minorities in the core) also witness liberation religion linked to revolutionary movements (Lincoln 1985). Future work is needed to explore these differences, but the point here is that general trends and diverse movements must be interpreted in the context of their underlying institutional structures.

Concluding Thoughts on the Sociology of Religion

Religious movements rarely can be reduced totally to political-economic processses; yet, the latter have profound effects on the structure and content of religion. Religion places everyday life and social order in a larger cosmos. As everyday life is transformed by the rational market and central bureaucratic state, religious change takes a particular direction. This is manifested in the growth of those religious movements that articulate a rationalized social order. The world as a whole has been rationalized so that economic growth, nationalism, and cultural individualism increasingly have been organized in statist structures. Thus, while stemming from similar social changes, various religious movements have tended historically toward defining individual and nation more in terms of the mystification of state and empowerment—what can be termed modern gnosticism. It has been argued that historical comparisons are crucial for understanding the nature of these religious movements as they come to grips with change in the context of an evolving world-historical system.

I developed an institutional model from a broad comparative-historical base. I then "tested" this model by looking closely at nineteenth-century United States, producing a somewhat counterintuitive interpretation of revivalism, nation building, and the market. To reiterate, revivalism was primarily an acceptance of the new order. It both legitimated and was legitimated by the individuated market and the new myth of rational individualism. It comprehensively worked individualism into a unified cosmic order of things, from family relations to individual action to national growth. Revivalism thereby became the plausibility structure for much change, including Republicanism. At base, Republicanism constituted a world in which the individual was autonomous and directly tied to the national state. Both the individual and the nation had to be freed from the constraints of communal market and traditional authority. The new moral community was to be a homogeneous national one composed of individuals.

The specific features of this order still had to be articulated in voluntary associations, in pulpit and pews, and at the election box. This process was complicated by the emergence of corporations, concentrated capital, and the growth of the laboring class, especially in the industrial sectors. These developments gave rise to myths of ineffectual individuals who were dependent on social organization and other external processes. In the face of this trend, and other new movements, revivalism and Republicanism were maintained, especially in those populations least affected by corporate capitalism.

I conclude by summarizing several implications for the general study of religion and society. The theory developed in this book presents an institutional view of religious symbols and of their relation to social life. Any institution must meet the rhetorical requirements of the larger cultural environment or lose legitimacy and social support. Social movements that presuppose the environmental ontology raise questions concerning an institution's legitimacy and attempt to organize that institution according to this cultural structure.

One important implication is that social movements are based on ontologies—theories of society. A movement gains adherents because it subscribes to a view of the social order that makes sense to particular populations. Revivalism made sense and was legitimated in those areas dominated by effectual individuation and myths of rationality and radical individualism. Republicanism likewise occurred where there was an underlying structure of individualism and the unified cosmos of revival religion.

This point underscores the importance of understanding the content of a social movement and the structure of its ontology. When this is done, the specific claims of a movement and the specific religious and political controversies of a period can be placed in the context of the theories of the social order that are at stake. It then is necessary to delineate structural affinities between a movement's ontology and the organization of the social world. Only then can the social bases of a movement and its claims be interpreted.

The institutional model further implies a rethinking of our approach to religion and the causes of religious movements. A reexamination of concepts such as disorganization, anxiety, anomie, and crisis is entirely appropriate and is relevant to collective behavior theory generally: Movements are not irrational reactions to stress, strain, and breakdown. Moreover, the model forces rationalistic theories such as resource mobilization to consider the cultural accounts that define the calculus of rationality. Religion itself does more than simply provide a ready-made social organization that facilitates mobilization. It also structures institutionalized accounts, and thereby provides the symbolic frame of and legitimacy for specific claims. Theories of social movements and political sociology, and especially the comparative-historical study of movements, require an aggressive sociology of religion.

Finally, the idea that the knowledge system of an institution is structured by an environment comprising other institutions or an underlying cultural ontology is distinct from extreme projectionist theories still prevalent in the interpretation of religion. The latter assume that there is a one-to-one correspondence between religion and a given sphere: family-sex (Freud), social organization (Durkheim, Swanson), or alienation from production/consumption (Marx). The theory I have delineated here rejects such reductions as illusions. Actors, when approaching the sacred, as they approach any sphere, carry with them particular conceptions of self and social and natural reality. These preconceptions affect the structure of religious knowledge. This study therefore is also a call for professional modesty: We are able to claim that a cultural or material structure affects a religious system, but to claim a sociological reduction is self-deceiving arrogance. For example, it is inappropriate to argue that the material and cultural environment of the nineteenth-century United States totally determined revivalism. Within the limits of sociological analysis, it can be concluded that nineteenth-century revival religion as an institution gained legitimacy from a rational, individualistic world that was itself intimately linked to the expansion of a rational market.

The institutional model sets a clear agenda. In order to construct a more general and complete theory it is necessary to incorporate more explicitly into the model the dynamics of "relatively autonomous" cultural-religious change. Earlier work, stemming largely from Weber's (1963) historical analyses of cultural-religious rationalization, attempted to describe the internal dynamics of religious evolution (e.g., Bellah 1964). Few have followed this lead, largely because of the inadequacies of developmental models and their tendency to ignore material changes. This remains a major theoretical task for institutional theory.

The institutional model, further, provides a basis for better understanding such cultural dynamics. In particular, the insistence on the coinherence of structure and action short-circuits the idealism/materialism polemic. The recognition of dialectical contradictions within the sociocultural order suggests the source or generator of autonomous change. Rather than some vague evolutionary process, contradictory poles lead to new syntheses which produce often heightened rationalization and contradictions. The dialectics are manifested in the conflict among institutions, groups, and movements; so while fairly abstract in its conceptualization of cultural structures and dynamics, the institutional model deals with the specific conflicts and movements of sociocultural change. Moreover, the concept of cultural environments enables us to articulate the specific mechanisms by which relatively autonomous change results in a family of movements and would provide the starting point for integrating these dynamics into a comparative-historical theory. The concept of a world cultural order points to the level at which autonomous change is most likely occurring. The dialectics of world and national institutions are especially powerful in generating change and conflict. Consequently, as part of the task of describing cultural dynamics, it is necessary to delineate more thoroughly the character, structure, and logic of the world order, its dialectical, contextual relation to the traditions, institutions, and movements of national societies, and its relation to movements contesting world identities and institutions.

Appendix: Technical Aspects of the Quantitative Analyses

Technical aspects of the quantitative analyses and more detailed tables of the statistical results are presented in this appendix. In order to facilitate cross-referencing with the text, the headings and subheadings of the appendix parallel those of chapter 5.

Research Design and Models

Panel models pose a problem of estimation when there is a high stability of the dependent variable over time, as is found for denominational memberships and voting behavior. Those causes of membership measured at time one (M_1) and at time two (M_2) that are not explicitly in the equation are for the most part the same. This means that the disturbances of M_1 and M_2 are correlated. Consequently, M_1 and all other independent variables correlated with it are correlated with the disturbances of M_2. This violation of ordinary least squares assumptions results in biased estimates of the coefficients of the independent variables in addition to their standard errors.

There is no way in a two-wave panel design to correct for this, but it is well to point out that (1) the estimator of the autoregression term, b_a, is biased upward; (2) while it is difficult to deduce the exact nature of bias in multivariate models, the b_i of an independent variable highly (positively or negatively) correlated with the lagged dependent variable has an opposite (negative or positive, respectively) correlation with b_a. In this light it should be noted for the present study that the time one dependent variable is primarily a control and not of direct substantive interest, multicollinearity of the other independent variables with it is not high, and the resulting bias is most often conservative. The major cases of bias are in the estimates of foreign born effects as discussed in the results.

Most studies in this area examine dependent variables that are weighted (i.e., divided) by population, total vote, total religious membership, or some other population-scaled variable. The rationale is simple: Greater adherence to a particular denomination or political party is trivially a function of the size of the population, the number of religious people per se, or the number of people voting. However, equations composed of such variables create problems. Simply put, the dependent variable, such as proportion voting Republican, is a joint variable of the Republican vote and of the total vote cast. Any positive relation between an independent variable and the dependent one can be due to either (1) a positive relation to the numerator or (2) a negative relation to the denominator. Similar problems, of course, are present no matter what the sign of the relation. This means that if, for example, an independent variable is positively related to voter turnout but not related to Republican vote, a negative relation will be introduced artificially. The same applies to weighting particular denomination memberships either by total religious membership or by total population.

These types of equations have been critiqued and various alternatives have been proposed (Freeman and Kronenfeld 1973; Fuiguitt and Lieberson 1974; Schuessler 1973; Firebaugh and Gibbs 1985). The solution employed here is to deal with raw variables and to enter population into the equation as an explicit control (Hannan 1979) as shown in equations (1) and (2), where "a_1" and "a_2" are constants, and "e_1" and "e_2" are error terms, t_1 and t_2 denote at what time point in the panel the variable is measured, and b_{ij} is the regression coefficient of the variable:

$$
\begin{aligned}
\text{Revival Religion } t_2 = \ & b_{11} \text{ Revival Religion } t_1 \\
& + b_{12} \text{ Individuation } t_1 \\
& + b_{13} \text{ Population } t_2 \\
& + a_1 + e_1
\end{aligned}
\tag{1}
$$

$$
\begin{aligned}
\text{Republican Vote } t_2 = \ & b_{21} \text{ Republican Vote } t_1 \\
& + b_{22} \text{ Individuation } t_1 \\
& + b_{23} \text{ Revival Religion } t_1 \\
& + b_{24} \text{ Population } t_2 \\
& + a_2 + e_2
\end{aligned}
\tag{2}
$$

These equations are straightforward models of the theoretical argument. However, there are several problems. One is simply that any variable not scaled to population will have artificially small effects. This can be solved by interacting such variables with population, as shown in equations (3) and (4). In other words, a characteristic of social organization that is not related to the size of the population will affect population-related variables partly as a function of the size of the population. This can be interpreted as a primitive diffusion factor.

$$
\begin{aligned}
\text{Revival Religion } t_2 = \ & b_{11} \text{ Revival Religion } t_1 \\
& + b_{12} \text{ Individuation } t_1 \times \text{ Population } t_2 \quad (3) \\
& + b_{13} \text{ Population } t_2 \\
& + a_1 + e_1
\end{aligned}
$$

$$
\begin{aligned}
\text{Republican Vote } t_2 = \ & b_{21} \text{ Republican Vote } t_1 \\
& + b_{22} \text{ Individuation } t_1 \times \text{ Population } t_2 \\
& + b_{23} \text{ Revival Religion } t_1 \quad (4) \\
& + b_{24} \text{ Population } t_2 \\
& + a_2 + e_2
\end{aligned}
$$

There are also several estimation problems with such equations caused by the violation of ordinary least squares assumptions: (1) All variables scaled to population have extremely high multicollinearity, that is the independent variables to the right of the equation are highly interrelated; (2) such variables are highly skewed because of a small number of counties with extremely large populations; and (3) the variance in the residuals of such an analysis are highly correlated with some of the independent variables. All three of these problems, however, can be solved by means of weighted least squares (see Wonnacott and Wonnacott 1970: 134–35; Meyer et al. 1979). If the equations are divided through by population at time two, multicollinearity, distributional irregularities, and heteroscedasticity are reduced. This results in equations (5) and (6), abbreviating population to Pop.

$$
\begin{aligned}
\text{Revivalism } t_2 \, / \text{ Pop. } t_2 = \ & b_{11} \text{ Revivalism } t_1 \, / \text{ Pop. } t_2 \\
& + b_{12} \text{ Individuation } t_1 \quad (5) \\
& + b_{13} \\
& + a_1 \, / \text{ Pop. } t_2 + e_1'
\end{aligned}
$$

Republican Vote t_2 / Pop. $t_2 = b_{21}$ Republican Vote t_1 / Pop. t_2
$\qquad\qquad\qquad\quad + b_{22}$ Individuation t_1
$\qquad\qquad\qquad\quad + b_{23}$ Revivalism t_1 / Pop. t_2 $\qquad$ (6)
$\qquad\qquad\qquad\quad + b_{24}$
$\qquad\qquad\qquad\quad + a_2$ / Pop. $t_2 + e_2'$

Since the error terms in equation (1) through (4) are heteroscedastic with respect to population, they have a population component built into them: $e = e' \times$ Population. In equations (5) and (6), $e' = e/$ Population. Therefore, e' provides a purified error term. In order to check on this manipulation, residuals for the weighted equations were calculated and their absolute values were correlated with various independent variables. In the revivalism equations the highest correlation is .18 with revivalism at time one; the correlation with population is −.11. In the Republican equations the highest relation is −.21 with total vote; the population correlation is .01. In addressing the issue of ratio variables, Firebaugh and Gibbs (1985) do not discuss weighted least squares, but they suggest a similar model: They suggest using only one variable as the weighting term and including the inverse of the weighting variable as a separate control.

It must be emphasized that the substantive equations that are interpreted are (3) and (4). Equations (5) and (6) are used as means to estimate them accurately. Thus, once equations (5) and (6) are estimated, they are multiplied through by population measured at time two, giving the substantive equations (3) and (4) and the appropriate coefficients. The estimated constant in equations (5) and (6) becomes the coefficient of population at time two, while the coefficient of the inverse of population becomes the constant, in the substantive equations. At the time this was done, the standard error for the population slope was not available, making significance tests for it impossible.

Concepts and Measures
Effectual Individuation
Manufacturing

A good indicator of effectual individuation in the manufacturing sector would be the predominance of self-employed entrepreneurs. The national censuses do not break down labor by self-employment for this period. However, this could be measured indirectly by dividing the total number of manufacturing establishments by the number of employed. This ratio is one if everyone is self-employed, and it approaches zero when all laborers work for one establishment. However, during this period this variable is very highly negatively correlated, −.80, with Industrialization (manufacturing production divided by manufacturing and agricultural production). This makes sense in that the "self-employment" ratio is merely the inverse of the number of employed per establishment; the latter itself is a good indicator of scale. During this period, the more an area's economy is devoted to industry, the more it is dominated by scale, and therefore the greater the number of workers employed by large establishments.

The influence of scale on production can be demonstrated by plotting the number of manufacturing establishments per capita in 1880 against 1880 manufacturing production per capita. At low levels of production there is a positive, linear relation, and at a given value of production within this range there is a small variation in the number (and thus size) of establishments. At higher levels, increments in production are not related to concomitant increases in the number of establishments, and at each level of production there is a large variation in the number (and thus size) of establishments. At these higher levels, production is more closely related to the size of the establishment than to the number of establishments. The overall correlation between production and number of establishments is moderate: $r^2 = .30$.

The negative relation between the index of effectual individuation and Industrialization sheds some light upon the process of industrialization, which usually is used to summarize a jumble of diverse elements. One large component of industrialization is the dramatic increase in the relevance of scale. However, it is desirable to separate out the abstract dimension of effectual individuation. It was thought that this could be done by splitting the sample on the industrialization measure. The more industrialized half is dominated by scale factors to a greater degree than the less industrialized counties. Therefore, in the latter, self-employment would not be as related to industrialization and would be a purer measure of effectual individuation. However, even in these counties the correlation is sometimes too high for both variables to be included in the same equation (over −.60). Consequently, Capital Per Manufacturing Establishment is used as an inverse index of effectual individuation in manufacturing.

Agriculture

Analyses using tenure as an independent variable were carried out. The type of tenure is reported in the United States beginning in 1880, although there are several problems with these data. One especially relevant to the present study is that mortgages are not reported on owned farms; systems dominated by mortgaged farms may in fact not be very dissimilar from systems characterized by renting. Lacking better data and with these problems firmly in mind, I used various indexes based on these three tenure systems. It is predicted that those counties dominated by average-size farms that were owned by the cultivator would be characterized by revival religion.

It can be shown by plotting the number of farms per capita against farm production per capita, that for this period, scale of production does not dominate the agrarian sector. For 1880, there is a positive linear relation throughout all levels of production, which means that any aggregate increment in production is not due to differences in the size of the farms but rather to increases in the number of farms in the county. This pattern still holds in 1890. The correlations between number of farms and production are relatively high: 1880, r^2 = .40; 1890, r^2 = .49. Thus, Production Per Farm is a valid measure of effectual individuation and Wages Per Farm is a valid inverse measure of it.

Table A1 shows the correlations among the various economic measures over time. The autocorrelations of the variables are moderately high, implying a relatively stable but not static market. For the total sample of counties, Capital Per Manufacturing Establishment is highly correlated with Industrialization—between .61 and .68; however, for counties low in industrialization the correlation drops to .24. Consequently, Capital Per Manufacturing Establishment is examined for the whole sample and then for those counties in the bottom half of Industrialization. The correlation of the two agrarian indicators for the entire sample of counties is .72, but after the exclusion of various counties described elsewhere and of those with missing values, the multicollinearity varies around .55, with some political equations reaching .65. As expected, Wages Per Farm is positively related to both Industrialization and the inverse measure of effectual individuation. Production Per Farm itself is not highly related to other measures. However, when Wages Per Farm is partialed out it becomes, as expected, significantly negatively related to Capital Per Manufacturing Establishment and Industrialization.

Revival Religion

Measuring increases in individualism cannot be done in the abstract. That is, a movement toward a more individualistic system means, in fact, a shift from one concrete historical system to another: from

Table A1 Correlation Matrix of Economic Variables[a]

	1	2	3	4	5	6	$\bar{X}$	SD
1. Industrialization '90	—						.48	.28
2. Industrialization '80	.93***	—					.43	.25
3. Capital/Mfg Establishment '90	.74***	.73***	—				10.50[b]	8.55[b]
4. Capital/Mfg Establishment '80	.61***	.68***	.64***	—			6.66[b]	6.86[b]
5. Prod/Farm '90[c]	.00	.03	.10	.04	—		6.77[d]	3.24[d]
	(−.43)***	(−.40)***	(−.23)***	(−.24)***	—			
6. Prod/Farm '80[c]	.08	.02	.16**	.02	.76***	—	6.75[d]	2.50[d]
	(−.27)***	(−.37)***	(−.11)*	(−.25)***	—	—		
7. Wages/Farm '70[e]	.35***	.36***	.32***	.26***	.75***	.72***	1.03[d]	.98[d]
	(.53)***	(.50)***	(.37)***	(.35)***	—	—		

[a]Correlations are Pearson coefficients and are based on all cases for which data are available. Some counties are excluded in the regression analyses. $N = 261$.

[b]In thousands.

[c]Controlling for Wages/Farm in parentheses.

[d]In hundreds.

[e]Controlling for Prod/Farm in parentheses.

* = $.01 < p \leq .05$.

** = $.001 < p \leq .01$.

*** = $p \leq .001$.

Catholicism to Protestantism, from Calvinism to Arminianism, from Arminianism to humanistic individualism. In this study we are concerned with the movement from a system based on a modified Calvinism to one constructed on Arminianism. The specific elements of the latter system, which I have labeled revival religion, are detailed in the text; they consist primarily of Arminianism and radical free will, rational methods of evangelism, perfectionism or holiness, and the postmillennial ideal of a perfectable nation. The task is to measure the degree to which a denomination adhered to these elements.

Two historians of religion rated the various denominations on the degree to which they adhered to these elements. While graciously willing to help and the source of many insights, these colleagues had a proper historian's skepticism. Also, I codified Richard Jensen's (1971) descriptions of denominational adherence to revivalistic pietism. Any superficiality in the ratings must be attributed to their inherent drawbacks and does not reflect on these colleagues. The ratings are presented in columns A, B, and C of table A2.

In addition, I read many histories of American religion from which I abstracted a fourth rating. The works consulted included, but were not limited to, Ahlstrom (1972), Carroll (1912), Cross (1950), Gaustad (1966), Kleppner (1970), Lipset (1964), Mayer (1956), Mead (1965), and Smith (1957). These authors, of course, are not responsible for the use I have made of their work, but for whatever is beneficial in my rating, I am largely indebted to them.

The four ratings were then combined into one overall rating of the denominations. In the case of discrepancies, I did not use a mechanical averaging process. I made personal judgments that I believe are justifiable. I report the rationale used for those denominations for which the discrepancies are large.

Adventist. Adventist groups emerged at mid-century and tended toward evangelism and individualism which was the basis of the rating of 3 by A. However, they were strictly premillennial and pessimistic in their theory of society. I felt this to be a most important factor in making them quite distinct from mainline revivalism; therefore the 0 rating.

Primitive Baptist. This Baptist sect was individualistic as was all of the denomination, but it adhered to radical Calvinism, denying free will, and also maintained an amillennial or premillennial eschatology. Therefore, a 0 rating was used.

Friends. There were several discrepancies in the scoring of the Quakers. It can be concluded that Quaker bodies in general should be a 1, but the ratings of the two main bodies are problematic. The tentative decision was based on the fact that the Hicksite group was more lenient

Table A2 Rating of Denominations on Revivalism

	A[a]	B[a]	C[a]	D[b]	E[c]
Adventist	3			0	0
Baptist groups in general	3	4	3	3	3
Northern & national convention	3	3	3	3	3
Southern & national convention	3	4	3	3	3
Freewill	3	4		4	4
Primitive	1	3		0	0
Christian Science	0	0		2	1
Christian (Christian Connection)	3	3	4	3–4	4
Churches of Christ	3	3		3	3
Congregational	2	3	4	4	3
Disciples of Christ	3	3	4	4	4
Dunkers	1	2			?
Evangelical Association	4	2	2	4	3
Friends in general		0–1			1
Hicksite	0	2		2	2
Orthodox	1	0		2	1
German Evangelical Synod of N.A.	3	0	2		?
Latter-day Saints	1	1–2		1	1
Lutheran groups in general	1	0–1	1	1	1
General Synod	2	0	3	1	1
General Council	1	0	2	1	2
Synodical Conference (Missouri)	1	0	0	0	0
United Norwegian Church of America	1	0	2	2	?
Norwegian Synod	1	0	1–2	0	0
Hauge's Norwegian	1	0	3	2	?
Iowa	1		1	1	1
Ohio	1		1	1	1
South	1		2	1	1
Methodist	4	4	4	4	4
Presbyterian groups in general	3	3	2	3	3
U.S.A. (Northern)	3			2–3	3
U.S. (Southern)	3			2–3	3
Cumberland	3	4	4	4	4
United	2	2		2	2
Protestant Episcopal	1	0–1	0–1	0–1	0
Reformed Church in America (Dutch)	1	1	1	1	1
Reformed Church in the U.S. (German)	1	1	1	1	1
Unitarian	0	0–1		3–4	3
United Brethren	2	2–3	4	4	3
Universalist	0	0–1		2–3	1
Roman Catholic	0	0	0	0	0
Jewish	0	0	0	0	0

Note: A five-point scale is used, from zero to four. Adapted from Thomas (1979).
[a]Rated by historians of American religion.
[b]Summary rating from various histories and descriptions.
[c]Combined rating used in the study.

with Arminianism and had tendencies toward the Unitarian idea of the inner light. The data used in the analysis contained only information on Quaker bodies in general.

Unitarians and Universalists. There were large disagreements in the scoring of these two denominations. This can be largely attributed to the fact that these groups were often at odds with the mainline Christian bodies including the revivalists: Unitarians tended to deny the deity of Jesus; the Universalists denied the necessity of belief in Jesus to be saved. This led the Universalists to downplay evangelism and thus the low rating of a 1. The Unitarians, on the other hand, moved toward revivalism during this period, creating a liberal evangelism. Unitarian moral humanism went well with revivalism's emphasis on free will, the universal availability of the Spirit, and the necessity of moral and social transformation. There were, of course, tensions within this synthesis between the rational humanism of an earlier day and the trend toward evangelism, and it should be emphasized that Unitarian evangelism was distinguished by the secular and liberal implications of its tradition. Nevertheless, it seemed to deserve the higher rating of 3 (see, especially, Smith 1957).

Lutherans. Several Lutheran groups presented problems. These ratings were constructed early in the project, and after much additional reading and study I consider only one rating to be a possible mistake: the scoring of the Lutheran General Council higher than the General Synod. These two bodies were extremely similar in belief and action and probably should be rated the same. However, rating Lutherans and other denominations dominated by immigrant groups presents a larger and more general problem. This is reflected in the number of discrepancies. The source of the problem is the necessity to take into account the tradition from which a group emerges. For example, all Lutherans were more liturgical and less revivalistic than most American Protestant groups. However, some groups such as the Hauge Norwegians moved toward a revivalistic pietism. It was a small movement relative to the stance of, say, the Methodists; however, relative to other Lutheran bodies it was dramatic. Should the Hauge Norwegian Synod be rated 3 or 4 by taking into account the traditional context of its shift, or should it be rated a 1, based on its stance on the four points and relative to a pure Methodism? The sources of the different ratings clearly disagreed on the solution. The ratings of immigrant groups and the Lutherans in general tended toward the second strategy. Only the General Synod and the General Council figure in the present analyses.

The primary bias resulting from these considerations is an underestimation and a general insensitivity of the ratings to revivalism within immigrant groups working within a dominant liturgical, non-revivalistic tradition. This measurement error attenuates the estimated relations of revivalism to other variables. It also magnifies an already high negative correlation between immigrant groups and revivalism. This bias can be reduced by excluding counties high in foreign-born groups. For the revivalism equations this made no real difference in the results. In the political equations the (negative) multicollinearity between revivalism and the number of immigrants was too great for both to be in the equation. After the exclusion of counties with large immigrant groups the correlation between the two variables was reduced to around $-.56$. This means the political analyses are not strictly applicable to homogeneous immigrant populations.

Unresolved ratings. Given the information available at the time, several immigrant denominations could not be assigned a summary rating: Dunkers, German Evangelical Synod of North America, and United Norwegian Church of America.

As stated in the text, two indexes are constructed from this data. The *Exclusive Index* sums the memberships of those denominations that were rated 4. The *Inclusive Index* sums the memberships of the various denominations, each weighted by its score on revivalistic piety.

The 1870 information is compiled by states and does not include those bodies that had small memberships in a given state. The 1890 census groups the information by denominations and includes their memberships in all states regardless of their predominance. Thus, there are data for more denominations at the latter point in time. This presented a problem in combining the data into indexes for the two different periods. Limiting the indexes to only those denominations with data in 1870 would be rather restrictive, and much information found in the 1890 census would be lost. This is especially true as the excluded denominations in 1870 were different for the different states. I decided to use all the information available. Thus, for 1870 those denominations are used for which there are data for at least three of the four states. All denominations are used in 1890. This means that the 1870 indexes will underestimate memberships, but this error will be extremely small since data are missing because the 1870 census did not report memberships for bodies within a given state because of the smallness of those denominations in that state. The composition of the indexes for both time points is presented in table A3.

Table A3 Composition of Two Indexes of Revivalism

Exclusive Index: 1870

Maine, Ohio, Iowa	"Christian" + Methodist
New York	Methodist

Exclusive Index: 1890

All states	Christian Connection + Disciples of Christ + Methodist

Inclusive Index: 1870

Maine	3 × Baptist + 4 × "Christian" + 3 × Congregational + 4 × Methodist
New York	3 × Baptist + 3 × Congregational + 4 × Methodist + 3 × Presbyterian
Ohio	3 × Baptist + 4 × "Christian" + 4 × Methodist + 3 × Presbyterian
Iowa	3 × Baptist + 4 × "Christian" + 3 × Congregational + 4 × Methodist + 3 × Presbyterian

Inclusive Index: 1890

All states	3 × N. Baptist + 4 × Freewill Baptist + 4 × Christian Conn. + 3 × Congreg. + 4 × Disc. Christ + 3 × Evangelical Assoc. + Latter-day Saints + Lutheran Gen. Synod. + 2 × Lutheran Gen. Confer. + 4 × Methodist, Episcopal + 4 × Methodist, Protestant + 3 × N. Presb. + 4 × Cumberland Presb. + 2 × United Presb. + Reformed Church in Amer. + Reformed Church in U.S. + 3 × Unitarian + 3 × United Brethren + Universalist

Because the Inclusive Index makes fuller use of the information, it was used in the political equations. Also, the Exclusive Index is very small relative to the entire population, making inferences from it to the whole county problematic. Analyses were performed using the Exclusive Index. In all cases, except for the cross-sectional analysis of 1880, it shows a pattern of causal effects on voting identical to the Inclusive Index, but the actual effects are much larger for the Exclusive Index. In the cross-sectional analysis the Exclusive Index has a negative effect on Republican Vote which is opposite that of the Inclusive Index.

As would be expected, both indexes are highly related to total Protestant memberships; the Exclusive Index less so than the Inclusive one. A few equations were run using Protestant Memberships in place of these two indexes. The findings are comparable; although the Exclusive Index results in much larger effects.

I should emphasize that these ratings and indexes are not the final word. More precise measurement of the immigrant groups and possibly more distinct differentiation among the major Protestant bodies are two directions for improvement.

Table A4 shows descriptive statistics and the intercorrelations of these measures. The high autocorrelation of both variables supports the assumption that seating capacity can be taken as an indirect measure of relative memberships. The two indexes are themselves highly correlated: .92 in 1870 and .85 in 1890. The mean of the Exclusive Index, as would be expected, is much lower than that of the Inclusive Index. This makes the exclusive measure more dependent on fluc-

Table A4 Correlation Matrix of Revival Variables

	Exclusive Index '90	Exclusive Index '70	Inclusive Index '90	$\bar{X}$	SD
Exclusive Index '90	—			.08	.04
Exclusive Index '70	.65 (229)	—		.20	.15
Inclusive Index '90	.85 (260)	.65 (226)	—	.59	.21
Inclusive Index '70	.62 (214)	.92 (214)	.71 (211)	1.34	.77

Note: All variables are divided by the corresponding population. Correlations are Pearson coefficients and are based on all cases for which data are available. Some counties are excluded in the regression analyses. N in parentheses. All relations are significant, $p \leq .001$.

tuations in case numbers. Therefore, the weight of the interpretation is put on the Inclusive Index.

Political Ideology

Table A5 shows descriptive statistics and the correlations of Republican Vote per capita over time. There is a high stability of the major party votes, which is consistent with the fact that party loyalties ran high throughout this period.

Control Variables
Total Memberships and Total Vote

The inclusion of a "total" variable presents problems of interpretation in that it includes, by definition, the dependent variable. This is partly offset by the Inclusive Index of revivalistic piety which weights the different memberships. It nevertheless remains impossible to give meaningful substantive interpretations to the coefficients of these controls. However, I felt that the arguments concerning total religiosity and voter turnout needed to be tested more explicitly. It has to be demonstrated that any effects of the independent variables are not mediated by or spuriously created by total denominational memberships or voter turnout. Population can be viewed as a proxy variable for Total Memberships and Total Vote; models without a total variable but controlling for the inverse of population are then statistically appropriate (Firebaugh and Gibbs 1985). For the revivalism models the equations were estimated first with just Population as a control and then a second time including Total Memberships. There were no differences between the equations; that is, the religiosity argument does not hold. The results without Total Memberships using Population as an indirect control are reported and interpreted in the text.

Table A5 Correlation Matrix of Republican Vote per Capita

	1896	1892	1888	1884	$\bar{X}$	SD
1896	—				.14	.02
1892	.93	—			.11	.02
1888	.87	.92	—		.12	.02
1884	.79	.83	.92	—	.12	.02
1880	.80	.81	.89	.92	.12	.02

Note: All variables are divided by the corresponding population.
Correlations are Pearson coefficients and are based on all cases for which data are available. Some counties are excluded in the regression analyses. $N = 261$. All relations are significant, $p \leq .001$.

It also is necessary to control for the effects of voter turnout in the electoral models. As noted in the text, including Total Vote as an explicit control makes no substantial difference in the results for the period from 1880 through 1892. Therefore equations using Population as an indirect control are reported in the text, and differences from equations with Total Vote are noted in footnotes and this appendix. Analyses for 1892–96 include an explicit control for Total Vote because of the important effects of voter turnout. Future work on improving the specification of both the revivalism and political models would control for the inverse of Total Memberships and Total Vote or simply the total variable minus the part—the dependent variable (Firebaugh and Gibbs 1985).

The Socioeconomic Context of Revivalism, 1870–1890: Results

The correlations among the religious, economic, and control variables are found in table A6. All are in the direction hypothesized. Additionally, there is very little multicollinearity, except for the relation between Industrialization and Capital Per Manufacturing Establishment. Foreign Born has a higher negative relation to Revivalism than expected; this most likely is due to the insensitivity of the ratings to subtle differences among immigrant religions. Equations were estimated in which the counties most dominated by foreign born were excluded. While the Foreign-Born effect is, of course, attenuated, the other coefficients in the model remain the same.

The core of the results are the regression equations. Table A7 presents the unstandardized slopes and the standard errors of the various independent and control variables in relation to the Exclusive Index of revivalism—the total memberships of denominations rated 4. Because there is a directional hypothesis for all variables, one-tailed tests of significance are used. The autoregression term is large and significant indicating stability of measurement over time. It has the same slope for both the total sample and the counties low in industrialization. Population has a smaller but nevertheless substantial effect. For both the whole sample and for the less industrialized counties Foreign Born has large negative effects on Revivalism, dominating the analysis. Equations (1) and (4) show that Industrialization (the proportion of production in manufacturing) has a negative effect on Revivalism and thus support the conventional lines of reasoning.

Equations (2) and (5) show that without controlling for Industrialization the inverse index of effectual individuation in manufacturing—Capital Per Manufacturing Establishment—has a significant

Table A6 Correlation Matrix of Revivalism, 1870–1890[a]

	1	2	3	4	5	6
1. Inclusive Rev Index '90[b]	—					
2. Inclusive Rev Index '70[b]	.68*** (211)	—				
3. Industrialization '90	-.11* (260)	-.07 (214)	—			
4. Foreign Born '90[b]	-.66*** (260)	-.65*** (214)	.11* (263)	—		
5. Capital/Mfg Establishment '80	-.20*** (258)	-.16** (214)	.61*** (261)	.21*** (261)	—	
6. Prod/Farm '80[c]	.19** (210)	-.05 (210)	-.25*** (210)	.02 (210)	-.25*** (210)	—
7. Wages/Farm '70[d]	-.28*** (210)	-.05 (210)	.39*** (210)	.27*** (210)	.32*** (210)	.72*** (261)

Note: Adapted from Thomas (1979).

[a] Correlations are Pearson coefficients and are based on all cases for which data are available. Some counties are excluded in the regression analyses. N in parentheses.

[b] Divided by Population, 1890.

[c] Controlling for Wages/Farm, 1870.

[d] Controlling for Prod/Farm, 1880.

$* = .01 < p \leq .05$.

$** = .001 < p \leq .01$.

$*** = p = .001$.

Table A7 Panel Analyses of Revivalism, 1870–1890: Exclusive Index[a]

Eq.	Capital/Mfg Establishment 1880 × Pop '90[b]	Prod/Farm 1880 × Pop '90[b]	Wages/Farm 1870 × Pop '90[b]	Industrialization 1890 × Pop '90	Foreign Born 1890	Pop 1890[c]	Revival Index 1870	Constant	N
				All Counties					
1.				−.04(.01)**	−.16(.03)**	.10	.12(.02)**	−80	229
2.[d]	−.05(.03)**				−.12(.03)**	.07	.15(.02)**	111	201
3.[e]		.04(.01)**	−.10(.05)**	−.04(.01)**	−.20(.04)**	.09	.11(.02)**	−46	175
			Counties in Bottom Half of Industrialization, 1880[f]						
4.				−.04(.02)**	−.27(.05)**	.12	.08(.02)**	−30	102
5.[d]	−.35(.16)**				−.19(.07)**	.09	.12(.03)**	272	74
6.[d]	−.34(.17)**			−.01(.03)	−.19(.07)**	.09	.12(.03)**	242	74
7.		.02(.02)	−.13(.06)**	−.03(.02)*	−.25(.05)**	.12	.09(.02)**	−59	102

Note: Adapted from Thomas (1979).

[a]Weighted least squares estimates of slopes; standard errors in parentheses; one-tailed test of significance: * = .05 < p ≤ .10; ** = p ≤ .05.

[b]In hundreds of thousands.

[c]Standard error not calculated.

[d]Counties with less than 18% production in industry in 1880 excluded.

[e]Counties with more than 69% production in industry in 1880 excluded.

[f]Counties with more than 38.3% production in industry in 1880 excluded.

negative effect on Revivalism, as predicted. Because of high multi-collinearity measures of effectual individuation and Industrialization cannot be in the equation for the entire sample simultaneously. In the less industrialized counties the correlation is around .24, and the results are shown in equation (6). The slope of Industrialization is decreased and not significant while the effect of Capital Per Manufacturing Establishment is not altered, remaining significant. As stated in the text, it therefore seems safe to infer that effectual individuation as inversely measured by the average amount of capital invested in a manufacturing establishment is a dimension distinct from industrialization.

Equations (3) and (7) of table A7 report the effects of the agrarian indexes: Production Per Farm and Wages Per Farm. For comparison purposes they are analyzed in the less industrial counties even though there is no problem of multicollinearity with Industrialization. Production Per Farm is a positive index of effectual individuation, and it has a positive effect on Revivalism. Wages Per Farm partials out factors of scale which may be entailed in the first index and is substantively interpreted as an inverse index of effectual individuation. As predicted, it has a negative effect on Revivalism. Thus, in support of hypothesis 1, effectual individuation within the agrarian sector as measured by these two variables has a positive causal relation to the acceptance of revivalistic pietism.

In analyses not reported, no index based on tenure had any effect on revivalism. This includes not only various ones designed to tap, in different ways, effectual individuation, but also indexes that measure economic interest and control over production. The only relation that approaches substantive or statistical significance is that the number of rented farms appears to have small positive effects, but the number of rented farms within any particular county is so small it is hard to infer the actual organization of a county's economy or pattern of material interest. It therefore at this point is impossible to make any interpretation about the causal factors involved.

The apparent failure of these indexes may be due in part to the deficiencies of the data. It may also be that the type of tenure is not an important factor in determining the attribution of individual autonomy and efficacy. It seems that productivity attributable to the individual or family farmer is a more important factor in the agrarian sector than ownership; this, of course, is qualified by the deficiencies of the tenure data.

Table A8 shows identical analyses for the Inclusive Index of revival religion—the sum of denominational memberships each weighted by its rating on revivalism. The autoregression term for this variable is

Table A8 Panel Analyses of Revivalism, 1870–1890: Inclusive Index[a]

Eq.	Capital/Mfg Establishment 1880 × Pop '90[b]	Prod/Farm 1880 × Pop '90[b]	Wages/Farm 1870 × Pop '90[b]	Industrialization 1890 × Pop '90	Foreign Born 1890	Pop 1890[c]	Revival Index 1870	Constant	N
				All Counties					
1.				-.17(.04)**	-.82(.16)**	.66	.12(.02)**	-769	211
2.[d]	-.23(.14)*				-.79(.18)**	.53	.14(.02)**	-222	194
3.[e]		.25(.07)**	-.52(.26)**	-.14(.06)**	-.96(.21)**	.52	.12(.02)**	-317	159
			Counties in Bottom Half of Industrialization, 1880[f]						
4.				-.16(.11)*	-1.2(.26)**	.72	.10(.02)**	-425	86
5.[d]	-1.8 (.72)**			.06(.15)	-1.0(.31)**	.59	.12(.03)**	1051	69
6.[d]	-1.9 (.79)**			-.12(.11)	-1.0(.31)**	.56	.12(.03)**	1427	69
7.		.21(.10)**	-.78(.33)**		-1.1(.26)**	.60	.11(.02)**	-334	86

Note: Adapted from Thomas (1979).

[a] Weighted least squares estimates of slopes; standard errors in parentheses; one-tailed test of significance: * = .05 < p ≤ .10; ** = p ≤ .05.

[b] In hundreds of thousands.

[c] Standard error not calculated.

[d] Counties with less than 18% production in industry in 1880 excluded.

[e] Counties with more than 69% production in industry in 1880 excluded.

[f] Counties with more than 38.3% production in industry in 1880 excluded.

very similar to that of the Exclusive Index, despite the difference in metric between the two. The other control variables have essentially identical effects on the Inclusive Index as on the Exclusive one. It should be noted that all the coefficients in the Inclusive Index equations are higher than the Exclusive Index ones simply because of the difference in metric. Equations (1) and (4) of table A8 replicate the negative effects of Industrialization. The statistical significance of the effect is lower for the less industrialized areas, but this is most likely due to the smaller number of cases as the slopes are similar.

Equations (2) and (5) show the negative effects of Capital Per Manufacturing Establishment on Revivalism. Equation (6) demonstrates that this relation remains when controlling for Industrialization while the latter drops to zero. Thus, the inference remains: Effectual individuation within the manufacturing sector is distinct from industrialization and has a positive effect on the acceptance of revival religion.

The analysis of the agrarian sector also replicates the previous results. The two measures of Production and Wages Per Farm have large positive and negative effects, respectively, on Revivalism, as shown in equations (3) and (7). Scales based on tenure have no discernable pattern of effects, and are not reported.

The Political Consequences of Revivalism, 1880–1896: Results

The correlations of the voting variables with the religious, economic, and control variables are shown in table A9. Variables are interpolated for off years. The only notable relation unique to the political analyses is the − .69 correlation between the Inclusive Index of revivalism and Foreign Born. In order to reduce this multicollinearity, counties with the top 25 percent of Foreign Born are excluded.

Detailed results of the political equations are reported in Tables A10 through A15. The substantive interpretations are discussed in the text; only technical points and amplifications are included here.

1880

Industrialization has a small positive relation to Republican Vote for the total sample (equations 1 and 3) and for the less industrialized counties (equations 4, 6, and 7) (table A10). Effectual individuation in manufacturing has no effect on Republican Vote as shown in equation (2), but the sign becomes the predicted negative for counties low in industrialization (equations 5 and 6). Equations (3) and (7) show that Production Per Farm has a positive effect but so does the variable Wages Per Farm. When Total Vote is included in equation (3), the

Table A9 Correlation Matrix of Republican Vote, 1880–1888[a]

	1	2	3	4	5	6	7
1. Rep Vote '88[b]	—						
2. Rep Vote '80[b]	.71*** (261)	—					
3. Inclusive Rev Index '80[b]	.35*** (209)	.53*** (209)	—				
4. Industrialization '88	-.10 (259)	-.03 (259)	-.12* (211)	—			
5. Foreign Born '88[b]	-.24*** (261)	-.42*** (261)	-.69*** (211)	.12* (261)	—		
6. Capital/Mfg Establishment '80	-.11* (259)	-.08 (259)	-.17** (211)	-.63*** (261)	.21*** (261)	—	
7. Prod/Farm '80[c]	.02 (208)	.13* (208)	-.01 (208)	-.27*** (208)	.02 (208)	-.25*** (208)	—
8. Wages/Farm '70[d]	-.04 (208)	-.12* (208)	-.10 (208)	.41*** (208)	.26*** (208)	.32*** (208)	.72*** (261)

[a]Correlations are Pearson coefficients and are based on all cases for which data are available. Some counties are excluded in the regression analyses. N in parentheses.

[b]Divided by population, 1888.

[c]Controlling for Wages/Farm, 1870.

[d]Controlling for Prod/Farm, 1880.

* = .01 < p ≤ .05.

** = .001 < p ≤ .01.

*** = p ≤ .001.

Table A10 Cross-sectional Analyses of Republican Vote, 1880[a]

Eq.	Inclusive Index Revival 1880	Capital/Mfg Establishment 1880 × Pop '80[b]	Prod/ Farm 1880 × Pop '80[b]	Wages/ Farm 1870 × Pop '80[b]	Industrialization 1880 × Pop '80	Foreign Born 1880	Pop 1880[c]	Con-stant	N
			All Counties						
1.	.022(.006)**				.01(.01)	.14(.05)**	.08	79	168
2.[d]	.023(.006)**	.00(.03)				.15(.05)**	.08	−47	155
3.[e]	.018(.006)**		.022(.016)*	.13(.05)**	.03(.02)*	.05(.06)	.05	280	137
			Counties in Bottom Half of Industrialization, 1880[f]						
4.	.021(.009)**				.01(.04)	.17(.08)**	.07	241	74
5.[d]	.027(.011)**	−.08(.14)				.22(.09)***	.06	209	61
6.[d]	.025(.010)**	−.16(.15)			.12(.07)**	.20(.09)**	.02	472	61
7.	.021(.008)**		.06(.02)**	.07(.07)	.03(.04)	.06(.07)	.01	611	74

[a]Weighted least-squares estimates of slopes; standard errors in parentheses; counties in which more than 18% of the population was foreign born in 1880 excluded; one-tailed test of significance: * = .05 < p ≤ .10; ** = p ≤ .05.

[b]In hundreds of thousands.

[c]Standard error not calculated.

[d]Counties with less than 18% production in industry in 1880 excluded.

[e]Counties with more than 69% production in industry in 1880 excluded.

[f]Counties with more than 38.3% production in industry in 1880 excluded.

beta for Production Per Farm is greater, $+.19$, while that of Wages Per Farm is negative and insignificant, $-.01$.

1880–1888; 1888–1892

Findings are substantively the same for the total sample and for less industrialized counties, so the latter are not reported (see table A11 and A12). When Total Vote is controlled, the only substantial difference is that in equation (1), Industrialization has a larger significant positive effect on Republican Vote, reinforcing the inference that Republican ideology was being adapted to urban big business.

1892–1896

Table A13 presents the effects of the independent variables on Republican Vote while table A14 shows the analysis of Democratic Vote. Both include Total Vote as a control for voter turnout. Foreign Born, as predicted, has a positive effect on Republican support while it is negatively related to Democratic success. Industrialization has the same effects and also is in line with the predictions. Equation (2) of table A13 shows a positive effect of Capital Per Manufacturing Establishment on Republicanism. However, this is reversed when the less industrialized counties are examined in equation (5). This negative effect is increased when Industrialization is controlled in equation (6). Thus, the positive effect found in equation (2) is a spurious result of the rather large positive relation of Industrialization to both Capital and Republican Vote. The negative relation of Capital with Democratic Vote in equation (2) of table A14 is also spurious; no significant relation is found when Industrialization is controlled as shown in equations (5) and (6) of table A14. Wages Per Farm does not differentiate the two parties; Production Per Farm shows positive effects on Republican success and small negative ones on Democratic Vote—equations (3) and (7) of both table A13 and table A14. When Total Vote is not included, equation (3) also shows a positive relation of Production Per Farm with Democratic Vote, but this model is less adequate.

Table A13 shows no effects of Revival Religion on Republican Vote. Table A14 shows a negative relation to Democratic Vote.

The revivalism effects obtained here are dramatically different from those previously found in the literature. The previous findings result from the use of ratio models that take the form of equation (7), even if only implicitly, in turnover tables.

Table A11 Panel Analyses of Three-Party Voting Pattern, 1880–1888, 1884–1888[a]

Eq.	Inclusive Index Revival Time 1	Capital/Mfg Establishment Time 1 × Pop '88[b]	Prod/Farm Time 1 × Pop '88[b]	Wages/Farm 1870 × Pop '88[b]	Industrialization 1888 × Pop '88	Foreign Born 1888	Pop 1888[c]	Party Vote Time 1	Constant	N
	Republican									
	1880	1880	1880					1880		
1.	−.008(.003)**				.004(.005)	−.028(.021)*	.04	.82(.03)**	−67	169
2.[d]	−.009(.003)**	.003(.012)				−.030(.022)*	.05	.83(.03)**	−136	156
3.[e]	−.008(.003)**		−.012(.007)**	.03(.02)*	.009(.006)*	−.005(.024)	.04	.82(.04)**	−54	136
	Democrat									
	1880	1880	1880					1880		
4.	−.014(.003)**				−.022(.007)**	.033(.029)	.06	.74(.05)**	−122	169
5.[d]	−.014(.004)**	−.014(.018)				.020(.032)	.05	.75(.05)**	48	156
6.[e]	−.014(.003)**		.042(.008)**	−.13(.03)**	−.012(.008)*	.019(.030)	.04	.79(.04)**	−110	136
	Prohibition									
	1884	1884	1884					1884		
7.	.002(.001)**				−.001(.001)	−.012(.005)**	.00	.94(.05)**	−32	169
8.[d]	.002(.001)**	.001(.003)				−.013(.005)**	.00	.93(.05)**	−19	153
9.[e]	.002(.001)**		.002(.002)	−.00(.01)	−.001(.002)	−.015(.006)**	.00	.92(.05)**	−37	135

[a]Weighted least-squares estimates of slopes; standard errors in parentheses; counties in which more than 19% of the population was foreign born in 1888 excluded; one-tailed test of significance: $* = .05 < p \leq .10$; $** = p \leq .05$.

[b]In hundreds of thousands.

[c]Standard error not calculated.

[d]Counties with less than 18% production in industry in 1880 excluded.

[e]Counties with more than 69% production in industry in 1880 excluded.

Table A12 Panel Analyses of Three-party Voting Pattern, 1888–1892[a]

Eq.	Inclusive Index Revival 1890	Capital/Mfg Establishment 1888 × Pop '92[b]	Prod/Farm 1888 × Pop '92[b]	Wages/Farm 1870 × Pop '92[b]	Industrialization 1892 × Pop '92	Foreign Born 1892	Pop 1892[c]	Party Vote 1888	Constant	N
					Republican					
1.	.018(.004)**				−.003(.003)	.09(.02)**	.01	.75(.03)**	163	184
2.[d]	.016(.004)**	−.012(.009)*				.10(.02)**	.01	.75(.02)**	142	156
3.[e]	.015(.004)**		.018(.005)**	−.05(.02)**	.001(.005)	.06(.02)**	−.01	.79(.03)**	157	153
					Democrat					
4.	.005(.004)*				.003(.003)	.07(.02)**	−.00	.87(.03)**	130	184
5.[d]	.003(.004)	.004(.010)				.07(.02)**	−.00	.86(.03)**	130	156
6.[e]	.003(.004)		.015(.005)**	−.06(.02)**	.008(.005)**	.05(.02)**	−.01	.88(.03)**	120	153
					Prohibition					
7.	.002(.001)**				.000(.001)	.007(.003)**	.00	.83(.03)**	−6	184
8.[d]	.002(.001)**	.015(.021)				.004(.004)	.00	.83(.03)**	−12	156
9.[e]	.001(.001)		.000(.001)	.002(.004)	−.000(.001)	.004(.005)	.00	.82(.03)**	−5	153

[a] Weighted least-squares estimates of slopes; standard errors in parentheses; counties in which more than 17% of the population was foreign born in 1892 excluded; one-tailed test of significance: * = .05 < p ≤ 10; ** = p ≤ .05.
[b] In hundreds of thousands.
[c] Standard error not calculated.
[d] Counties with less than 18% production in industry in 1888 excluded.
[e] Counties with more than 75% production in industry in 1888 excluded.

Table A13 Panel Analyses of Republican Vote, 1892–1896[a]

Eq.	Inclusive Index Revival 1892	Capital/Mfg Establishment 1892 × Pop '96[b]	Prod/Farm Farm 1892 × Pop '96[b]	Wages/Farm 1870 × Pop '96[b]	Industrialization 1896 × Pop '96	Foreign Born 1896	Pop 1896[c]	Total Vote 1896	Rep Vote 1892	Constant	N
				All Counties							
1.	−.000(.004)				.015(.004)**	.07(.02)**	−.00	.02(.03)	1.1(.03)**	132	171
2.[d]	−.002(.004)	.01(.01)			.020(.005)**	.04(.02)**	.02	−.02(.03)	1.1(.04)**	−96	141
3.[e]	−.001(.004)		.013(.005)**	−.04(.01)**	.020(.005)**	.04(.02)**	.00	−.02(.03)	1.1(.03)**	123	144
			Counties in Bottom Half of Industrialization, 1892[f]								
4.	.004(.006)				.009(.008)	.12(.03)**	−.02	.08(.07)	1.0(.05)**	131	82
5.[d]	.004(.007)	−.047(.025)**				.11(.04)**	−.02	.10(.08)	1.1(.07)**	−39	52
6.[d]	.004(.007)	−.057(.026)**			.017(.013)*	.12(.04)**	−.02	.10(.08)	1.0(.07)**	17	52
7.	.004(.006)		.006(.007)	−.03(.02)*	.016(.010)*	.11(.04)**	−.03	.09(.08)	1.0(.06)**	133	82

[a]Weighted least squares estimates of slopes; standard errors in parentheses; counties in which more than 15% of the population was foreign born in 1896 excluded; one-tailed test of significance: * = .05 < p ≤ .10; ** = p ≤ .05.

[b]In hundreds of thousands.

[c]Standard error not calculated.

[d]Counties with less than 18% production in industry in 1892 excluded.

[e]Counties with more than 77% production in industry in 1892 excluded.

[f]Counties with more than 47% in production in industry 1892 excluded.

Table A14 Panel Analyses of Democratic Vote, 1892–1896[a]

Eq.	Inclusive Index Revival 1892	Capital/Mfg Establishment 1892 × Pop '96[b]	Prod/Farm 1892 × Pop '96[b]	Wages/Farm 1870 × Pop '96[b]	Industrialization 1896 × Pop '96	Foreign Born 1896	Pop 1896[c]	Total Vote 1896	Dem Vote 1892	Constant	N
				All Counties							
1.	-.02(.01)**				-.037(.008)**	-.09(.04)**	-.03	.42(.06)**	.73(.06)**	-102	171
2.[d]	-.01(.01)	-.03(.02)*				-.06(.04)*	-.08	.42(.06)**	.93(.07)**	82	141
3.[e]	-.02(.01)**		.002(.011)	-.11(.03)**	-.046(.010)**	-.05(.05)	-.05	.53(.08)**	.77(.07)**	-182	144
				Counties in Bottom Half of Industrialization, 1892[f]							
4.	-.05(.01)**				-.049(.016)**	-.26(.06)**	.12	.11(.12)	.51(.09)**	-204	82
5.[d]	-.04(.01)**	.01(.05)				-.20(.08)**	.07	.06(.12)	.73(.10)**	103	52
6.[d]	-.04(.01)**	.02(.05)			-.022(.025)	-.21(.08)**	.08	.07(.13)	.71(.10)**	27	52
7.	-.04(.01)**		-.02(.02)	-.04(.04)	-.060(.021)**	-.19(.07)**	.09	.23(.14)*	.52(.09)**	-249	82

[a]Weighted least squares estimates of slopes; standard errors in parentheses; counties in which more than 15% of the population was foreign born in 1896 excluded; one-tailed test of significance: * = .05 < p ≤ .10; ** = p ≤ .05.

[b]In hundreds of thousands.

[c]Standard error not calculated.

[d]Counties with less than 18% production in industry in 1892 excluded.

[e]Counties with more than 77% production in industry in 1892 excluded.

[f]Counties with more than 47% in production in industry 1892 excluded.

$$\text{Party Vote } t_2 \text{ / Total Vote } t_2 = b_1 \text{ Party Vote } t_1 \text{ / Total Vote } t_1$$
$$+ \, b_2 \text{ Revivalism } t_1 \text{ / Population } t_1 \quad (7)$$
$$+ \, B_i V_i + a + e$$

Party Vote would be Republican or Democrat, V_i is a set of other independent and control variables and B_i the corresponding b's, "a" is the constant, and "e" is the error term. This model is implicit in turnover tables employing percentages.

I estimated raw equations, similar to the ones used in the present study, using Total Vote as the dependent variable. The main causal variable on voter turnout throughout the period is Revivalism. Total Vote itself is not statistically related to Republican Vote in 1896, as seen in table A13. The cross-sectional correlation between Total Vote per Capita (*TOT/POP*) and Republican Vote divided by Total Vote (*REP/TOT*) is negative ($r = -.36$, $p < .001$), as would be expected. Consequently, there is a strong negative bias built into b_2 of equation (7), the coefficient of Revivalism, because of Revivalism's positive relation to Total Vote—the denominator of the dependent variable. This is independent of Revivalism's relation to Republican Vote.

In equations with Democratic Vote as the dependent variable, the relation of Revivalism to Total Vote in the denominator produces the same negative bias in b_2. As shown in table A14, however, Total Vote has a strong positive relation to Democratic Vote. This relation is so great that there actually is a positive relation between Democratic Vote per Total Vote (*DEM/TOT*) and Total Vote Per Capita (*TOT/POP*) ($r = .40$, $p < .001$). This means two things. First, without an explicit control for Total Vote, there will be a baseline positive bias in the estimates of Revivalism's effects on Democratic Vote (Revivalism positively affects Total Vote which positively affects Democratic Vote). For example, equations were estimated without Total Vote included but otherwise identical to the ones reported in the text. While the Revivalism Index still had insignificant effects on Republican Vote, it had small positive effects on Democratic Vote for certain equations, reflecting this positive bias. Second, this bias is magnified when Total Vote is in the denominator of ratio variables. The negative bias induced by the relation between Revivalism and Total Vote in the denominator is more than offset by the positive relation between Total Vote in the denominator and Democratic Vote in the numerator.

Equations (1) and (2) of table A15 present estimations of ratio models. The results replicate conventional findings: Revivalism is negatively related to Republican Vote while positively related to Democratic Vote. Equations (3) and (4) control for Total Vote. The effect on Republican

Table A15 Panel Analyses of Percentage Party Vote, 1892–1896

Eq.	Inclusive Index Revival 1890/ Pop '90	Industrialization 1896	Foreign Born 1896/ Pop '96	Total Vote 1896/ Pop '96	Party Vote 1892/ Pop '92	Con- stant	N
			Republican				
1.	−.06(.02)**	.09(.01)**	.08(.07)		1.1(.03)**	−.03	171
			Democrat				
2.	.05(.03)**	−.16(.02)**	−.05(.13)		.93(.06)**	.08	171
			Republican, Controlling for Total Vote				
3.	−.023(.015)*	.07(.01)**	.11(.06)**	−.67(.10)**	1.1(.03)**	.15	171
			Democrat, Controlling for Total Vote				
4.	−.01(.03)	−.13(.02)**	−.10(.12)	1.1(.18)**	.87(.05)**	−.14	171

Note: Dependent Variables: Party Vote / Total Vote Counties in which more than 15% of the population was foreign born in 1896 excluded; one-tailed test of significance: * = .05 < p ≤ .10; ** = p ≤ .05.

Vote is dramatically reduced while Revivalism's relation to Democratic Vote becomes nonsignificantly negative. These results are close to the findings of the equations reported in the text. I conclude that previous findings appear to be artifactual.

This demonstration underscores the fact that even the simplest turnover tables carry with them implicit models which may, or may not, build in certain biases. The underlying model should be analyzed in the context of the relations of all the variables in order to ascertain such bias. The specifications of the models in the present study are by no means the last word. Controlling for voter turnout by including Total Vote has its own problems due to the fact that it includes by definition the dependent variable—party vote. A better specification for future work would be total vote minus the dependent variable or party vote (see Firebaugh and Gibbs 1985).

Notes

Chapter Two

1. The sociological analysis of conversion also has made impressive progress during this period and converges with macroanalyses. A crisis does not appear to be necessary or sufficient for effecting conversion or one's joining a movement (Heirich 1977; Snow and Machalek 1984; Wuthnow 1985). Moreover, many scholars have explored the way in which language and cultural accounts shape conversion and commitment (Snow and Machaleck 1984; Staples and Mauss 1987). I do not deal with these issues in the present study but simply note the convergence and implications for future integrative work.

2. People tend not to apprehend the entire cultural order nor do they necessarily consciously work it out into a logically consistent system. They perceive and appropriate types and rules only as they are relevant or specified within concrete action situations (Mills 1940).

3. Cultural order is described as a worldview (*Weltanschauung*, world perspective) more frequently than an ontology. I use the term "ontology" to stress a central point of my model: a fundamental aspect of a cultural order is a theory of reality or a set of implicit assumptions about what exists. For any worldview, certain things exist and are objectively given. Moreover, subtle nuances are observed about the nature of existence of these entities. I purposely undermine any distinction between recipelike everyday knowledge and intellectual metaphysics or social thought. A structure of existence, then, underlies and is implicit in all worldviews. It is true that this aspect has been recognized, but the use of worldview has tended to draw attention to the social psychological aspects of individual beliefs and styles of cognition. I use the term "worldview" because of its common use, because the social psychological aspects are important, and because it does encompass the idea of ontology. Nevertheless, I more frequently use the term "ontology" to focus attention on the assumed structure of existence underlying any cultural order. (For a discussion of these terms see Berger and Luckmann 1966; Berger and Pullberg 1965; Thomas et al. 1987; for a similar critique of worldview see Wuthnow 1987). Culture as a theory of reality or existence can be specified, depending on the analytic focus, as cosmology, theory of nature, of society,

of the individual, and so on. I use the term "ideology," following common usage, to refer to cultural theories of society and polity as they are used in practice and sometimes in conflict to define and legitimate social organization and policy.

4. Geertz (1973) describes how a religious system synthesizes a society's worldview and ethos, where the latter entails a morality as well as a character and quality of life. He emphasizes that they are mutually supportive and that the ontology is not merely invented to legitimate an already existing ethos. Berger et al. (1972) argue that assumptions about reality are crucial to understanding definitions of justice.

5. Distinguishing social spheres is somewhat arbitrary. A theorist will make particular distinctions because of practical or analytic interest. The present analytic distinction, therefore, does not imply that social activity is composed of objectively given disparate sectors.

6. If and how sociocultural integration exists is a central issue in sociology. Phenomenology leaves the integration of interpretative rules as problematic. Various "action" approaches such as network, exchange, or public choice theories view it as arising from the rational action of individuals. Functional theories argue that norms are integrated by a distinct level of general abstract values and goals which individuals internalize through socialization. Conflict theories attribute integration to the hegemony of vested interests. With the institutionalist perspective, I am suggesting that while choice, personal belief, and interest are oriented to the cultural order, the cultural order is not reducible to them (See Meyer, Boli, and Thomas 1987).

7. The relation of rules and metaphors is a technical issue that is still being explored. I do not mean to equate their use. The reproduction of the underlying structure (what I will refer to as isomorphism) seems to be a product of the construction and application of rules. Nevertheless, people tend to move from applying rules to using the structure as a whole metaphorically and equating categories and structures across institutional spheres. This goes against the common view that the use of metaphors is more fundamental than that of rules. I use metaphor to refer to the underlying cultural structure when calling attention to the process of holistically equating structures of everyday life. I use myth to refer to the same underlying structure when referring to the practice of treating it as an explanation or account that in principle can be elaborated as a story or narrative.

8. "Underlying, basic, fundamental, and ground" are themselves metaphors based on spatial imagery and connote lying beneath. "Higher, broad, and overarching" are spatial metaphors connoting existing above. Mixing these metaphors helps guard against being too rigidly spatial.

9. It is debatable as to which term is best, "environment" or "context." The concept of environment has the advantage of linking the analysis of texts and symbols to theories of social organization. It includes symbols, organizations, resources, and groups. It also encourages an analytic distinction between figure and ground. Its main disadvantage is that it can make the cultural

context seem too distinct from the institution being examined. The advantage of the concept of context is precisely that in the hermeneutical tradition it underscores the fundamental unity of the institution or symbol structure one is examining and the broader culture. Its disadvantage is that it forces us to treat institutions only as texts somewhat divorced from organizations, resources, and groups. In this work, I use the two terms interchangeably, in part to explore the extent to which the two different approaches and literatures can be linked. I use the term "environment" more often because, following Weber, I want to relate isomorphic structures to organizations, groups, and sectors of society.

10. Most terms were coined by structuralists (e.g., Levi-Strauss 1962; Barthes 1972; Leach 1976): homology, isomorphism, resemblance, correspondence, metaphoric. For example, Bourdieu (1984) shows how distinctions in art, music, food, and dress are patterned by class structure and thus are "homologous." Theorists of formal organization argue that formal rules and structures are "isomorphic" with the organizational environment (e.g., Meyer and Scott 1983; Scott 1987). For a critical treatment of "isomorphic legitimation," see Wuthnow (1987).

11. Conceptualizing formal organization as a ritual coding of cultural rules complements anthropological studies of ritual and provides a basis for understanding the power of religious rituals and symbols to codify a cultural order. Rituals cannot be taken as superstitious, inaccurate instrumental activity any more than rational, technical organization can be taken solely as efficient instrumental activity. Both include task-oriented and ceremonial aspects (e.g., Goffman 1967). As with formal organization, rituals specify the sociocultural myth and constitute an immediate frame of activity. They concretize and make visible the ontology in practical everyday action (e.g., Berger 1969; Douglas 1966; Gluckman 1962; Turner, 1967 1974). Thus religious rituals are not manifestations of a different type of system. We should not be surprised that in modern society sacralized rituals play a special role in framing the cultural ontology (Ellul 1975).

12. The present discussion focuses on the movement from culture to specification in formal organization. The relation between the underlying structure and formal rules is itself reciprocal and dialectical just as has been emphasized for the relation of culture and social organization in general. There is no deterministic relation between the cultural order and specific rules of organization and interaction. Different elements may be emphasized over others, and different themes taken as more or less primary. Nevertheless, the coding of the cultural order within a particular formal organization and its rules of interaction, narrows the range and flexibility of that order.

13. This is what Schattschneider (1960) argues when he refers to political rules and organization as the "mobilization of bias" (Zelditch et al. 1983; Thomas, Walker, and Zelditch 1986). Bias is activated apart from explicit manipulation by groups, factions, or elites. Still, much conflict occurs and movements compete over positions of power—whether in a political party or

a church. Such movements challenge groups in power but not the organization. Dissident factions claim legitimacy and rights to greater power by using the same institutional context as those in power. Thus, institutions, as distinct from "regimes" or factions in power, are able to absorb tremendous amounts of change (e.g., Thomas and Meyer 1987). We will see that a movement within an institution finds leverage for mobilizing support in its competition with groups in power if it is able to make use of changes in the cultural order.

14. This point illustrates the notion that sociologists tend to accept either a sectarian (charismatic) or church (organizational) view of institutionalization. Many observers of revivalism (e.g., Hammond 1979) appear to use the former's assumption (and that of the revivalists themselves) that formal organization marks a loss of vitality. Parsons (1963) seems to accept the "church" position that institutionalization is a sign of successfully building movement values into society. The institutional model takes a third view suggested by Berger (1954), that charisma is institutionalized or stored within formal organization.

15. In many cases a particular institution or organization is "chartered" as managing the cultural environment of another institution or organization. For example, a religious organization may be the legitimate manager of the political sphere, as was the case in early New England. More indirectly, a religious organization may be defined as a superior interpreter of reality. Therefore, the state must defer to it on certain issues, as can be seen at various points in the relationship between church and state in European history; or at least the issues of the state must be phrased and discussed in quasi-religious terms. Also, political organization may structure religious content as with a civil religion. In other cases an institution might be compartmentalized and isolated from the influence of others. The pattern of specific linkages and buffers will channel these ripple effects.

16. An ethos is associated with a status group and its "lifestyle" (Weber 1946, 180–95, 268). Much of Weber's sociology of religion maps the relations between groups and religious content through the mediatorial role of the ethos of each (1963).

17. I have emphasized the causal nature of this process. It is commonplace to suggest that while social structures are causally integrated, cultural systems are integrated in a logico-meaningful way within a discursive textual web of meaning (Sorokin 1937; Geertz 1973). It goes too far totally to detach culture from causal processes. For example, in any story the author is constrained in writing the ending by how he or she has developed the plot, the characters, and the mood. If a skeptical mood has been established, and if the characters are portrayed as self-aggrandizers, an altruistic ending is not credible. Conscious violation of "conventions" of logico-meaningful consistency are themselves interpreted as "anti-stories" rather than as mistakes (see, e.g., Lasch 1979). Social change involves contextual meaning *and* causation. Once a structure is set up as a ground, other elements must fit it or be modified. The

acceptance of a cultural element as legitimate or not is causally affected by its relation to the structure that is used to interpret it. Of course as in all fields, causality is inferred by the observer.

18. Walzer (1965) underscores the aspect of Weberian theory that considers movements: The world view of Calvinism formed the basis of the Puritan movement which articulated a new political order and played a key role in the English Civil War. Similarly, Geertz (1968, 1973) argues that the Majumi party in Indonesia was a movement that used a literalist Islam to frame centralized nation-state authority—only in this case the transformation of cultural structure had its origins in colonialism.

19. Competition arises not only from internal dissenting factions and from other movements, but also from countermovements by those in power who are resisting change. Such movements make concessions to the new order but put across more moderate proposals of change, usually in terms of preserving the power structure. Countermovements usually gain force after a movement attains a certain degree of success and support. Scholars have yet to distinguish the conditions that allow one countermovement to successfully coopt the goals and support of a movement from another that fails.

20. Whereas Marx and Engels together argue that these contradictions are due to the capitalist class manipulating culture in its own interest, in his early writings Marx argues that the contradictions between institutional spheres are due to alienation rather than class conflict:

> The nature of alienation implies that each sphere applies a different and contradictory norm, that morality does not apply the same norm as political economy, etc., because each of them is a particular alienation of man; each is concentrated upon a specific area of alienated activity and is itself alienated from the other. (1963, 173)

Luckmann (1967) characterizes modern society precisely by this compartmentalization of "part-time" norms. Daniel Bell (1976) points out parallel contradictions in postindustrial capitalism: the rational discipline of work versus the antinomian celebration of leisure. Yet, he does not deal adequately with the fact that disciplined production and antinomian consumption feed on each other as two movements of the same dialectic: Routinized release has never been subversive of structures of disciplined work, authority, and technology (see, for example, Gluckman 1954; Douglas 1966; see especially Ellul 1975).

21. Hypocrisy is built into the system when moral-religious duties are prescribed for the laboring class, while any personal obligation of the capitalist is left to private piety or the pursuit of self-interest for the "collective good" (Bendix 1956). Using another example of compartmentalizing contradictions from the culture of individualism in the technological age: (a) Scientific myths of origin describe cosmic competition and define individuals as valueless molecular arrangements; (b) everything from economic liberties to citizens' rights

to middle-class lifestyles to revolutions are legitimated in terms of the ultimate value of individual life. These contradictions are compartmentalized: (a) The degrading aspects of evolution are invoked in the continual ideological combat with traditional authority such as religion, communal organization, families, and social thought that views value as immanent in the individual and society; (b) the celebration of the individual and of evolutionary progress is invoked to legitimate new structures such as state authority, professional privilege, and technology (e.g., Ellul 1975).

22. That laboring classes accept a particular cultural order might be viewed as false consciousness by some objective standard. This study does not reject this possibility out of hand as does Weber (1946; cf. Habermas 1975), although standards are available other than material interest. It underscores the fact that action that rejects legitimated structures also rejects the legitimating cultural order. In Marxist categories, revolutionary praxis carries within itself critical theory. Critical theory as an alternative institutional order is crucial to the organization and mobilization of collective action against a system.

23. The failure to do this has led to seriously inaccurate interpretations of important political-religious movements. For example, movements that are repressed tend to be driven into marginal, lower class, and powerless populations; they are then misinterpreted as growing out of the peculiar needs of an oppressed people or of structural conditions for failure.

Chapter Three

1. Consider the following statistics which document both growth and expanding markets. The total value of exports jumped from 72 million dollars in 1830 to 124 million in 1840, reaching 334 million dollars by 1860. Cotton from the South and cotton products and goods from northern textile factories comprised the bulk of U.S. exports as well as a large part of coast-to-coast trade. In 1833, 560,000 bales were produced whereas 1,534,000 were turned out in 1840 (North 1961, 232–33, tables A-VII, A-VIII). The value of receipts of produce from the interior at New Orleans was 26 million dollars in 1830, 50 million in 1840, and 197 million dollars in 1850. The Erie Canal, which reduced freight cost within New York State by 85 percent, had a national impact by the late thirties. In 1836, the total tonnage on the canal from the (Mid-) West was 54,000 tons. In 1840 there were 158,000 tons and 842,000 by 1850 (North, 1961, 250–51, tables A-IX, B-IX; Cochran and Miller 1961, 7; also see Heilbroner 1977). Moreover, the percentage of people residing in towns of 2,500 or more increased from 7.2 percent in 1820 to 15.5 percent in 1850 (U.S. Bureau of the Census 1970, pt. 1, 11–12, Series A 57–72).

2. Some companies established manufacturing towns that controlled the everyday activity of their employees. For example, Lowell, Massachusetts, employed women for two-year periods, housing them in barracks. Such towns were the focus of popular literature. Nevertheless, they were relatively few

in number. Moreover, the early and short-lived labor movements were in part reactions against the company towns and their "un-republican" control of the individual (see Kasson 1976; Ryan 1981).

3. The military is a fourth important aspect of this social change. (Tilly 1975, 1984; Collins 1978, 1986). In his history of power, Mann (1986) identifies these four, although he views them as social networks rather than institutions. I am implicitly including power and the military under state processes. Distinguishing them makes for a more precise theory; however, the military, while relevant to changes in nineteenth-century United States, does not play a key role. I therefore have streamlined my model, which could easily be extended to treat military factors more fully (cf. Giddens 1987).

4. I use the generic term rationalization to refer to the more precise phrase instrumental or practical rationalization. This does not imply that traditional societies are in any way irrational for there are other types of rationality. Generally, rationality can refer to any process by which a culture is made more coherent, consistent, and articulated relative to integrating principles. One type, substantive rationality, is common in traditional societies and refers to the articulation of cultural theories around substantive goals—the good and the moral—rather than efficient means. There is an extended literature on the nuances of the concept of rationality (e.g., Kalberg 1980; Roth and Schluchter 1979; Schluchter 1981; and Campbell 1982).

5. In this view, the market and state constitute an infrastructure of rationality as myth, and as they spread geographically and sociologically, so the myth of rationality comes to dominate culture. Other secondary institutions also play a role in consolidating the infrastructure of rationality. For example, Berger, Berger, and Kellner (1973) map out technological and bureaucratic "packages" that, as they are adopted by Third World countries, carry with them cultural conceptions of rationality or "modernity."

6. Authority relations and kin groupings are sacred in the sense that they are valued as ends rather than as rational means to attaining some abstract end. Cosmic stability and welfare are equated with (are immanent in) the smooth running of the social order. Such societies might be characterized by high levels of substantive rationality in that cultural theories are greatly elaborated within them.

7. Of course, not all feudal systems are identical and historical systems have varied in this respect. Most notably, Medieval Europe was unique in that Christianity to a certain extent considered the individual soul to be of utmost value. Even sacral qualities of the church mediated the personal relation between God and the individual. This factor provided a major source of rationalization (e.g., Meyer, Boli, and Thomas 1987).

8. Rights in part served to protect "society" from centralized authority. Yet, their structural support of central authority was great. In fact, it was often the case that the monarch actively promoted the Estates and their corresponding rights so that authority could be rationalized (e.g., Poggi 1978; Tilly 1975).

9. The collective is celebrated within nationalism. This creates a large potential for resacralization of the polity: The polity as well as state authority may be resacralized when the larger values of the people and nation are equated with the specific organizational arrangements of the state (e.g., communism) or economy (e.g., fascism).

10. Of course, state formation and nation building are not disparate processes. The construction and expansion of central bureaucratic structures tends to increase nationalism and nation building, and nation building eventually leads to central bureaucracies under certain conditions. Nevertheless, the differences are important to observe.

11. For example, the amount of capital reinvested in buildings and equipment in the nation was 0.4 billion dollars in 1870 and 2.0 billion dollars by 1890 (constant 1958 dollars; U.S. Bureau of the Census 1970, pt. 2, 683, Series P 107–22). In the North and Midwest, the average capital invested in a manufacturing establishment was 8,000 dollars in 1860, increasing to 12,000 in 1880 and reaching 22,000 dollars by 1900 (U.S. Bureau of the Census 1900b, clxxii, Table LXX). In 1900, "combinations" employed 8.4 percent of the wage earners in industry, accounting for 14.1 percent of production (U.S. Bureau of the Census 1900b, lxxxi, table XXVI). In the textile industry, by 1860 the average establishment in the Northeast had almost 7,000 spindles and 163 power looms; compare this to Thomas Jefferson's domestic facilities in 1814 of four jennies and 112 spindles (Kasson 1976, 25). Western textile factories were smaller and southern ones smaller yet (North 1961, 161; Clark 1929, U.S. Bureau of the Census 1860, x–xiii). Industrial combinations by 1900 employed 20 percent of all wage earners within the iron and steel industry, accounting for 28.4 percent of all production.

12. In the North during the twenty years from 1870–90 the average value of farm implements and machinery of a farm increased 15 percent from 124 to 143 dollars per farm. In the ten years from 1890 to 1900 the value of implements and machinery went up by 26 percent to 180 dollars (U.S. Bureau of the Census 1900a, xxx, table XIII). The acceleration after the 1890 enumeration is due, in part, to a more exact enumeration.

13. Mechanization in the eastern states, especially in dairy areas, and in midwestern corn areas did not reduce the amount of labor required to harvest a crop nor did it make large tracts of land more profitable than smaller ones. Rather, it refined and extended the farming process through such innovations as selective breeding, new fertilizers, insect control, and cream separators. The initial effects of scale in the West are manifested in the relative size of farms and mortgages. From 1870 to 1890 the average size of farms in the North Atlantic states decreased from 104 to 95 acres per farm; the average North Central and Midwestern farm increased from 124 to 133 acres per farm (U.S. Bureau of the Census 1900a, xxi, table III). Farms with mortgages in the Middle Atlantic and East North Central states remained stable at 37 to 41 percent of all farms operated by the owner; in the wheat dominated West North Central region, the percentage hovered at 47 (U.S. Bureau of

the Census 1910, 160, table 3). In the South, trends in the number and size of farms and in the number of mortgages were influenced by the political consequences of the Civil War. Plantation estates were broken up, leading to dramatic increases in the number of farms and decreases in the average size, but the overall landed estate system was maintained as evidenced by increases in dependent tenancy.

14. Farmers, bearing rational demands from an essentially irrational position, formed various grassroots cooperatives and alliances, from the Granger and Farmer Alliance movements of the 1860s and 1870s to the populists of the early nineties. Their protests were commonly directed at the urban middlemen and financial interests that were their links to the long-distance market. The greater support for protest movements and alliances in wheat areas (Hays 1957) was due to an interaction between mechanization and the related fact that as an export crop wheat was more closely linked to the world economy and under the control of a greater number of largely incomprehensible variables.

15. Generally, all corporate capitalistic systems construct an ineffectual individual, but late capitalistic systems (industrialized core countries in the twentieth century) are more rationalized and individuated and marked by individualistic nationalism than early or dependent corporate capitalism (agrarian peripheral countries). This contrast is complicated by the world polity that tends to create structural-cultural convergence: Peripheral states tend to take on structures of the core without "experiencing" effectual individualism. Two mechanisms account for this consequence. First, dependent regions tend to imitate a worldwide model (dominated by the core) resulting in a diffusion of cultural forms. Second, the world polity as an environment is highly rationalized. The fact that dependent regions operate within a highly rationalized world system coupled with their limited internal rationalization creates a great potential for movements that push for more complete rationalization (Meyer 1987; Thomas and Meyer 1987, 1984). These are the nation-building and state formation movements of the twentieth century in the Third World. They initially tend to be millenarian and peasant rebellions, but because of the dynamics of the world polity, late capitalism, and dependent development, movements and their ontologies tend toward revolutionary, statist forms (Ramirez and Thomas 1987).

16. It is not accurate to say that definitions of individuality do not exist at all before the individuation of social exchange, for the latter presupposes the existence of differentiated entities. For example, medieval Christendom established rather elaborate definitions of the individual emphasizing personal responsibility and sacredness. The transformations that took place in the sixteenth and seventeenth centuries, therefore, did not introduce de novo conceptions of the individual. Rather, as these prior individualistic cultural elements gave rise to the expansion of rational exchange and authority, the cultural order became more radically centered on completely sovereign persons (Thomas et al. 1987).

17. Holding these two views simultaneously allows us to make arguments concerning the flow of causation from one institution to another without reifying the necessary analytic distinction between them and without constructing a reductionist argument.

18. Early in the nineteenth century, the English industrial revolution resulted in dramatic increases in world trade within English hegemony. Large amounts of capital came to be centralized in the hands of British commercial and financial interests who sought out profitable investment markets in peripheral regions of the world, including the United States. The result was a large flow of British capital into peripheral industry and transportation, especially the financing of railroads (Hobsbawm 1968).

19. Many observers have analyzed the pattern of conflicts of interest that emerge within such a system in general and in nineteenth-century United States in particular (e.g., Stinchcombe 1961; Rubinson 1978: Wiley 1967). These studies add much to our knowledge of change during the nineteenth century, and they are discussed more fully in the analyses of specific movements and issues in chapters 4 and 5.

20. This interpretation does not assume a determinism that would preclude different types of revivalism or different implications of revivalism for political movements. In particular, the institutional model suggests that the early revivals throughout the country were somewhat similar. As the organization of everyday life diverged between the South and the rest of the country, the framing of individualism, nationalism, and progress also diverged. Great similarities remained because both included increased rationalization. Therefore, we can categorize northern and southern revivalism as being of the same family of movements. However, given the limits of rationalization within a plantation system, they differed in emphasis and more sharply in political-economic impact. In some respects the meaning of southern revivalism gradually became distinct from that of the North. Future work is necessary to map the divergent evolution of southern revivalism and its political implications (cf. Loveland 1980).

Chapter Four

1. These developments were reinforced by the Constitution and pluralism, as well as by French rationalism. There was also an increase in nonconformist groups ranging from Baptists to Quakers and Unitarians who probably had more in common with the rationalists and deists with their emphasis on the divine light.

2. Smith is quoting from a series of unsigned articles in the *Christian Spectator*, 1835, which he attributes to Taylor.

3. There was a very close connection between mechanistic natural laws and human freedom: God "never violates the great laws of moral action or contravenes the freedom of the subject!" (Smith 1980, 12). Notice that freedom (from God's sovereignty) was at the cost of being governed by impersonal

laws and thus manipulable by others. This view parallels the dialectic of impersonality and freedom of rational organization.

4. Reverend R. W. Van Schoick, "A Revival of Every Charge," *The New York Christian Advocate,* 22 March 1888.

5. Not all nineteenth-century revivalists agreed that revivals could be generated. For example, one critical evangelical wrote that the "taking of revivals out of God's hand is done by those who claim a special charge to vindicate the divine agency in revivals, while they will not allow the free and *sovereign* Spirit to shape them as he pleases" (*The New-York Evangelist,* 12 January 1833).

6. The idea of a second experience evolved into the concept of the "baptism of the Spirit" as a work subsequent to regeneration, which is a characteristic component of the Pentecostal-Holiness movements of the twentieth century.

7. Perfectionism led naturally to the belief that perfected saints could trust as revelation whatever impulse or impression they felt. At this point holiness fed into the antinomian thread, making external authority and doctrines seem less necessary when the individual could directly and perfectly follow the Spirit. Conservative versions of holiness, as espoused by Finney, did not imply sinlessness as much as entire dedication, but the more radical versions embraced the logical conclusion of sinlessness. Cross describes this branch of holiness as arguing that "the regenerate were guided by the Holy Spirit through the prayer of faith and must follow the impulses to the exclusion of all external authority" (1950, 239). Through the conflict between the conservative and radical positions the modal definitions of perfectionism within revivalism were continually being reconstructed.

8. The third main school is *a*millennialism. It interprets the reign of Christ as allegorical: Christ currently reigns in the hearts of the regenerate and through the church. A future millennial reign is either denied or considered unimportant. This view was held by Saint Augustine as well as most Reformers. Their inattention to the millennium makes it difficult to know exactly what was thought by groups such as the Puritans, but eighteenth-century North Americans such as Edwards can be classified as postmillennial. The postmillennialism of the revivalists marked a dramatic departure from even its eighteenth-century counterpart.

9. Revivalists were quite aware of the temptations inherent in technological progress and prosperity. Each advance in secular history carries with it greater temptation and a greater fall if the temptation is given in to. People, they believed, must recognize history as a spiritual battle and must continually seek the higher life in order truly to regenerate the world. Bushnell took great pains to distinguish the difference between secular evolutionary theories of history and the Christian theory of the millennium. In the latter, God's goals "is to develop in us a character of external uprightness; developing also, in that manner, as a necessary consequence, grand possibilities of social order and well-being; though, when we thus speak, we include the fact of sin and the engagement with it of a supernatural grace, to lift us from the otherwise remediless fall of nature" (Bushnell, 1863, 384, quoted in Tuveson, 1968, 64).

The millennium is the Kingdom of God, and the power behind it must come from heaven, working first in the personal piety of individuals and then spilling outward to the regeneration of society. Yet, with these qualifications, and once subsumed under the supernatural theory of history and infused with the proper piety, technological, economic, and political advances were viewed as giant steps toward the millennium.

10. From Edward Beecher, "The Nature, Importance, and Means of Eminent Holiness throughout the Church," *The American National Preacher* 10, 1835, quoted in Smith (1957, 105).

11. Because sovereignty was located in the people, revivalists did not view as coercive the nation's freely choosing moral reform through *democratic processes* (see Hammond 1979, 66). Free choice independent of coercive authority is also reflected in revivalism's framing the shift from patriarchal households. Children would not be saved through the convenental authority of father, but freely through the persuasion and affection of mother. Revivalism thus helped shape an important part of the new individualism: the concept of the child (although still viewed as not fully rational) as a relatively autonomous moral agent with complex emotions and psychology. Intergenerational bonds became rooted in the language of individualism (Ryan 1981).

12. The sacralization of political documents was not simply nationalistic propaganda, and the core of this system was not the literature produced by elites nor the speeches of presidents on which the civil religion literature focuses. Coming from men in power, these statements take on an aura of artificiality. However, this system was generated most forcefully within the folk tradition that centered on the creation of a sanctified nation; and at this level the more superficial elite pronouncements were often attacked as being insubstantial. For example, the *New York Christian Advocate* (23 April 1863) praised Lincoln's declaration of a day of fasting and humiliation, but also castigated the whole operation as falling short of the demands of God's justice. It may have been adequate for civil religion but not for revivalistic pietism.

13. Reverend Schoick, "A Revival in Every Charge," *The New York Christian Advocate*, 22 March 1888. W. S. H. Hermans, "The Tone of the Christian Scriptures on the Subject of Christian Perfection," *The New York Christian Advocate*, 1 March 1888.

14. Talcott Parsons (1963) seems to be writing within this tradition, giving it a modern twist, when he argues that secularization of industrial society is the fulfillment of Christianity because Christian values are now institutionalized in secular life.

15. For example, the *New York Christian Advocate* on 26 April 1888, editorialized in favor of "Christian socialism." Further articulations of its position appeared necessary; it ran an editorial on 22 September 1892 that attacked the "so-called Christian socialists," and later (20 October 1892) gave a call for individuals to "Christianize their ledgers."

16. Early southern revivalism shared the various elements described here. After about 1830, southern Evangelicalism backed off from the extreme

positions of its northern counterpart on almost all points. Arminianism prevailed, but not in the extreme self-willed form of the new measures and perfectionism of the North, especially among the Baptists and Presbyterians but also among the Methodists (Ahlstrom 1972; Loveland 1980). Southern Evangelicals, while just as millennialistic, "did not infuse that belief with the urgency and optimism that many nothern Evangelicals did" (Loveland 1980, 162), and they emphasized local communal unity over any national calling (McLoughlin 1978). Loveland (1980, 125) summarizes by stating that southern Evangelicals were very far from accepting the "dominant American ideology" of human instrumentality, self-reliance, confidence in the rule of the people, and progress. Moreover, the transformation of moral perfectionism and reform into social reform never occurred in the South. The moral fervor of revivalism increasingly evolved into a quietistic pietism with an almost exclusive focus on emotional experience and personal lifestyle (Loveland 1980; Ahlstrom 1972; McLoughlin 1978). These differences resulted in part from the nature of everyday life within a plantation system but also from depoliticization by authorities in order to preclude any criticism of slavery (Loveland 1980; Mathews 1977; Thomas 1965).

17. The imagery of the skeptical male farmer (merchant, shopkeeper, lawyer, or clerk) rejecting Calvinism and coming to embrace revivalism fits the details of personal life, although it does not capture possible generational dynamics (Ryan 1981). Women organizing a revival brought unsaved children (through their teens and twenties) and husbands (who commonly justified their skepticism by references to unjust Calvinism). The small but steady increase in the percentage of male church members resulting from revivals was made up of many husbands, but mostly sons and other single young males (pp. 79–80).

18. Many observers find it puzzling that southern revivalism, so similar in moral and religious fervor to that of the North, would look so different and have such different social implications by midcentury. The institutional model begins with the fact that both the South and the rest of the country experienced economic growth and market penetration. However, growth in the South took the form of an exporting plantation system. The *in*effectual individuation of such a system limits rationalization, including individualism and nationalism (cf. Moore 1966). It is understandable, then, that revivalism flourished in the South, framing the rationalization of everyday life. At the same time, given the limits of rationalization within an exporting plantation system, it is understandable that southern revivalism never embraced the "extremes" of individual self-reliance, rational method, perfectionism, and an optimistic postmillennialism.

Revivalism can be viewed as a family of movements, each articulating a rationalized polity and ontology, but each a significantly different version. The particular version that this study focuses on did not survive in the South. Interestingly, the quietism and emotionalism of southern evangelicalism predates fundamentalism and Pentecostalism, which arose at the turn of the twentieth century in the face of corporate capitalism (ineffectual individuation) and forced disestablishment. This would account in part for southern influence in twentieth-century evangelical-fundamentalism.

19. Pritchard (1976) has focused mainly on the revivals in the 1820s and 1830s which accompanied rapid economic growth. But what about the Second Great Awakening at the turn of the nineteenth century? McLoughlin attempts to integrate these periods into one coherent interpretation and there is no possible argument for material disruption in the 1790s. Thus, the disorganization must be more cultural than material. One observer's period of calm before rapid change is another's period of crisis. Concepts of strain and disorganization, as well as the related concept of relative deprivation, are imprecise, making specification for testing extremely difficult. What tests have been carried out show little evidence of crisis effects on conversion (Snow and Machalek 1984) or collective political action (e.g., Snyder and Tilly 1972; Tilly 1978). General theoretical problems were discussed in chapter 2 (see also Ramirez 1987).

20. This kind of argument illustrates the functional, somewhat teleological, logic of conflict theory (cf. Giddens 1981; Stinchcombe 1968). It is especially hard to falsify. If laborers are the first and foremost to participate in revivals, then it is due to alienation or disorganization. If owners have high levels of participation, then it is an attempt to control labor. If both classes take part, then this shows the success of the elite in manipulating revivals as a means of imposing false consciousness on the workers: "A significant minority of working men participated willingly. . . . And that, of course, is the most total and effective social control of all" (Johnson 1978, 138).

21. Johnson raises the issue himself (on the third to the last page of the book!). The Rochester revival "was a religious solution, addressed to religious problems. The revival will remain unexplained until we know how social problems became translated into specifically religious unrest" (p. 139). His solution is particularly unsatisfying in its circularity: "But if we are to render his [the master's] turn to religion intelligible, we must understand that he experienced disobedience and disorder as religious problems" (p. 140). He closes the text with a vivid description that captures the institutional aspect of revivalism but that, in its hedging, betrays the imprecision of the functional-conflict interpretation:

> Thus a recent industrial capitalism became attached to visions of a perfect moral order based on individual freedom and self-government, and old relations of dependence, servility, and mutuality were defined as sinful and left behind. The revival was not a capitalist plot. But it certainly was a crucial step in the legitimation of free labor. (p. 141)

22. The crisis perspective provides a ready-made account of high female participation. For example, rapid economic change stripped the family of production and excluded women from economic and political activity. Women

therefore constituted a powerless, alienated enclave that found escape (or attempted to wield symbolic power) through traditional religion. This interpretation ignores the already high female church memberships well before these changes and revivalism. The institutional model follows those interpretations such as Ryan's (1981; see also Cancian 1987) that focus on the active role of women in change. In particular, while alienated in important ways from production and politics by increased gender inequalities, the female role was transformed into the manager and creator of moral and spiritual value. Moreover, this role, like religion, was not privatized, as yet. Women organized para-church, para-family missionary and moral reform associations that had public agendas. Women worked alongside the preacher and lawyer, albeit subordinately, in the project of constructing the moral tone of the new order. High female participation in these constructive aspects of religion was not escapist but creative, leading to the formation of new roles, moral citizenship, and a new nation. Only later was the innovative work and organization of women coopted by male-dominated structures and political parties, and were women and the family privatized (Cancian 1987; Ryan 1981; Ginzberg 1986), a fate religion would meet still later.

23. The pattern of interests is complicated as the very same interest that is supporting the cultural order in one instance may find itself fighting that order in another. For example, local economic elites and especially yeoman farmers often came into conflict with national industrial and commercial classes and with transportation interests such as the railroads. These interests were greatly legitimated by ideologies of individualistic nationalism. Was the revivalism of Rochester shopkeepers therefore a false consciousness imposed on them by national elites? Probably not, although both classes manipulated the cultural order for their own interests.

24. The Whigs were not based in a coalition of rich, propertied gentry and urban industrial elites, but drew broad support from across many classes (although there was greater support by all classes in industrial areas); and Democractic support was not primarily from lower classes (Benson 1961, 140–50).

25. It is in the context of social mobility that the West as myth was constructed: Labor could always move from a crowded, monopolistic East and find land. Free labor in the new territories was essential to the continued plausibility of this myth (Moore 1966).

26. According to Republicanism, slavery degraded not only the black, but also labor generally so that it had to be done away with in order to protect white labor—an emphasis which often took on racist overtones (Foner 1970, 1980). This political stance was reinforced by worldwide trends away from slavery, for any faction will add to its legitimacy by conforming to world political models (Meyer 1987). This was not the moral assertiveness of abolitionism but the rational political calculation of Republicanism (Hammond 1979). The transition from religious moral fervor to political ideology is discussed in detail by Ginzberg 1986. This transition was manifested in the

Republican belief that slave owners controlled the federal government—the slave power conspiracy. The threat of slavery was transformed from an evil menace resulting almost mechanically from the violation of moral principles to the conscious attempt of a reactionary class to control the state.

27. These changes are manifested in the various constitutional amendments, civil rights acts, and Supreme Court rulings of the late 1860s and 1870s that specified federal powers supporting the primacy of national citizenship (Benedict 1974; Spackman 1976).

28. As already noted, a somewhat similar revivalism in the South framed a dramatically different political-economic view, which belies any deterministic linkages. Yet, it should be noted further that revivalism, even in its moderated form within southern Evangelicalism, was a force of individualistic nationalism. It could be argued that it is precisely because of this general "impulse" that southern Evangelicalism became quietistic and apolitical, both willingly and at the insistence of authorities: A politicized revivalism would always have the potential of criticizing southern society in general and slavery in particular.

29. This difference has important methodological implications. Hammond's position would not readily accept membership data of revivalist denominations as a measure of revivalistic pietism. The institutional model would view this measure as acceptable as long as it could be shown that the denomination carries a revivalistic ontology and ethos. Ethnoculturalists use membership data because identification with an ethnocultural group is almost interchangeable with membership in the representative denomination.

Chapter Five

1. Important technical aspects of the quantitative analyses are presented in the Appendix. The chapter is designed so that reading through it without reference to the Appendix is sufficient for a complete assessment of the substantive purpose and findings of the study. The Appendix presents a more complete discussion of methodological issues and a more detailed report of the statistical results. The headings and subheadings of the chapter and the Appendix are generally the same to facilitate cross-references.

2. Alternatively, many of the results could be interpreted by focusing on the *rise and diffusion of in*effectual individualism.

3. This variable also is a direct indicator of *in*effectual individuation in the face of rising inefficacy. Given the historical situation, these different views are two sides of the same coin. Because I am here primarily concerned with effectual individuation, I will continue to refer to this variable as a negative index of efficacy. Also, at the initial stage of market penetration—or within any individuated system not dominated by scale—this variable could possibly be seen as an indicator of economic value that would be a direct measure of effectual individuation. However, within a scale-dominated system it can be interpreted only as an index of individual inefficacy.

4. This was facilitated by the data files of the Inter-University Consortium for Political and Social Research (ICPSR).

5. See Christiano (1988) for an assessment of the census enumerations of religious bodies. A weakness with the use of memberships is the possibility of undercounting adherents to a denomination that is relatively unconcerned with official membership tallies. One could also underestimate groups with unusually exclusive standards. However, by the second half of the nineteenth century, such divergent definitions of membership were rare.

6. An exception is the Roman Catholic Church for which memberships are consistently larger than seating capacity. However, it scores zero on the revivalism rating and thus does not figure in any index described below.

7. I use quotation marks to refer to the specific denomination with the name "Christian." New York had so few "Christians" in 1870 that none were reported for any of its counties.

8. This is not to say that gubernatorial or congressional elections are unimportant. Nor is it argued that the parties present homogeneous ideologies. Other factors such as party conventions need to be examined in order to acquire a more complete picture of the political situation. However, I am interested specifically in conceptions of the national polity present in each party. National presidential elections provide the natural starting point.

9. All controls are measured at the second point in time in the panel models.

10. For the manufacturing equations for 1880, the cutoff corresponds to under 18 percent of production in manufacturing while for the agricultural equations it is under 31 percent of production in agriculture.

11. In 1880 the median of Industrialization is .383. This means that half of the counties have more than 38.3 percent of their total agricultural and manufacturing production in the manufacturing sector.

12. Part of the high relation between foreign-born populations and revivalism is an inadequacy in the measurement of the latter (see the Appendix).

13. Because of the Exclusive Index's low mean it is hard to make inferences about the cultural organization of an entire county. Also, it is too sensitive to fluctuations in the number of cases across analyses. Therefore only the Inclusive Index is used as an independent variable in the political analyses. For nonmeasured years, variables are interpolated (e.g., Revivalism 1880, 1884, 1888, and 1892—using 1906 measurement).

14. When controlling for voter turnout, Production Per Farm has much larger positive effects and Wages Per Farm has an insignificant negative effect, more in line with the hypothesis. Support for hypothesis 2 nevertheless remains mixed.

15. The latter result is most likely due to the rise of the Populist party in 1892. This party is not analyzed because it had significant strength only in this one election. The number of Foreign Born also did not differentiate the major parties, with large positive effects on both.

16. The concept of realignment refers to a major and enduring shift of groups from one party to another. The models here are concerned with changes over time, but if a group shows movement to a different party this does not necessarily imply realignment. For example, in the eighties revivalist populations shifted to Prohibitionism. However, cross-sectionally the major

alignment was still with the Republican party. A realignment constitutes changes, and relatively permanent ones, in cross-sectional associations.

17. This line of argument can be looked at with respect to the use of religious symbols. Revivalistic religious symbols were closely linked to individualistic nationalism—if not the Republican party itself. The political theory of revivalism *was* Republicanism. To use these symbols to express a totally divergent theory of the polity would be nonsensical and immoral, and would require long-term and possibly violent change before it would compete viably with Republicanism. This interpretation is supported by the fact that many revivalistic ministers, at both the national and grassroots levels, publicly attacked Bryan for blasphemously taking the sacred symbols of Christianity and using them to sell his theories and schemes (McSeveney 1972; Fite 1971, 1821; Jensen 1971, 284; Bryan 1897). One may venture to say that Bryan was no more, or less, mercenary than the traditional Republican revivalists in using religious symbols rhetorically for political ends. The point, however, is that the symbols integrated into revival religion were firmly linked to the individualistic Republican ideology. Any change that violated this linkage by ripping these symbols out of their context and tying them to an alien theory was indeed sacrilege, but it was the citizen and the nation-state that were blasphemed, not God.

18. Recall that for the 1892–96 analysis the equations include Total Vote as a control; the important role of this variable will be a focus of the following discussion.

19. A substantive interpretation of this discussion, one which would salvage, at least partially, conventional interpretations, is that in 1896 revivalistic groups formed a political movement away from the Republican party causing politicization and an overall increase in voter turnout. This is not credible in light of two facts: (1) Revivalism has high positive effects on total vote throughout this period, and (2) during this period total vote varies in its causal effects on party vote. Revivalistic pietism as a cultural institution politicized a population in which it prevailed, including the "non-revivalist" as much as the revivalist, supporting the general thrust of the institutional interpretation that revival religion provided a framework for participation in the national polity.

Chapter Six

1. When societal structures are out of sync with the world cultural environment, there is much potential conflict. Movements emerge which attempt to "revitalize" traditional culture, often by reworking it in terms of world culture. Decoupling and compartmentalization mediate these contradictions.

2. Much of the discussion of the Radical branch is based on Williams (1962).

3. See Moore's (1966) discussion of the Puritans' role in the English Civil War. Their role was reflected in and reinforced by their conception of a covenant between a nation and God (e.g., Zaret 1985).

4. This is not to say that there was no nation building during the French Revolution. There was much celebration of the people (e.g., Michelet [1847] 1967), much sacralization (Hunt 1984); and even "revival" (Desan 1988). One group in particular, the urban laborers or sans cullottes, has remained problematic in sociological analyses. Skocpol (1979) has pointed out that it cannot be viewed as a proletarian movement, but she avoids interpreting it by shifting attention to rural peasant rebellion. One possibility is to view it as the group most incorporated into the rational economic organization benefiting from inflated urban wages. They were in support of rationalizing economy and polity and therefore provided support for the more radical Jacobins (cf. Moore 1966; Tilly 1964). That is, in a revolutionary period dominated by state-formation forces, their seemingly anomolous participation was the result of their relation to nation-building forces.

5. Voegelin is here citing Marx (1963, 164, 166).

6. There is a very large and insightful literature on cultural change and new religious movements; any review that would do it justice is beyond the scope of this work. (For overviews see Barker 1982; Bromley and Hammond 1987; Hammond 1985; Robbins 1988; Robbins, Shepherd, and McBride 1985; Snow and Machalek 1984). Social scientific theories tend to be built on and reproduce the same ideological-cultural themes. Sociological interpretations of new religious movements have focused on the various antinomian trends in the United States and other core countries. The standard interpretation of these movements—from Jonestown to the Moral Majority to the New Age Movements—is that they are escapes from the disorderly and alienating reality of rapid technological change. Or, they are seen as real critiques of Western rationalistic materialism, impersonality, and modernization. To this is added the conflict notion that the United States is losing world hegemony, and groups attempt to resist this loss by revitalizing the traditional American cultural order. I am suggesting that new religious movements are more optimistic, actively embracing cultural transformations usually from world dynamics by reconsituting the individual and the nation (see Robertson 1985; Robertson and Chirico 1985).

7. Lewis (1947) has argued that in their beginnings, science and technology shared with magic, including gnostic forms of the occult, a common structural orientation in their quest for power, control, and the transformation of humanity's relation to nature. Thus, a certain level of mystification is inherent to them.

8. Recall the usage of the terms. Rationality is being used to refer to instrumental, practical rationality. Substantive rationality is an increased systematization of an order around goals or entities and is nonrational from the point of view of instrumental rationality. Irrationality is an explicit rejection of both traditional substantive and instrumental rationality: Statements about reality are couched neither in traditional realist categories nor "Western" instrumentalist, positivistic ones.

9. The study of early Christian gnosticism that has become so popular within the university focuses on the self-transcendent and antistructural rhetoric of gnosticism. This not only is incomplete, it has been used to foster an inaccurate picture of the historic gnostics as being repressed, marginal individuals who aggregated into an egalitarian social movement. Pagels's (1979) popular book is an extreme example of this interpretation. In fact, gnosticism appears to have been a movement of intellectuals attempting to formulate an elite caste within Christianity. The early church's opposition to it, which Pagels tries to make so problematic, is grounded not only in the radically different cosmologies, but sociologically it "was nothing else than a struggle against the aristocracy of the intellectuals, such as is common to ascetic religions, with the object of preventing their seizing of leadership in the church. This struggle was crucial for the success of Christianity among the masses . . . " (Weber 1961, 363).

10. There are several research programs that support or complement this interpretive structure (see Thomas 1987b): Several typologies are based on movement ontologies (Robbins, Anthony, and Richardson 1978; Anthony and Ecker 1987); several studies link the new religious movements to a general rationalized culture (Campbell 1982; Wuthnow 1985, 1987); theorists have come to conceptualize conversion as a "seeking" framed within cultural accounts (Snow and Machalek 1984; Richardson 1985; Staples and Mauss 1987); some studies interpret movements within a resource mobilization perspective while perserving the importance and impact of their content and claims (Liebman and Wuthnow 1983; Lincoln 1985); most collections note that new religions depict an impersonal order (Wuthnow 1978), emphasize the self, subjective experience, and mystical union (Ahern 1983; Hood 1985; Johnson 1981) and are technological in nature (Barker 1982; Richardson, Stewart, and Simmonds 1979; Wilson 1982; Wuthnow 1985); and there are several recent studies of global dynamics, the work of Robertson especially emphasizing the role of religious movements in constituting changes in self and nation in the face of globalization (Robertson 1985; Robertson and Chirico 1985).

References

Ahern, Geoffrey. 1983. Esoteric "new religious movements" and the Western esoteric tradition. Pp. 165–76 in *Of gods and men: New religious movements in the West*, ed. E. Barker. Macon, Ga.: Mercer Univ. Press.

Ahlstrom, Sydney. 1972. *A religious history of the American people.* New Haven: Yale Univ. Press.

Anderson, Perry. 1974. *Lineages of the absolutist state.* London: Verso.

Anthony, Dick, and Bruce Ecker. 1987. The Anthony typology: A framework for assessing spiritual and consciousness groups. Pp. 35–105 in *Spiritual choices*, ed. D. Anthony, B. Ecker, and K. Wilber. New York: Paragon.

Badie, Bertrand, and Pierre Birnbaum. 1983. *The sociology of the state.* Chicago: Univ. of Chicago Press.

Bailyn, Bernard. 1955. *The New England merchants in the seventeenth century.* New York: Harper Torchbooks.

Barker, Eileen, ed. 1982. *New religious movements: A perspective for understanding society.* New York: Edwin Mellen Press.

Barthes, Roland. 1972. *Mythologies.* New York: Hill & Wang.

Bell, Daniel. 1973. *The coming of post-industrial society.* New York: Basic Books.

———. 1976. *The cultural contradictions of capitalism.* New York: Basic Books.

Bellah, Robert N. 1964. Religious evolution. *American Sociological Review* 29:358–74.

———. 1970. *Beyond belief.* New York: Harper & Row.

———. 1975. *The broken covenant.* New York: Seabury Press.

Bendix, Reinhard. 1956. *Work and authority in industry.* Berkeley: Univ. of California Press.

———. 1964. *Nation building and citizenship: Studies of our changing social order.* Garden City, N.Y.: Anchor Books.

———. 1978. *Kings or people.* Berkeley: Univ. of California Press.

Benedict, Michael L. 1974. Preserving the Constitution: The conservative bias of radical reconstruction. *Journal of American History* 61 (June): 65–90.

Benson, Lee. 1961. *The concept of Jacksonian democracy: New York as a test case.* Princeton: Princeton Univ. Press.

―――. 1972. *Toward the scientific study of history.* New York: J. B. Lippincott Co.

Berger, Joseph, M. Zelditch, Jr., B. Anderson, and B. P. Cohen. 1972. Structural aspects of distributive justice: A status value formulation. Pp. 119–46 in *Sociological theories in progress,* vol. 2, ed. J. Berger, M. Zelditch, Jr., and B. Anderson. New York: Houghton Mifflin.

Berger, Peter. 1954. The sociological study of sectarianism. *Social Research* 21: 467–85.

―――. 1963. A market model for the analysis of ecumenicity. *Social Research* 30:77–94.

―――. 1967. A sociological view of the secularization of theology. *Journal for the Scientific Study of Religion* 6:3–16.

―――. 1969. *The sacred canopy: Elements of a sociological theory of religion.* Garden City, N.Y.: Doubleday.

Berger, Peter, B. Berger, and H. Kellner. 1973. *The homeless mind.* New York: Vintage Books.

Berger, Peter, and Thomas Luckmann. 1966. *The social construction of reality.* Garden City, N.Y.: Anchor Books.

Berger, Peter, and S. Pullberg. 1965. Reification and the sociological critique of consciousness. *History and Theory* 4:196–211.

Berthoff, Rowland. 1982. Peasants and artisans, Puritans and Republicans: Personal liberty and communal equality in American history. *Journal of American History* 69:579–98.

Blau, Peter. 1964. *Exchange and power in social life.* New York: Wiley.

Bloch, Marc. 1961. *Feudal society.* Chicago: Univ. of Chicago Press.

Boli, John. 1987a. World-polity sources of expanding state authority and organization, 1870–1970. Pp. 71–91 *Institutional structure: Constituting state, society, and the individual,* by G. M. Thomas, J. W. Meyer, F. O. Ramirez, and J. Boli. Newbury Park, Calif: Sage.

―――. 1987b. Human rights or state expansion? Cross-national definitions of constitutional rights, 1870–1970. Pp. 133–49 in *Institutional structure: Constituting state, society, and the individual,* by G. M. Thomas, J. W. Meyer, F. O. Ramirez, and J. Boli. Newbury Park, Calif.: Sage.

Bourdieu, Pierre. 1984. *Distinction: A social critique of the judgement of taste.* Cambridge, Mass.: Harvard Univ. Press.

Braudel, Fernand. 1981. *The structure of everyday life.* New York: Harper & Row.

Bromley, David G., and Phillip E. Hammond, eds. 1987. *The future of new religious movements.* Macon, Ga.: Mercer Univ. Press.

Bruchey, Stuart. 1968. *The roots of American economic growth, 1607–1861.* New York: Harper Torchbooks.

Bryan, William Jennings. 1897. *The first battle: The story of the campaign of 1896.* Chicago: W. B. Conkey Co.

Burke, Kenneth. 1950. *A rhetoric of motives.* Berkeley: Univ. of California Press.

Bushman, Richard L. 1967. *From Puritan to Yankee: Character and the social order in Connecticut, 1690–1765.* New York: W. W. Norton & Co.

Bushnell, Horace. 1863. *Nature and the supernatural, as together constituting one system of God.* 5th ed. New York: Charles Scribner's Sons.

Campbell, Colin. 1982. The new religious movements, the new spirituality, and post-industrial society. Pp. 232–42 in *New religious movements: A perspective for understanding society,* ed. E. Barker. New York: Edwin Mellon Press.

——. 1987. *The romantic ethic and the spirit of modern consumerism.* New York: Basil Blackwell.

Cancian, Francesca M. 1987. *Love in America: Gender and self development.* Cambridge: Cambridge Univ. Press.

Carroll, H. K. 1912. *The religious forces of the United States.* New York: Charles Scribner's Sons.

Carroll, Michael P. 1975. Revitalization movements and social structure: Some quantitative tests. *American Sociological Review* 40:389–401.

Chirot, Daniel. 1986. *Social change in the modern era.* New York: Harcourt Brace Jovanovich.

Chirot, Daniel, and Charles Ragin. 1975. The market, tradition, and peasant rebellions: The case of Romania in 1907. *American Sociological Review* 40:428–44.

Christiano, Kevin. 1988. *Religious diversity and social change in turn-of-the-century American cities.* Cambridge: Cambridge Univ. Press.

Clark, V. S. 1929. *History of manufactures in the United States.* 3 vols. New York: McGraw-Hill.

Clasen, Claus-Peter. 1972. *Anabaptism: A social history, 1525–1618.* Ithaca: Cornell Univ. Press.

Cochran, Thomas C., and William Miller. 1961. *The age of enterprise: A social history of industrial America.* New York: Harper Torchbooks.

Cohn, Norman. 1957. *The pursuit of the millennium.* New York: Oxford Univ. Press.

Collins, Randall. 1978. Some principles of long-term social change: The territorial power of states. Pp. 1–34 in *Research in social movements, conflicts, and change,* ed. L. Kriesberg. Greenwich, Conn.: JAI Press.

——. 1986. *Weberian sociological theory.* Cambridge: Cambridge Univ. Press.

Cross, Whitney R. 1950. *The burned-over district: The social and intellectual history of enthusiastic religion in western New York, 1800–1850.* New York: Harper Torchbooks.

Davis, Winston Bradley. 1977. *Toward modernity: A developmental typology of popular religious affiliations in Japan.* Ithaca: Cornell Univ., East Asia Papers.

Desan, Suzanne. 1988. Redefining revolutionary liberty: The rhetoric of religious revival during the French revolution. *Journal of Modern History* 60(March):1–27.

Diamond, William. 1941. Urban and rural voting in 1896. *American Historical Review* 46:281–305.

Douglas, Mary. 1966. *Purity and danger*. London: Routledge & Kegan Paul.

――――. 1973. *Rules and meanings: The anthropology of everyday knowledge*. Baltimore: Penguin Books.

――――. 1986. *How institutions think*. Syracuse, N.Y.: Syracuse Univ. Press.

Douglas, Mary, and Steven Tipton, eds. 1983. *Religion and America: Religion in a secular age*. Boston: Beacon Press.

Dooyeweerd, Herman. [1936] 1978. *The Christian idea of the state*. Nutley, N.J.: Craig Press.

――――. 1969. *A new critique of theoretical thought*. 4 vols. Philadelphia, Pa.: Presbyterian and Reformed Publishing Co.

Durkheim, Emile. 1933. *The division of labor in society*. New York: Free Press.

――――. 1958. *Professional ethics and civic morals*. New York: Free Press.

――――. 1972. *Selected writings*. Edited by Anthony Giddens. Cambridge: Cambridge Univ. Press.

Durkheim, Emile, and M. Mauss. 1963. *Primitive classification*. Chicago: Univ. of Chicago Press.

Edwards, Jonathan. [1736] 1974. A faithful narrative of the surprising work of God in the conversion of many hundred souls. Pp. 344–64 in *The works of Jonathan Edwards*, vol. 1. Carlisle, Pa.: Banner of Truth Trust.

――――. [1742] 1974. Some thoughts concerning the present revival of religion in New England. Pp. 365-430 in *The works of Jonathan Edwards*, vol. 1. Carlisle, Pa.: The Banner of Truth Trust.

Ellul, Jacques. 1964. *The technological society*. New York: Vintage Books.

――――. 1967. *The political illusion*. New York: Alfred Knopf.

――――. 1975. *The new demons*. New York: Seabury Press.

――――. 1978. *The betrayal of the West*. New York: Seabury Press.

Finney, Charles. [1835] 1960. *Lectures on revivals of religion*. Edited by William G. McLoughlin. Cambridge, Mass.: Harvard Univ. Press.

――――. 1980. *The promise of the Spirit*. Compiled and edited by Timothy L. Smith. Minneapolis, Minn.: Bethany House.

Firebaugh, Glenn, and Jack G. Gibbs. 1985. User's guide to ratio variables. *American Sociological Review* 50:713–22.

Fite, G. C. 1971. The election of 1896. Pp. 1787–1826 in *History of American presidential elections*, vol. 2, ed. A. M. Schlesinger, Jr., and F. L. Israel. New York: Chelsea House.

Foner, Eric. 1970. *Free soil, free labor, free men*. New York: Oxford Univ. Press.

――――. 1975. Politics, ideology, and the origins of the American Civil War. Pp. 15–34 in *A nation divided*, ed. George M. Fredrickson. Minneapolis, Minn.: Burgess.

――――. 1980. *Politics and ideology in the age of the Civil War*. New York: Oxford Univ. Press.

Freeman, John, and J. Kronenfeld. 1973. Problems of definitional dependency. *Social Forces* 52:108–21.

Fuiguitt, G., and S. Lieberson. 1974. Correlation of ratios or difference scores having common terms. Pp. 128–44 in *Sociological methodology, 1973–74*, ed. H. Costner. San Francisco: Jossey-Bass.

Gamson, William A. 1975. *The strategy of social protest*. Homewood, Ill.: Dorsey Press.

Gaustad, Edwin S. 1966. *A religious history of America*. New York: Harper & Row.

Geertz, Clifford. 1968. *Islam observed: Religious development in Morocco and Indonesia*. Chicago: Univ. of Chicago Press.

──────. 1973. *The interpretation of cultures*. New York: Basic Books.

──────. 1980. *Negara: The theatre state in nineteenth-century Bali*. Princeton: Princeton Univ. Press.

Giddens, Anthony. 1981. *A contemporary critique of historical materialism*. Berkeley: Univ. of California Press.

──────. 1987. *The nation-state and violence:* Vol. 2 of *A contemporary critique of historical materialism*. Berkeley: Univ. of California Press.

Gierke, Otto. [1881] 1958. *Political theories of the middle age*. Boston: Beacon Press.

Ginzberg, Lori D. 1986. "Moral suasion is moral balderdash": Women, politics, and social activism in the 1850s. *Journal of American History* 73 (3):601–22.

Glock, Charles Y. 1964. The role of deprivation in the origin and evolution of religious groups. Pp. 24–36 in *Religion and social conflict*, ed. R. Lee and M. Marty. Oxford: Oxford Univ. Press.

Gluckman, Max. 1954. *Rituals of rebellion in southeast Africa*. Manchester: Manchester Univ. Press.

──────. 1962. *Essays on the ritual of social relations*. Manchester: Manchester Univ. Press.

Goffman, Erving. 1963. *Stigma: Notes on the management of spoiled identity*. Englewood Cliffs, N.J.: Prentice-Hall.

──────. 1967. *Interaction ritual: Essays on face-to-face behavior*. Garden City, N.Y.: Anchor Books.

──────. 1974. *Frame analysis*. New York: Harper & Row.

Habermas, Jurgen. 1975. *Legitimation crisis*. Boston: Beacon Press.

Hackett, David G. 1988. The social origins of nationalism: Albany, New York, 1754–1835. *Journal of Social History* 21 (Summer): 659–82.

Hammarberg, Melvin. 1974. Indiana farmers and the group basis of the late nineteenth-century political parties. *Journal of American History* 61:91–115.

Hammond, John L. 1979. *The politics of benevolence: Revival religion and American voting behavior*. Norwood, N.J.: Ablex.

Hammond, Phillip E., ed. 1985. *The sacred in a secular age*. Berkeley: Univ. of California Press.

Handy, Robert T. 1984. *A Christian America*. Oxford: Oxford Univ. Press.

Hannan, Michael T. 1979. Issues in panel analysis of national development: A methodological overview. Pp. 17–33 in *National development and the world system: Educational, economic, and political change, 1950–1970,* ed. J. W. Meyer and M. T. Hannan. Chicago: Univ. of Chicago Press.

Hays, Samuel P. 1957. *The response to industrialism, 1885–1914.* Chicago: Univ. of Chicago Press.

————. 1967. Political parties and the community-society continuum. Pp. 152–81 in *The American party system,* ed. W. N. Chambers and W. D. Burnham. Oxford: Oxford Univ. Press.

Heilbroner, Robert L. 1977. *The economic transformation of America.* New York: Harcourt Brace Jovanovich.

Heirich, Max. 1977. Change of heart: A test of some widely held theories about religious conversion. *American Journal of Sociology* 83:653–80.

Hirsch, M. D. 1971. The election of 1884. Pp. 1561–82 in *History of American presidential elections,* vol. 2, ed. A. M. Schlesinger, Jr., and F. L. Israel. New York: Chelsea House.

Hobsbawm, E. J. 1959. *Primitive rebels.* New York: W. W. Norton & Co.

————. 1968. *Industry and empire: The Pelican economic history of Britain,* vol. 3. London: Penguin Books.

Hofstadter, Richard. 1962. *Anti-intellectualism in American life.* New York: Alfred A. Knopf.

Hood, Ralph W., Jr. 1985. Mysticism. Pp. 285–97 in *The sacred in a secular age,* ed. P. E. Hammond. Berkeley: Univ. of California Press.

Hudson, Winthrop. 1953. *The great tradition of the American churches.* New York: Harper.

Hughes, Everett C. 1945. Dilemmas and contradictions of status. *American Journal of Sociology* 50:353–59.

Hunt, Lynn. 1984. *Politics, culture, and class in the French Revolution.* Berkeley: Univ. of California Press.

Hunter, James D. 1983. *American Evangelicalism.* New Brunswick, N.J.: Rutgers Univ. Press.

Illich, Ivan. 1970. *Deschooling society.* New York: Harper & Row.

Jenkins, J. C. 1983. Resource mobilization theory and the study of social movements. *Annual Review of Sociology* 9:527–53.

Jensen, Richard J. 1971. *The winning of the Midwest: Social and political conflict, 1888–1896.* Chicago: University of Chicago Press.

————. 1978. Party coalitions and the search for modern values: 1820–1970. Pp. 11–40 in *Emerging coalitions in American politics,* ed. S. M. Lipset. San Francisco: Institute for Contemporary Studies.

Johnson, Benton. 1981. A sociological perspective on new religion. Pp. 51–66 in *In gods we trust: New patterns of religious pluralism in America,* ed. T. Robbins and D. Anthony. New Brunswick, N.J.: Transaction Books.

Johnson, Paul E. 1978. *A shopkeeper's millennium.* New York: Hill & Wang.

Jonas, Hans. 1958. *The Gnostic religion.* Boston: Beacon Press.

Jung, Carl. 1933. *Modern man in search of a soul.* New York: Harcourt, Brace & World.

Kalberg, Steven. 1980. Max Weber's types of rationality: Cornerstones for the analysis of rationalization processes in history. *American Journal of Sociology* 85:1180–1201.

Kasson, John. 1976. *Civilizing the machine: Technology and republican values in America, 1776–1900.* New York: Penguin Books.

Key, V. O., Jr. 1955. A theory of critical elections. *The Journal of Politics* 17:3–18.

Key, V. O., Jr., and Frank Munger. 1959. Social determinism and electoral decisions: The case of Indiana. In *American voting behavior,* ed. E. Burdick and A. Brodbeck. Glencoe: Free Press.

Kleppner, Paul. 1970. *The cross of culture: A social analysis of midwestern politics, 1850–1890.* New York: Free Press.

———. 1973. The Greenback and Prohibition parties. Pp. 1549–81 in *History of U.S. Political Parties,* vol. 2, *1860–1910,* ed. A. M. Schlesinger, Jr. New York: Chelsea House.

———. 1978. From ethnoreligious conflict to "social harmony": Coalitional and party transformations in the 1980s. Pp. 41–59 in *Emerging coalitions in American politics,* ed. S. M. Lipset. San Francisco: Institute for Contemporary Studies.

———. 1979. *The third electoral system, 1853–1892.* Chapel Hill: Univ. of North Carolina Press.

Lasch, Christopher. 1979. *The culture of narcissism.* New York: Warner Books.

Leach, Edmund. 1976. *Culture and communication: The logic by which symbols are connected.* Cambridge: Cambridge Univ. Press.

Lenski, Gerhard E. 1961. *The religious factor.* Garden City, N.Y.: Doubleday.

Levi-Strauss, Claude. 1962. *Totemism.* Boston: Beacon Press.

———. 1963. *Structural anthropology.* New York: Basic Books.

———. 1969. *The elementary structures of kinship.* Boston: Beacon Press.

Lewis, C. S. 1947. *The abolition of man.* New York: Macmillan.

Liebman, Robert, and R. Wuthnow, eds. 1983. *The new Christian Right: Mobilization and legitimation.* Chicago: Aldine.

Lincoln, Bruce, ed. 1985. *Religion, rebellion, revolution.* New York: St. Martin's Press.

Lipset, Seymour Martin. 1963. *The first new nation.* Garden City, N.Y.: Anchor Books.

———. 1964. Religion and politics in the American past and present. Pp. 69–126 in *Religion and social conflict,* ed. R. Lee and M. Marty. New York: Oxford Univ. Press.

———. 1968. *Revolution and counterrevolution.* Garden City, N.Y.: Anchor Books.

Loveland, Anne C. 1980. *Southern Evangelicals and the social order, 1800–1860.* Baton Rouge: Louisiana State Univ. Press.

Luckmann, Thomas. 1967. *The invisible religion.* London: Macmillan.

McCarthy, John D., and M. N. Zald. 1977. Resource mobilization and social movements: A partial theory. *American Journal of Sociology* 83:1212–41.

McLoughlin, William G., Jr. 1959. *Modern revivalism: Charles Grandison Finney to Billy Graham.* New York: Ronald Press.

———. 1967. Is there a third force in Christendom? *Daedalus* 96 (Winter):43–68.

———. 1978. *Revivals, awakenings, and reform: An essay on religion and social change in America, 1607–1977.* Chicago: Univ. of Chicago Press.

McSeveney, Samuel T. 1972. *The politics of depression: Political behavior in the Northeast, 1893–1896.* New York: Oxford Univ. Press.

Mann, Michael. 1986. *The sources of social power,* vol. 1, *A history of power from the beginning to A.D. 1760.* Cambridge: Cambridge Univ. Press.

Marcuse, Herbert. 1964. *One-dimensional man.* Boston: Beacon Press.

Marsden, George M. 1980. *Fundamentalism and American culture: The shaping of twentieth-century Evangelicalism, 1870–1925.* Oxford: Oxford Univ. Press.

———. 1987. *Reforming fundamentalism: Fuller theological seminary and the new evangelicalism.* Grand Rapids, Mich.: William B. Eerdmans.

Marx, Karl. 1963. *Early writings.* Edited by T. B. Bottomore. New York: McGraw-Hill.

———. 1967. *Capital.* Vol. 1. New York: International Publishers.

———. 1973. *Grundrisse.* New York: Vintage Books.

Mathews, Donald G. 1977. *Religion in the Old South.* Chicago: Univ. of Chicago Press.

Mayer, F. E. 1956. *The religious bodies of America.* Saint Louis, Mo.: Concordia Publishing House.

Mead, Frank S. 1965. *Handbook of denominations in the United States.* New York: Abingdon Press.

Mead, Sydney E. 1954. Denominationalism: The shape of Protestantism in America. *Church History* 23 (December):291–320.

Meyer, John W. 1984. Review of *The Politics of Benevolence,* by John Hammond. *American Journal of Sociology* 89:1265–67.

———. 1987. The world polity and the authority of the nation-state. Pp. 41–70 in *Institutional structure: Constituting state, society, and the individual,* by G. M. Thomas, J. W. Meyer, F. O. Ramirez, and J. Boli. Newbury Park, Calif.: Sage.

Meyer, John W., J. Boli, and C. Chase-Dunn. 1975. Convergence and divergence in development. *Annual Review of Sociology* 1:233–46.

Meyer, John W., J. Boli, and G. M. Thomas. 1987. Pp. 12–37 in *Institutional structure: Constituting state, society, and the individual,* by G. M. Thomas, J. W. Meyer, F. O. Ramirez, and J. Boli. Newbury Park, Calif.: Sage.

Meyer, John W., M. T. Hannan, R. Rubinson, and G. M. Thomas. 1979. National economic development in the contemporary world system, 1950–1970: Social and political factors. Pp. 85–116 in *National development and the world system: Educational, economic, and political change, 1950–1970,* ed. J. Meyer and M. Hannan. Chicago: Univ. of Chicago Press.

Meyer, John W., and Brian Rowan. 1983. Institutionalized organizations: Formal structure as myth and ceremony. Pp. 71–97 in *Organizational environ-*

ments: Ritual and rationality, ed. J. W. Meyer and W. R. Scott. Newbury Park, Calif.: Sage.

Meyer, John W., and W. Richard Scott, eds. 1983. *Organizational environments: Ritual and rationality.* Newbury Park, Calif.: Sage.

Michelet, Jules. [1847] 1967. *History of the French Revolution.* Chicago: Univ. of Chicago Press.

Miller, Perry. 1961. From covenant to revival. Pp. 322–68 in *The shaping of American religion,* ed. J. W. Smith and A. L. Jamison. Princeton: Princeton Univ. Press.

Miller, W. L. 1961. American religion and American political attitudes. Pp. 81–118 in *Religious perspectives in American culture,* ed. J. W. Smith and A. L. Jamison. Princeton: Princeton Univ. Press.

Mills, C. Wright. 1940. Situated actions and vocabularies of motive. *American Sociological Review* 5:904–13.

Moore, Barrington, Jr. 1966. *Social origins of dictatorship and democracy.* Boston: Beacon Press.

Moorhead, James H. 1984. Between progress and apocalypse: A reassessment of millennialism in American religious thought, 1800–1880. *Journal of American History* 71:524–42.

Neitz, Mary Jo. 1981. Revivals, awakenings, and reform by . . . William G. McLoughlin. *American Journal of Sociology* 87 (November):729–32.

Niebuhr, H. Richard. 1929. *The social sources of denominationalism.* New York: Meridian Books.

———. 1937. *The kingdom of God in America.* New York: Harper & Row, Torchbooks.

———. 1951. *Christ and culture.* New York: Harper & Row.

Noll, Mark A., N. O. Hatch, and G. M. Marsden. 1983. *The search for Christian America.* Westchester, Ill.: Crossway Books.

North, Douglass C. 1961. *The economic growth of the United States, 1790–1860.* Englewood Cliffs, N.J.: Prentice-Hall.

Owen, John [1658] 1967. Of the mortification of sin in believers: The necessity, nature and means of it. Pp. 1–86 in *The works of John Owen.* Carlisle, Pa.: Banner of Truth Trust.

Pagels, Elaine. 1979. *The Gnostic Gospels.* New York: Vintage Books.

Paige, Jeffrey M. 1975. *Agrarian revolution: Social movements and export agriculture in the underdeveloped world.* New York: Free Press.

Parsons, Talcott. 1951. *The social system.* New York: Free Press.

———. 1963. Christianity and modern industrial society. In *Sociological theory, values, and sociocultural change,* ed. E. Tiryakian. New York: Free Press.

———. 1966. *Societies: Evolutionary and comparative perspectives.* Englewood Cliffs, N.J.: Prentice-Hall.

Poggi, Gianfranco. 1978. *The development of the modern state.* Stanford: Stanford Univ. Press.

———. 1983. *Calvinism and the capitalist spirit: Max Weber's Protestant ethic.* Amherst, Mass.: Univ. of Massachusetts Press.

Polanyi, Karl. 1944. *The great transformation.* Boston: Beacon Press.

Pritchard, Linda K. 1976. Religious change in nineteenth-century America. Pp. 297–330 in *The new religious consciousness,* ed. C. Y. Glock and R. N. Bellah. Berkeley: Univ. of California Press.

————. 1979. Pulling back from the brink of a breakthrough. *Journal for the Scientific Study of Religion* 18 (December):438–40.

Ramirez, Francisco O. 1987. Comparative social movements. Pp. 281–96 in *Institutional structure: Constituting state, society, and the individual,* by G. M. Thomas, J. W. Meyer, F. O. Ramirez, and J. Boli. Newbury Park, Calif.: Sage.

Ramirez, Francisco O., and G. M. Thomas. 1987. Structural antecedents and consequences of statism. Pp. 111–29 in *Institutional structure: Constituting state, society, and the individual,* by G. M. Thomas, J. W. Meyer, F. O. Ramirez, and J. Boli. Newbury Park, Calif.: Sage.

Ramirez, Francisco O., and J. Weiss. 1979. The political incorporation of women. Pp. 238–49 in *National Development and the world system,* ed. J. Meyer and M. Hannan. Chicago: Univ. of Chicago Press.

Richardson, James T. 1985. The active vs. passive convert: Paradigm conflict in conversion recruitment research. *Journal for the Scientific Study of Religion* 24:163–79.

Richardson, James T., M. W. Stewart, and R. B. Simmonds. 1979. *Organized miracles: A study of a contemporary, youth, communal, fundamentalist organization.* New Brunswick, N.J.: Transaction Books.

Robbins, Thomas. 1988. The transformative impact of the study of new religions on the sociology of religion. *Journal for the Scientific Study of Religion* 27 (March): 12–31.

Robbins, Thomas, D. Anthony, and J. Richardson. 1978. Theory and research on today's "new religions." *Sociological Analysis* 39:95–122.

Robbins, Thomas, W. Shepherd, and J. McBride, eds. 1985. *Cults, culture, and the law.* Chico, Calif.: Scholars Press.

Robertson, Roland. 1978. *Meaning and change: Explorations in the cultural sociology of modern societies.* New York: New York Univ. Press.

————. 1985. The relativization of societies, modern religion, and globalization. Pp. 31–42 in *Cults, culture, and the law,* ed. T. Robbins, W. Shepherd and J. McBride. Chico, Calif.: Scholars Press.

Robertson, Roland, and J. Chirico. 1985. Humanity, globalization, and worldwide religious resurgence: A theoretical exploration. *Sociological Analysis* 46:219–42.

Roth, Guenther, and W. Schluchter. 1979. *Max Weber's vision of history: Ethics and methods.* Berkeley: Univ. of California Press.

Rubinson, Richard. 1978. Political transformation in Germany and the United States. Pp. 39–74 in *Social change in the capitalist world economy,* ed. B. H. Kaplan. Beverly Hills, Calif.: Sage.

Ryan, Mary P. 1981. *Cradle of the middle class: The family in Oneida County, New York, 1790–1865.* Cambridge: Cambridge Univ. Press.

Schattschneider, E. E. 1960. *The semisovereign people.* Hinsdale, Ill.: Dryden Press.

Schlesinger, Arthur M. 1933. *The rise of the city, 1878–1898.* New York: Macmillan.

Schluchter, Wolfgang. 1981. *The rise of Western rationalism: Max Weber's developmental history.* Berkeley: Univ. of California Press.

Schuessler, K. 1973. Ratio variables and path models. In *Structural equation models in social science,* ed. A. Goldberger and O. Duncan. New York: Seminar Press.

Schutz, Alfred. 1967. *The phenomenology of the social world.* Chicago: Northwestern Univ. Press.

Scott, W. Richard. 1987. *Organizations: Rational, natural, and open systems.* Englewood Cliffs, N.J.: Prentice-Hall.

Simmel, Georg. 1978. *The philosophy of money.* London: Routledge & Kegan Paul.

Sizer, Sandra S. 1978. *Gospel hymns and social religion.* Philadelphia: Temple Univ. Press.

Skocpol, Theda. 1979. *States and social revolutions.* Cambridge: Cambridge Univ. Press.

Skowronek, Stephen. 1982. *Building a new American state: The expansion of national administrative capacities, 1877–1920.* Cambridge: Cambridge Univ. Press.

Smelser, Neil. 1962. *Theory of collective behavior.* New York: Free Press.

Smith, Jonathan Z. 1976. A pearl of great price and cargo of yams: A study in situational incongruity. *History of Religions* 16:1–19.

Smith, Timothy L. 1957. *Revivalism and social reform in mid-nineteenth century America.* New York: Abingdon Press.

———. 1980. Introduction: How Finney helped Americans discover the new covenant: Righteousness through grace. Pp. 9–33 in *The promise of the Spirit,* by C. Finney. Minneapolis, Minn.: Bethany House Publishers.

Snow, David A., and Richard Machalek. 1984. The sociology of conversion. *Annual Review of Sociology* 10:167–90.

Snyder, David, and Charles Tilly. 1972. Hardship and collective violence in France, 1830 to 1960. *American Sociological Review* 37:520–32.

Sorokin, Pitirim A. 1937. *Social and cultural dynamics.* 3 vols. New York: American Book Company.

Spackman, S. G. F. 1976. American federalism and the Civil Rights Act of 1875. *Journal of American Studies* 10 (Dec.):313–28.

Staples, Clifford L., and A. L. Mauss. 1987. Conversion or commitment? A reassessment of the Snow and Machalek approach to the study of conversion. *Journal for the Scientific Study of Religion* 26:133–47.

Stinchcombe, Arthur L. 1961. Agricultural enterprise and rural class relations. *American Journal of Sociology* 67:165–76.

———. 1968. *Constructing social theories.* Chicago: Univ. of Chicago Press.

Strayer, Joseph R. 1970. *On the medieval origins of the modern state.* Princeton: Princeton Univ. Press.

Sweet, William Warren. 1944. *Revivalism in America: Its origin, growth and decline.* New York: Charles Scribner's Sons.

———. 1948. *The American churches: An interpretation.* New York: Abingdon-Cokesbury Press.

Swidler, Ann. 1981. Love and adulthood in American culture. Pp. 120–47 in *Themes of work and love in adulthood,* ed. N. J. Smelser and E. H. Erikson. Cambridge, Mass.: Harvard Univ. Press.

Thomas, George M. 1979. Rational exchange and individualism: Revival religion in the U.S., 1870–1890. Pp. 351–72 in *The religious dimension,* ed. R. Wuthnow. New York: Academic Press.

———. 1987a. Cultural contradictions and religious-political movements in the nineteenth-century United States. Pp. 61–80 in *Rethinking the nineteenth century: Contradictions and movements,* ed. F. O. Ramirez. Westport, Conn.: Greenwood Press.

———. 1987b. Rational ontology and new religious movements. Unpublished paper, Department of Sociology, Arizona State University.

Thomas, George M., and John W. Meyer. 1984. The expansion of the state. *Annual Review of Sociology* 10:461–82.

———. 1987. Regime changes and state power in an intensifying world state system. Pp. 92–110 in *Institutional structure: Constituting state, society, and the individual,* by G. M. Thomas, J. W. Meyer, F. O. Ramirez, and J. Boli. Newbury Park, Calif.: Sage.

Thomas, George M., John W. Meyer, Francisco O. Ramirez, and John Boli. 1987. *Institutional structure: Constituting state, society, and the individual.* Newbury Park, Calif.: Sage.

Thomas, George M., Henry A. Walker, and Morris Zelditch, Jr. 1986. Legitimacy and collective action. *Social Forces* 65:378–404.

Thomas, John L. 1965. Romantic reform in America, 1815–1865. *American Quarterly* 17:656–81.

Thrupp, Sylvia L. 1970. *Millennial dreams in action.* New York: Schocken Books.

Tillich, Paul. 1959. *Theology of culture.* New York: Oxford Univ. Press.

Tilly, Charles. 1964. *The vendée.* Cambridge: Harvard Univ. Press.

———, ed. 1975. *The formation of national states in Western Europe.* Princeton: Princeton Univ. Press.

———. 1978. *From mobilization to revolution.* Menlo Park, Calif.: Addison-Wesley Publishing Co.

———. 1984. Social movements and national politics. Pp. 297–317 in *State-making and social movements,* ed. C. Bright and S. Harding. Ann Arbor, Mich.: Univ. of Michigan Press.

Tilly, Charles, L. Tilly, and R. Tilly. 1975. *The rebellious century, 1830–1930.* Cambridge, Mass.: Harvard Univ. Press.

Tocqueville, Alexis de. 1945. *Democracy in America.* New York: Vintage Books.

Trollope, Anthony. [1860] 1951. *North America.* New York: Alfred A. Knopf.

Turner, Ralph H. 1982. Collective behavior and resource mobilization as approaches to social movements: Issues and continuities. Pp. 1–24 in *Research in social movements, conflicts, and change*, vol. 4, ed. Louis Kriesberg. Greenwich, Conn.: JAI Press.

Turner, Victor W. 1967. *The forest of symbols*. Ithaca: Cornell Univ. Press.

———. 1974. *Dramas, fields, and metaphors*. Ithaca: Cornell Univ. Press.

Tuveson, Ernest Lee. 1968. *Redeemer nation: The idea of America's millennial role*. Chicago: Univ. of Chicago Press.

Tyack, David. 1974. *The one best system*. Cambridge: Harvard Univ. Press.

Tyler, Alice F. 1944. *Freedom's ferment*. New York: Harper & Row.

U.S. Bureau of the Census. 1860. *Eighth Census*. (Manufactures). Washington, D.C.: U.S. Government Printing Office.

———. 1900a. *Twelfth Census*. Vol. 5 (Agriculture). Washington, D.C.: U.S. Government Printing Office.

———. 1900b. *Twelfth Census*. Vol. 7 (Manufactures). Washington, D.C.: U.S. Government Printing Office.

———. 1910. *Thirteenth Census*. Vol. 5 (Agriculture). Washington, D.C.: U.S. Government Printing Office.

———. 1970. *Historical Statistics of the U.S., Colonial Times to 1970*. 2 parts. Washington, D.C.: U.S. Government Printing Office.

Voegelin, Eric. 1968. *Science, politics, and Gnosticism*. Chicago: Gateway.

Wallace, Anthony C. 1956. Revitalization movements. *American Anthropologist* 58:264–81.

Wallerstein, Immanuel. 1974a. The rise and future demise of the world capitalist system: Concepts for comparative analysis. *Comparative Studies in Society and History* 16:387–415.

———. 1974b. *The modern world-system: Capitalistic agriculture and the origins of the European world-economy in the sixteenth century*. New York: Academic Press.

Walton, John. 1984. *Reluctant rebels: Comparative studies of revolution and underdevelopment*. New York: Columbia Univ. Press.

Walzer, Michael. 1965. *The revolution of the saints*. New York: Atheneum.

Weber, Max. 1930. *The Protestant ethic and the spirit of capitalism*. New York: Charles Scribner's Sons.

———. 1946. *From Max Weber: Essays in sociology*. Translated and edited by H. Gerth and C. W. Mills. New York: Oxford Univ. Press.

———. 1961. *General economic history*. New York: Collier Books.

———. 1963. *The sociology of religion*. Boston: Beacon Press.

———. 1968. *Economy and society*. Edited by G. Roth and C. Wittich. Berkeley: Univ. California Press.

Weisberger, Bernard A. 1958. *They gathered at the river*. New York: Quadrangle.

Wesser, Robert F. 1971. The election of 1888. Pp. 1615–52 in *History of American presidential elections*, vol. 2. ed. A. M. Schlesinger, Jr., and F. L. Israel. New York: Chelsea House.

Wiley, Norbert. 1967. America's unique class politics: The interplay of the labor, credit, and commodity markets. *American Sociological Review* 32:529–41.

Williams, George H. 1962. *The radical reformation*. Philadelphia: Westminister Press.

Wilson, Bryan. 1982. *Religion in sociological perspective*. Oxford: Oxford Univ. Press.

Wolf, Eric R. 1969. *Peasant wars of the twentieth century*. New York: Harper & Row.

Wolfe, Tom. 1976. The "Me" decade. *New York*, 23 Aug.

Wonnacott, R. J., and Wonnacott, T. H. 1970. *Econometrics*. New York: John Wiley & Sons.

Wuthnow, Robert. 1978. *Experimentation in American religion*. Berkeley: Univ. of California Press.

———. 1980. World order and religious movements. Pp. 57–75 in *Studies of the modern world-system*, ed. A. Bergesen. New York: Academic Press.

———. 1985. The cultural context of contemporary religious movements. Pp. 43–56 in *Cults, culture, and the law*, ed. T. Robbins, W. Shepherd, and J. McBride. Chico, Calif.: Scholars Press.

———. 1987. *Meaning and moral order: Explorations in cultural analysis*. Berkeley: Univ. of California Press.

Zald, Mayer N. and John D. McCarthy, 1987. *Social movements in an organizational society*. New Brunswick, N.J.: Transaction Books.

Zaret, David. 1985. *The heavenly contract: Ideology and organization in prerevolutionary Puritanism*. Chicago: Univ. of Chicago Press.

Zaretsky, Eli. 1976. *Capitalism, the family, and personal life*. New York: Harper & Row.

Zelditch, Morris, Jr., William Harris, George M. Thomas, and Henry A. Walker. 1983. Decisions, nondecisions, and metadecisions. Pp. 1–32 in *Research in social movements, conflicts, and change*, vol. 5, ed. Louis Kriesberg. Greenwich, Conn.: JAI Press.

Zelizer, Viviana A. 1981. The price and value of children: The case of children's insurance. *American Journal of Sociology* 86:1036–56.

Index